Ancient Greek Myth in World Fiction since 1989

Bloomsbury Studies in Classical Reception

Bloomsbury Studies in Classical Reception presents scholarly monographs offering new and innovative research and debate to students and scholars in the reception of Classical Studies. Each volume will explore the appropriation, reconceptualization and recontextualization of various aspects of the Graeco-Roman world and its culture, looking at the impact of the ancient world on modernity. Research will also cover reception within antiquity, the theory and practice of translation, and reception theory.

Also available in the Series:
Ancient Magic and the Supernatural in the Modern Visual and Performing Arts, edited by Filippo Carlà and Irene Berti
Greek and Roman Classics in the British Struggle for Social Change, edited by Henry Stead and Edith Hall
Imagining Xerxes, Emma Bridges
Ovid's Myth of Pygmalion on Screen, Paula James
Victorian Classical Burlesques: A Critical Anthology, Laura Monros-Gaspar

Ancient Greek Myth in World Fiction since 1989

Edited by
Justine McConnell and Edith Hall

Bloomsbury Academic
An imprint of Bloomsbury Publishing Plc
B L O O M S B U R Y
LONDON • OXFORD • NEW YORK • NEW DELHI • SYDNEY

Bloomsbury Academic

An imprint of Bloomsbury Publishing Plc

50 Bedford Square
London
WC1B 3DP
UK

1385 Broadway
New York
NY 10018
USA

www.bloomsbury.com

BLOOMSBURY and the Diana logo are trademarks of Bloomsbury Publishing Plc

First published 2016

British Library Cataloguing-in-Publication Data
A catalogue record for this book is available from the British Library.

ISBN: HB: 978-1-47257-937-9
PB: 978-1-47257-938-6
ePDF: 978-1-47257-940-9
ePub: 978-1-47257-939-3

Library of Congress Cataloging-in-Publication Data
A catalog record for this book is available from the Library of Congress.

Series: Bloomsbury Studies in Classical Reception

Typeset by RefineCatch, Broad Street, Bungay, Suffolk
Printed and bound in India

Contents

Acknowledgements

The genesis of this book lies in a conference organized by Edith Hall with the help of Katie Billotte at the British Academy in London in July 2012. We are grateful for the support of the British Academy, and warmly thank all those who attended the conference and made it such a success. We are also grateful for the support of the Arts and Humanities Research Council and the Leverhulme Trust on separate projects which have run concurrently with the development of this book.

We are grateful to Charlotte Loveridge, who first expressed interest in publishing this volume, and to Alice Wright, Lucy Carroll, and Anna MacDiarmid at Bloomsbury, as well as to our copy-editor, Lisa Carden. We wish to thank the following in particular for their help and support in various ways: Fiona Macintosh, Sebastian Matzner and Stephen Tuck.

Contributors

Giorgio Amitrano taught Japanese Language and Literature at the 'Orientale' University of Naples until 2012. He has been the director of the Italian Cultural Institute of Tokyo since 2013. His translations of Japanese literature into Italian include works by Kawabata Yasunari, Murakami Haruki, Yoshimoto Banana, Nakajima Atsushi, Inoue Yasushi and Miyazawa Kenji. He was awarded the Noma Award for the Translation of Japanese Literature and the Grinzane Cavour Prize (Lifetime Achievement Award) in 2001 and 2008 respectively.

Helen Eastman is Artistic Associate of the Archive for the Performance of Greek and Roman Drama at Oxford University and Director of the Cambridge Greek Play. She has worked as a director of theatre and opera throughout Europe and has written a number of plays and librettos. She founded the Live Canon ensemble. She is about to be the Peter Wall Institute Artist in Residence and Visiting Scholar at The University of British Columbia. Her research has focused on classical reception in contemporary theatre and poetry.

Sofia Frade is Lecturer in Classics at the University of Lisbon, Portugal. Her research interests focus on the politics of Greek tragedy and performance reception in Portugal. She is the author of *Heracles and Athenian Propaganda: Politics, Imagery and Drama* (Bloomsbury, forthcoming).

Adam Ganz is Reader in Screenwriting at Royal Holloway, University of London, as well as being a professional screenwriter and director for radio, film and television. His research focuses on audiovisual narrative, on the television development process, and on the collaboration between author and audience. His dramas for radio include *The Chemistry Between Them* (2014), *The Gestapo Minutes* (2013), *Nuclear Reactions* (2010) and *Listening to the Generals* (2009).

After teaching at Reading, Oxford, Durham and Royal Holloway universities, **Edith Hall** took up a Chair in Classics at King's College London in 2012. She is also co-founder and Consultant Director of the Archive of Performances of Greek and Roman Drama (APGRD) at Oxford. Her latest book is *Introducing the Ancient Greeks* (W. W. Norton, 2014). She has recently been awarded the Erasmus Medal of the European Academy for her research.

Lorna Hardwick is Emeritus Professor Classical Studies at the Open University UK and an Honorary Research Associate of the Archive of Performances of Greek and Roman Drama at Oxford. With James Porter she is series editor of the Classical Presences series (Oxford University Press). Recent publications have included essays on the relationship between translation and reception of Greek epic, drama and historiography and the implications for subsequent cultural histories. She is currently working on a second edition for Cambridge University Press of her *Reception Studies* (2003).

William Maynard Hutchins, who is a professor at Appalachian State University in North Carolina, was educated at Berea College, Yale University and the University of Chicago. He was awarded a National Endowment for the Arts grant for literary translation in 2005–2006 and a second in 2011–2012. He was co-winner of the 2013 Saif Ghobash/Banipal Prize.

Anna Ljunggren is Professor of Russian at Stockholm University. Her main area of research is nineteenth- and twentieth-century poetry. She has also conducted a project dedicated to contemporary Russian prose at the turn of the millennium. She is originally from St Petersburg, where she gained her MA in Romance languages, and she taught for a number of years in the United States.

Fiona Macintosh is Professor of Classical Reception and Director of the APGRD at the University of Oxford. Her publications include *Dying Acts* (Palgrave Macmillan, 1994), *Greek Tragedy and the British Theatre 1660–1914* (with Edith Hall; Oxford University Press, 2005) and *Sophocles' Oedipus Tyrannus* (Cambridge University Press, 2009). She has edited numerous APGRD volumes, most recently *The Oxford Handbook of Greek Drama in the Americas* (with Kathryn Bosher, Justine M^c^Connell and Patrice Rankine; Oxford University Press, 2015).

Sebastian Matzner is Lecturer in Comparative Literature at King's College London. His research focuses on interactions between classical and modern literature, particularly in relation to literary and critical theory, the history of sexualities, and the theory and poetics of intercultural encounters across time. His doctoral thesis, *The Forgotten Trope: Metonymy in Poetic Action*, won the University of Heidelberg's Prize for Classical Philology and Literary Theory and is forthcoming as a monograph.

Justine M^c^Connell is a Leverhulme Early Career Fellow at the University of Oxford, currently working on contemporary African, Caribbean and ancient

Greek poetics. She is author of *Black Odysseys: The Homeric Odyssey in the African Diaspora* (Oxford University Press, 2013), and co-editor of *Ancient Slavery and Abolition: from Hobbes to Hollywood* (with Edith Hall and Richard Alston; Oxford University Press, 2011) and *The Oxford Handbook of Greek Drama in the Americas* (with Kathryn Bosher, Fiona Macintosh and Patrice Rankine; Oxford University Press, 2015).

Simon Perris is Senior Lecturer in Classics at Victoria University of Wellington, New Zealand. He has published numerous articles on Greek tragedy, classical reception and New Zealand literature. His book, *The Gentle, Jealous God: Reading Euripides'* Bacchae *in English* (2016), is also published by Bloomsbury.

Patrice Rankine completed his doctorate in Classics at Yale University with a dissertation on the tragedies of Seneca. He has since developed interdisciplinary interests in the redeployment of classical themes among modern authors, particularly as it pertains to African American literature and identity. His first book, *Ulysses in Black: Ralph Ellison, Classicism, and African American Literature* (University of Wisconsin Press, 2006), was named one of *Choice* magazine's outstanding academic books. His second book is *Aristotle and Black Drama: A Theater of Civil Disobedience* (Baylor University Press, 2013). His other publications include *The Oxford Handbook of Greek Drama in the Americas* (Oxford University Press, 2015), co-edited with Kathryn Bosher, Fiona Macintosh and Justine McConnell.

Margaret Reynolds is Professor of English at Queen Mary, University of London. Her books include a critical edition of Elizabeth Barrett Browning's *Aurora Leigh* (W. W. Norton, 1992), *The Sappho Companion* (Chatto & Windus, 2000) and *The Sappho History* (Palgrave Macmillan, 2003). She is the presenter of BBC Radio 4's 'Adventures in Poetry'.

Efrossini Spentzou teaches Latin and Classical Reception at Royal Holloway, University of London. She is the author of *Readers and Writers in Ovid's Heroides: Transgressions of Gender and Genre* (Oxford University Press, 2003), *Reflections of Romanity: Discourses of Subjectivity in Imperial Rome* (with Richard Alston; Ohio State University Press, 2011) and *The Roman Poetry of Love: Elegy and Politics in a Time of Revolution* (Bloomsbury, 2013). She is also co-editor of *Cultivating the Muse: Struggles for Power and Inspiration in Classical Literature* (with Don Fowler; Oxford University Press, 2002). Currently she is editing (with William Fitzgerald) a volume on *The Production of Space in Latin Literature* (Oxford University Press, 2017).

Introduction

Justine M[c]Connell

Barry Unsworth, the British Booker Prize-winning author, was, in a sense, the creative catalyst for this volume. While researching the late-twentieth-century revival of Euripides' *Iphigenia at Aulis* on international stages, Edith Hall was led from drama to fiction by reading Unsworth's 2002 novel, *The Songs of the Kings*.[1] Unsworth's novel pinpointed one of the major features in the revival of Euripides' long-neglected tragedy: the prevalence of political 'spin' that dominated media discourse in the 1990s and in the run-up to the second Iraq War; in Unsworth's novel, this led directly to Iphigenia's death under the influence of ancient 'spin doctors' such as Odysseus.[2] So when Edith, together with Katie Billotte, began to plan a conference on ancient Greek myth in contemporary fiction, Unsworth was first on their list of invitees. With characteristic generosity, he accepted with enthusiasm, but fate tragically intervened and he died from cancer at the age of 82 in June 2012, just a month before the British Academy conference which gave rise to this volume.

Unsworth's reflections on *The Songs of Kings* and his use of myth in fiction resonate throughout the diverse chapters of this volume nevertheless. As he described:

> My novel is partly about how stories are made, it's a kind of story about story and so various analogies between fiction and epic song were bound to occur. One of the main technical problems was to transpose the gravity-defying, arbitrary world of myth to the plodding factual world of fiction.[3]

This technical obstacle will have likewise confronted the authors whose work is considered in this volume, with a variety of solutions being found. These worlds to which myth is transposed range across Asia, Africa, Europe, Oceania and the Americas, and from the early nineteenth century's Greek War of Independence (1821–1832) to the contemporary era of *The Wire*'s Baltimore, and into a dystopic future. All the works were created in the post-Cold War era, which can be seen to inflect their composition and their appropriation of Greek myth, and in many instances to raise questions regarding the appropriateness of gazing at historical events through a mythical lens.

In his famous essay 'Odysseus' Scar' (1946), Erich Auerbach remarked that recent events both before and during the Second World War underlined 'how unfit [historical themes] are for legend'. Yet he conceded that their very complexity often compelled historians to resort to what he saw as the simpler, less nuanced technique of mythic storytelling.[4] Within this same context of Nazism, both Bernhard Schlink and Jonathan Littell were accused of inappropriate 'kitsch' in their use of myth to grapple with historical reality, as Sebastian Matzner (Chapter 10) and Edith Hall (Chapter 11) respectively show, particularly given the German literary-cultural discourse of *Vergangenheitsbewältigung* ('coming to terms with the past'). Yet there is also no doubt that myth can give a protective veneer to literature which opposes a repressive regime, and thus enables a critical resistance, as Helen Eastman (Chapter 14), Patrice Rankine (Chapter 1) and Margaret Reynolds (Chapter 13) all demonstrate in their contributions.

Before considering the reasons for a resurgence of Greek myth in fiction after 1989, the other half of our title demands some explication. 'World fiction' naturally evokes a subset of 'world literature', which, although it has long been a contested term, has in recent years once again become the lynchpin of intense scholarly debate and scrutiny. First coined by Christoph Martin Wieland in the undated notes to his translation of Horace's *Epistles*,[5] Goethe brought the concept *Weltliteratur* to prominence back in 1827 when he declared, 'National literature is now a rather unmeaning term; the epoch of world literature (*Weltliteratur*) is at hand, and everyone must strive to hasten its approach';[6] and many agreed. But exactly what 'world literature' should mean is less clear. It is fraught with political problems that pivot around accusations of its entwinement with global capitalism (*n+1*), unwieldy size (Moretti), loss of nuance resulting from its refusal to acknowledge 'untranslatability' (Apter), and uncertain criteria for inclusion (if, as Damrosch suggests, it is about a mode of circulation and reading rather than an infinite canon of works, does every literary work have the potential to be 'world literature'?).[7]

It is, without doubt, an important concept. In our globalized age, contemporary 'national' literature scarcely makes sense. Not only has the migration of peoples around the world ensured that many of us trace our roots via multiple routes (to deploy a homophony first advanced by Paul Gilroy),[8] but also, as the cultural theorist Stuart Hall argued, 'all of us are composed of multiple social identities, not of one'.[9] The local persists (indeed, Hall argues that it can intensify under the conditions of globalization),[10] but it is also nearly always deeply affected by the global. Even prior to the current wave of globalization, 'national literature' had proved to be an insufficient concept, as Goethe's *Weltliteratur* signifies. For his notion was one which, as Maire and Edward Said noted, 'transcends national literatures without, at the same time, destroying their individualities'.[11] Goethe was not so naïve as to believe that *Weltliteratur* would be welcomed by all with cosmopolitan open arms; rather he suggested its aim was:

> Not that the nations shall think alike, but that they shall learn how to understand each other, and, if they do not care to love one another, at least they will learn to tolerate one another.[12]

Goethe sought this kind of tolerance in the wake of the bloody Napoleonic Wars. For Auerbach, writing less than a decade after the Second World War, *Weltliteratur* would likewise have a role to play. He saw culture the world over becoming 'standardized': 'To be sure, national wills are stronger and louder than ever, yet in every case they promote the same standards and forms for modern life.'[13] It is this very merging that *Weltliteratur* can articulate in Auerbach's conception of it: 'this coalescence, so rendered and articulated, will become their myth.'[14] Just as world literature itself is born out of a 'coalescence', so in this volume we frequently see a similar kind of development happening in the myths that are retold. The Greek myths merge and combine with folklore from other times and places, as the chapters by William M. Hutchins (Chapter 2), Simon Perris (Chapter 3), Giorgio Amitrano (Chapter 6), Anna Ljunggren (Chapter 9) and Helen Eastman (Chapter 14) demonstrate. Coalescence, seen in these new castings of myth and in these modern works of literature, becomes the very force at the heart of these novels: it is the myth (as Auerbach envisaged it) that drives them.

Literary classical reception can always be seen as a subset of the 'world literature' paradigm because, by necessity, the ancient myths cross linguistic and cultural boundaries to take their place in the more modern works. Even if the physical geography remains more or less the same – a modern Greek reception of classical Greece, or a contemporary Italian reception of ancient Rome, for instance – boundaries both linguistic and cultural are traversed as a result of the vast changes occasioned by more than two thousand years of intervening history. Such border crossings are integral to *Weltliteratur*, binding classical reception studies innately to world literature. However, the criticisms of Eurocentrism that have plagued studies of world literature (most forcibly articulated by René Etiemble in 1974, and more recently – alongside parallel criticisms of Anglo-American domination – by Gayatri Spivak)[15] are naturally accentuated by a focus on Greek myth and literature, not to mention the fact that all the chapters in this book are written in English. The latter is tempered only to a degree by the linguistic range of the works under examination, including Arabic, French, German, Russian, modern Greek, Japanese and Brazilian Portuguese, as well as English (by American, Australasian, Canadian and South African writers). The former, meanwhile, has its roots in the fact that the notion of world literature developed at the very same time as European imperialism was asserting its dominance over, and claiming a superiority over, the non-European world.[16]

Focusing on works created after 1989 further highlights the inadequacy of categorizing works of fiction according to national tradition: the themes and approaches that emerge cross national boundaries with slight regard for them, yet without losing their singularity.[17] All of the works are in dialogue with Greek myth, no matter where they were composed or by whom; their other influences are not restricted to their own national traditions, either: the Canadian Theresa Kishkan is particularly influenced by the Irish writers Joyce and Synge (Chapter 8), for instance, while the Russian Viktor Pelevin foregrounds the Argentine Jorge Luis Borges in his novel (Chapter 9). The geographical range of this book – which includes works by Brazilian, French, German, Japanese, Indian, North American, Maori, African, Russian, Greek, Irish, and Arabic writers – is intended to offer a scope that demonstrates the total porousness of national boundaries in contemporary literature. At the same time, the turn to a concept of world literature in the wake of conflict reverberates with the circumstances which led Goethe to develop the paradigm in the first place in the decades following the Napoleonic Wars. Cultural alliances, however uneasy or resistant, are built in the very act of appropriating ancient Greek myth for another time and space.

Notwithstanding Pascale Casanova's influential model of world literature and a 'world republic of letters', which is premised on competition between nations and their national literatures, this volume's focus on world literature seeks to challenge the conventional categorization of works of fiction according to national tradition.[18] Nonetheless, this book offers a geographic reach that illuminates the remarkable renaissance of fiction which engaged with Greek myth in the wake of the Cold War – a trend seen the world over – at a time when there was a renewed impetus towards cultural globalization and cosmopolitanism.[19] This is particularly important for classical reception studies because the relationship between the genres of modern fiction and ancient Greek tragedy has often been observed but seldom theorized. The details of any particular 'reception' of Greek tragedy have tended to dominate to such an extent that the theoretical nature of the relationship has suffered relative neglect. As Edith Hall has argued, critics have frequently been guilty of a slippage between Greek tragedy and Greek myth, and thereby failed to perceive the importance of the dramatic form as inspiration.[20] Yet it is that very form which has, in many cases, provided the key to modern writers' engagement with antiquity because it foregrounds 'the question of rival subjectivities – the radically different ways in which individual subjects can each experience the "same" events'.[21]

The interplay between Greek tragedy and prose fiction is as old as the novel itself. The eighteenth-century novel, written during the heyday of neoclassical theatre, enjoyed reminding its readers of the Greek myths they had seen dramatized. In the great nineteenth-century age of realism, however, novelists became interested in more philosophical aspects of Greek tragedy, as many critics have noted. The form of Greek tragic theatre, especially the collective voice of the chorus which seems reflected in some of Thomas Hardy's communities, for example, is a factor. But what, broadly speaking, attracted Thackeray, Eliot, Hardy and a host of less well-known novelists, were the ethical seriousness and metaphysical scope they perceived in the works of the ancient Greek tragedians.

A century later, since the fall of the Berlin Wall there has been a remarkable renaissance of interest in ancient Greek myth, derived both from Greek drama and other ancient sources, in fiction all over the world. While Greek myth and literature were key constituents in nineteenth-century realist and early twentieth-century modernist fiction, they faded in significance mid-century, at a time when V. S. Pritchett warned that the novel as a form would be inadequate to the cultural 'processing' of recent atrocities. However, the creative energies released by the end of the Cold War, the rise of the postcolonial novel, and the terrible recent conflicts in the Balkans, Iraq, Afghanistan and Africa, which the collapse of the Soviet Union contributed to and impacted on, played a role in a remarkable renaissance of significant fiction which engaged once more with the Greeks.

Among these other ancient sources, it is striking how many of the works examined in this volume engage with epic (see the chapters by Ganz, Hardwick, Ljunggren, McConnell, Macintosh, Matzner, Reynolds and Spentzou). As repositories of myth, the prominence of epic may be unsurprising, but it is also likely that epic's role as the narrative of nation-building (as well as empire) contributed to its popularity in the aftermath of the Cold War. While epic does not shine the same kind of spotlight on rival subjectivities that drama does, it offers another facet of great importance to fiction after 1989. As the world sought to reconfigure itself in a new way, Greek epic could be appropriated, adapted and renewed; once claimed in these ways, it offered a path which writers could choose to either tread or consciously veer away from. In addition, the flexibility of epic, which was foregrounded by Milman Parry and Albert Lord's groundbreaking work in Yugoslavia in the 1930s, the uncertainty over the authorship of the Homeric epics, and the unfixed nature of oral traditions, combine to form a particular encouragement to diverse and multiple engagements with the myths that the epics contain. Finally, as Barry Unsworth's *The Songs of the Kings* illustrates, works of classical reception have an extraordinary capacity to cross generic boundaries, so that myth, epic, drama and the novel can all enter into dialogue with each other in new and different forms. The focus on fiction in this volume (including that seen on the small screen) allows us to shine a spotlight on one of the most popular and accessible forms of storytelling that exists in the contemporary era.

The diverse ways in which ancient Greek myth has been used in fiction internationally since 1989 become apparent in the panorama of collected essays presented in this volume: whether as a framing device, or a filter, or via resonances and parallels, Greek myth has proven fruitful for many writers of fiction since the end of the Cold War. Yet their engagement with it has been by no means homogeneous, and this volume examines the varied ways that writers from around the world have turned to classical antiquity to articulate their own contemporary concerns.

Adopting a broadly chronological structure, the collection opens with Patrice Rankine's exploration of classical myth in the modern Brazilian novel. He demonstrates that the deployment of classical myth in Brazilian fiction over the course of the twentieth century shifted from a monumental to a multivalent approach. After 1989, classical myth retreats into the background, consumed (to deploy the metaphor of the 1922 Brazilian modernist movement that privileged a symbolic anthropophagy) and incorporated along with a number of other influences.

A parallel kind of multiplicity of inspiration is seen in the works of the Libyan writer Ibrahim al-Koni, who was shortlisted for the 2015 Man Booker Prize. William M. Hutchins, al-Koni's primary translator into English, argues in his chapter that the fusion of Tuareg myths with ancient Greek and Egyptian ones is essential to al-Koni's Arabic fiction. His books consistently display an interest in these myths (particularly those relating to Athena, Atlantis, Typhon and Odysseus) and invoke them in fresh and original ways.

The exploration of mythopoesis, and the diverse ways in which modern writers from around the globe have combined traditions and tales from ancient Greece with myths, old and new, from other countries continues in Simon Perris's discussion of two novels by the prominent Maori writer, Witi Ihimaera.

Mythmaking is a recurrent theme in Ihimaera's work, particularly in his combination of New Zealand history, Maori mythology, his own family history and ancient Greek myth and tragedy. As Perris argues, *The Matriarch* (1986; revised 2009) and *The Dream Swimmer* (1997) both engage with classical material albeit in markedly different ways.

The fourth chapter returns to Brazil once more, with Sofia Frade's consideration of Luiz Antonio de Assis Brasil's 1990 novel, *Videiras de Cristal* (*Crystal Vines*). The historical tale of the nineteenth-century religious leader, Jacobina Maurer, which the novel relates, is retold as if it were a Greek tragedy. The chapter also demonstrates the 'chain of receptions', a term first coined by Charles Martindale in *Redeeming the Text* (1993), which emerges as a prominent element in many of the works considered in this volume. For Assis Brasil, it was Chico Buarque and Paulo Ponte's 1975 musical, *Gota d'Água* (a version of the Medea story set in a Brazilian favela) that proved to be a crucial intertext in his novel.

Lorna Hardwick turns to translation (in the broadest sense) in Chapter 5, theorizing it as a 'relationship of exchange, resistance, and interpenetration'. Examining literature that has emerged at, and made an impression on, periods of radical transition, Hardwick focuses on novels by the German writer, Christa Wolf (*Medea: Stimmen* from 1996) and South African author, Zakes Mda (whose *Ways of Dying* was published one year earlier), to demonstrate the multivalent use of myth in fiction. These writers, Hardwick argues, acknowledge myth's capacity to offer distance from a painful history which enables critique of that past, while simultaneously observing myth's capacity to repress.

Giorgio Amitrano turns to Japanese literature in his chapter, illuminating the use of the Oedipus myth in *Umibe no Kafuka* (*Kafka on the Shore;* 2002) by prize-winning novelist Murakami Haruki. Tracing a more extensive historical lineage of Greek myth in Japanese fiction, dating back to the second half of the nineteenth century, Amitrano reveals the ways in which ancient Greece came to be seen as a model of civilization and a founding myth for democracy in Japan. This exploration includes analysis of important works by Yano Ryūkei, Mishima Yukio and Kurahashi Yumiko which engage with Greek myth, drama, and even the ancient novel.

The next chapter turns the volume's gaze away, temporarily, from literary fiction to the small screen and HBO's highly acclaimed television series *The Wire* (2002–2008). Adam Ganz demonstrates that *The Wire* has a more complex relationship with Greek myth, epic and tragedy than has been recognized. The connection between the two was signposted by the series' creator, David Simon, but as Ganz argues, this dialogue pervades the show to such an extent that it features in its exploration of the US constitution, civic community, ancient and contemporary heroism and societal forces no less implacable than the ancient Greek gods.

Fiona Macintosh's chapter brings us back to literary fiction, as she examines Canadian poet and novelist Theresa Kishkan's *A Man in a Distant Field* (2004). Arguing for a bifurcated reception of Homer's *Odyssey* alongside that most influential of modern engagements with Homeric epic, James Joyce's *Ulysses*, Macintosh reveals the ways in which this dual dialogue enables Kishkan to reflect on Ireland's brutal history of the nineteenth and early twentieth centuries, while also figuring it as a complex, composite place with multiple voices and manifold agendas. In an instance of meta-reception, Kishkan's protagonist undertakes his own form of classical reception by translating the *Odyssey*. The process of doing so helps him salvage some meaning out of the chaos of his own life, as he grows to recognize correspondences between his life and that of the ancient hero.

Chapter 9 sees Anna Ljunggren turn to Viktor Pelevin's novel, *Shlem uzhasa* (*The Helmet of Horror*), published in Russian in 2005, and in English the following year. The novel takes the form of an internet chat, with the online 'thread' recreating Ariadne's thread in the Minotaur's labyrinth. The anonymity that can be fostered in these new virtual communities is embodied in the theme of masking, which creates a link between anonymity and carnival, and enhances the novel's submerged myth of the Minotaur.

The following chapter focuses on Bernhard Schlink's 2006 novel *Die Heimkehr* (*Homecoming*), with Sebastian Matzner arguing that the prominence of the *Odyssey* within the novel should be seen as a staged failure rather than as the accidental deficiency that many critics perceived it to be at the time of publication. Matzner draws on multiple Odyssean intertexts (including those by Theodor Adorno and Max Horkheimer, as well as Schlink's own earlier work) to show how the perceived narrative shortcomings created by the excessive presence of Odyssean models highlight the problematic nature of the 'mythical turn' in modern fiction, particularly in (dangerously?) comforting redemptive narratives of the German nation in the most recent stages of *Vergangenheitsbewältigung*.

Edith Hall's chapter similarly focuses on the Germany of the Second World War by its exploration of Jonathan Littell's 2006 novel *Les Bienveillantes* (*The Kindly Ones*). Hall argues that Greek myth in this work of 'docufiction' operates both as a hermeneutic tool for exploring psychological motivation and as a framing device to control the horror of recalled reality, while ultimately showing that its abuse in imperial propagandist self-fashioning caused Greek myth to have played all too real a part in motivating history. Two myths – the hounding of Orestes by the Erinyes, and the erotic self-fixation of Narcissus – shape the narrative of Littell's novel at every turn.

Efrossini Spentzou examines Isidoros Zourgos' *Aidonopita* (*A Nightingale's Pie*) from 2008 in Chapter 12. The novel focuses on a much earlier period of war – that of the nineteenth-century Greek War of Independence – as seen through the eyes of an American Philhellene. As Spentzou argues, Zourgos offers an anti-heroic reading of the foundational epics of Greek identity, which exposes the colonizing myths surrounding modern Greece and denies any complacent narratives of belonging, thereby encouraging reassessment of conflicts between east and west.

Margaret Reynolds turns to Australia and two twenty-first-century works that reflect on local violence and the impact of war through the lens of Homer's *Iliad* and ancient myth: David Malouf's *Ransom* (2009), and Chloe Hooper's *The Tall Man* (2008). Reading each book alongside Simone Weil's famous essay, '*The Iliad*: or, The Poem of Force' (1940), which Malouf has described as being in his mind as he wrote, Reynolds examines the ways in which the Homeric epic can help tell a tale even as horrific as the systemic violence towards Aboriginal peoples and the death in police custody of an innocent man, killed by 'the tall man' of Hooper's tale.

Helen Eastman's contribution explores a new twenty-first-century hero-type, with a feminist as well as a social agenda, that has begun to emerge from the intersection of Greek mythical archetypes and fiction writing. The teenaged female fighting both for her family and for the values of her civilization, modelled on the figure of Antigone, can be seen in Joydeep Roy-Bhattacharya's 2012 novel *The Watch*, set in contemporary Afghanistan, and Suzanne Collins' *The Hunger Games* trilogy. Despite their shared engagement with an Antigone archetype, their creative responses to ancient Greek myth are very different, as Eastman demonstrates. In parallel to the kinds of mythopoesis analysed in Rankine's, Perris's, and Hutchins's chapters in particular, *The Hunger Games* engages in mythmaking of a different sort, a temporal rather than cultural kind, with its envisioning of a futuristic dystopia.

Finally, I turn to Dinaw Mengestu's *How to Read the Air* (2010) in order to explore the ways in which this Ethiopian-born American novelist has structured his novel as a 'Telemachy', and in doing so positions himself in a genealogy with a number of other young diaspora writers of his generation. Engaging not only with the *Odyssey* but with earlier Homeric receptions seen in the works of Ralph Ellison and Derek Walcott, Mengestu once more embodies the 'chain of receptions' that has been seen as fundamental to the works of Kishkan, Schlink and Malouf. In these novels, the intervening works can be as influential on the contemporary fiction as the ancient works that they appropriate.

An edited volume such as this gives us the opportunity to work collaboratively to tackle one of the often-cited difficulties of studying 'world literature': its sheer size. Indeed, this is the very solution that Etiemble proposed to the problem of approaching the immensity and the Eurocentrism of 'world literature'.[22] In working together and crossing disciplinary boundaries, we have an opportunity to make a foray into this field; in considering ancient Greek myth in world fiction since 1989, we acknowledge and affirm Auerbach's statement: 'our philological home is the earth: it can no longer be the nation.'[23]

Bibliography

Apter, Emily (2013), *Against World Literature: On the Politics of Untranslatability*. New York: Verso.

Auerbach, Erich (1969 [1952]), 'Philology and *Weltliteratur*', trans. Maire and Edward Said, *Centennial Review*, 13 (1): 1–17.

Auerbach, Erich (1971), *Mimesis: The Representation of Reality in Western Literature*, trans. Willard R. Trask, 3–23. Princeton, NJ: Princeton University Press.

Buescu, Helena Carvalhão (2011), 'Pascale Casanova and the Republic of Letters', in Theo D'haen, David Damrosch and Djelal Kadir (eds), *The Routledge Companion to World Literature*, 126–135. Abingdon: Routledge.

Casanova, Pascale (2004), *The World Republic of Letters*, trans. M. B. DeBevoise. Cambridge, MA: Harvard University Press.

Damrosch, David (2003), *What is World Literature?* Princeton, NJ: Princeton University Press.

Editors (2013), 'World Lite: What is Global Literature?,' *n+1* 17 (Fall) – https://nplusonemag.com/issue-17/the-intellectual-situation/world-lite/

Etiemble, René (1974), 'Faut-il réviser la notion de Weltliteratur?, in *Essais de literature (vraiment) générale*, 15–34. Paris: Gallimard.

Gilroy, Paul (1993), *The Black Atlantic: Modernity and Double Consciousness*. Cambridge, MA: Harvard University Press.

Goethe, Johann Wolfgang von (1850), *Conversations of Goethe with Eckermann and Soret*, 2 vols, trans. John Oxenford. London: Smith, Elder & Co.

Goethe, Johann Wolfgang von (1973), 'Some Passages Pertaining to the Concept of World Literature', in Hans-Joachim Schulz and Philip Rhein (eds), *Comparative Literature: The Early Years*, 3–11. Chapel Hill, NC: University of North Carolina Press.

Hall, Edith (2005), 'Iphigenia and Her Mother at Aulis: A Study in the Revival of a Euripidean Classic', in John Dillon and S. E. Wilmer (eds), *Rebel Women: Staging Ancient Greek Drama Today*, 3–41. London: Methuen.

Hall, Edith (2009), 'Greek tragedy and the politics of subjectivity in recent fiction', *Classical Receptions Journal*, 1 (1): 23–42.

Hall, Stuart (1991), 'Old and New Identities, Old and New Ethnicities', in Anthony D. King (ed.), *Culture, Globalization, and the World-System: Contemporary Conditions for the Representation of Identity*, 41–68. Basingstoke: Macmillan.

Hall, Stuart (1999), 'A Conversation with Stuart Hall', *The Journal of the International Institute* 7 (1) (Fall) – http://hdl.handle.net/2027/spo.4750978.0007.107

Hannerz, Ulf (2006), 'Two Faces of Cosmopolitanism: Culture and Politics', *Dinámicas interculturales*, 7: 5–29.

Moretti, Franco (2000) 'Conjectures on World Literature', *New Left Review*, 1 (Jan–Feb): 54–68.

Park, Sowon S. (2015), 'The Adaptive Comparative', *Comparative Critical Studies*, 12 (2): 183–196.

Reynolds, Matthew, Mohamad-Salah Omri and Ben Morgan (2015), 'Introduction – Comparative Criticism: Histories and Methods', *Comparative Critical Studies*, 12 (2): 147–159.

Spivak, Gayatri Chakrovorty (2003), *Death of a Discipline*. New York: Columbia University Press.

Unsworth, Barry (2002), *The Songs of the Kings*. London: Hamish Hamilton.

Weitz, Hans-J. (1987), '"Weltliteratur" zuerst bei Weiland', *Arcadia*, 22: 206–208.

Young, Robert J.C. (2011), 'World Literature and Postcolonialism', in Theo D'haen, David Damrosch and Djelal Kadir (eds), *The Routledge Companion to World Literature*, 213–222. Abingdon: Routledge.

1

From Anthropophagy to Allegory and Back: A Study of Classical Myth and the Brazilian Novel

Patrice Rankine

Let it be remembered that events narrated in this chronicle – full of veracity, albeit lacking in brilliance – took place during the worst years of the military dictatorship and the most rigid censorship of the press. There was a hidden reality, a secret country that didn't get into the news. The newsrooms of newspapers and radio and television stations found themselves restricted to covering generally unexpected events. Their editorial pages were reduced to unconditional praise for the system of government and those who governed.

Jorge Amado[1]

In the epigraph above, the narrator of *The War of the Saints*, written by Jorge Leal Amado de Faria (Jorge Amado) in 1988, sets his narrative – 'lacking in brilliance' but filled (ostensibly) with the stuff of social and cultural narrative – against a backdrop of the 'hidden reality', the 'secret country that didn't even get into the news'. In the passage that follows the epigraph, the narrator goes on to elaborate on the 'total prohibition of any reportage that carried the slightest allusion to the daily imprisonments, torture, political murders, and violation of human rights'.[2] Historical events under the regime remained outside of the official accounts of newspapers. The narrator of *The War of the Saints* seems to implicitly criticize journalists for their reportage of 'recipes', 'poems, ballads, odes, sonnets by classical poets, and stanzas from *The Lusiads*' (that is, from Luís Vaz de Camões' 1572 Homeric-Virgilian epic of the Portuguese colonial conquests), and yet the narrative is no weightier, politically potent or consequential than those topics. In fact, given the repeated – though subtle – references to classical stories such as Theseus, or to figures like Aphrodite and Menelaus, the novel might be read in epic terms alongside the Portuguese *The Lusiads*, rather than as an insignificant, quotidian tale. Nevertheless, as is the case with literature under many repressive regimes throughout history,[3] the façade of myth and fairytale – the allegory – to some extent conceals the potential subversiveness of the material.

The War of the Saints privileges cultural over political accounts. At the same time, the third-person omniscient narrator's complaint masks the extent to which the cultural practices reveal a great deal about the military dictatorship and its aftermath. Herein lies the paradox of Amado's story. *The War of the Saints*, set approximately ten years before its publication, seemingly does no more to reveal the mysteries of the 'hidden reality' or 'secret country' where 'strikes, demonstrations, picketing, protests, mass movements, and guerrilla attacks' occur than would other books and articles published during the period, texts for which the narrator hints his disapproval. The story of the clash between the folk cultures 'on the ground', as it were, and the Catholic, national narrative of *ordo e progresso* – 'order and progress' – the slogan emblazoned in the globe on Brazil's flag – holds a key to the hidden, secret truth. The 'war' between local and national culture, or between culture and politics, itself occurs in the aftermath of the military regime, although Amado – somewhat uniquely – succeeded in advancing culture over politics even before 1989. Indeed, the difficulty of foregrounding political themes under the regime is one reason why classical myth was a primary mode of expression in the Brazilian novel before 1989: as an allegorical cover for real events.

The status of Brazilian public discourse in 1989 is apparent in the clash in *The War of the Saints*: a clash between, on the one side, the Yoruba goddess Yansan and the practices that celebrate her and other *orixás*, the African 'saints' that came to Brazil along with the slaves;[4] and, on the other side, accepted, state-sanctioned, Catholic practices embodied in saints like Paul, Lazarus and Barbara. *The War of the Saints* has many of the features of other Brazilian novels written after 1989, such as J. G. Noll's *Hotel Atlantico* (1989), as well as *The Discovery of America by the Turks* (1994), another novel by Amado with which I am concerned in this essay.

Even before the military dictatorship that began in 1964,[5] these features included an essentially apolitical narrative focus because Brazilian authoritarian rule has not historically been confined to the dictatorship, but arrived as early as the birth of the Republic in 1890.[6] After 1964, however, military tactics became professionalized, everyday instances rather than exceptional or temporary responses to crises.

The second feature of Brazilian fiction after 1989, along with the continued apolitical nature of commercially successful books, is the retreat of classical myth from monumental to multivalent status. The longer arch of twentieth-century Brazilian fiction helps to contextualize this claim. In 1922, Brazilian modernists declared anthropophagy (*omophagia*) as a literary mode during the Week of Modern Art; Oswaldo de Andrade's *Anthropophagia Manifesto* (1928) was one of the key documents to emerge. Brazilian artists would come to see the country, which was founded in 1500 in competition with native inhabitants who were mythically purported to eat the human flesh of their defeated enemies, as having a native artistic mode of consuming material from outside. Brazilians would become themselves by consuming the forms, stories and styles of expression of others. The blending of these was to be Brazil's unique contribution to humanity. Classical myth would be only one of many outside influences to be symbolically eaten. Between 1964 and 1989, however, there are several examples of its centrality in providing a cover for political and cultural discussion, ranging from Chico Buarque's *Gota de Água* (1975) to Marcel Camus' 1959 film, *Orfeu Negro* (revisited in 1999 through Carlos Diegues' *Orfeu*). This monumental classicism allowed culture to rise to the level of national politics, and Amado was bolder in his use of local cultural practices, such as African religious retentions in Brazil, over classical myth, although remnants of the classics remain.[7] It is worth noting that many of Amado's more socialist-leaning novels were published prior to 1964.[8] For writers working under the regime, such as Moacyr Scliar, the consumption of the Greco-Roman classics would seem at times wholesale rather than involve taking the form of an integration into the whole being that comes with anthropophagy. After 1989, Brazilian novelists do not abandon a diet of classical vitals, but the novels with which I am concerned here do appear to return to a deployment of classical myth alongside other cultural influences more like the pre-1964 model of anthropophagy.

If an apolitical narrative and the role of the classics in it were two features of the Brazilian novel, a third aspect that continues after 1989 – perhaps in heightened fashion – would be the degree to which the stories upset the conventions of the traditional *Bildungsroman*. The protagonists of the novels discussed in this chapter might each be called anti-heroes, or at least picaresque. This description applies to the hero of Scliar's *The Centaur in the Garden* (1980), whose animalistic nature leads him to infidelity and other foibles. The heroes of Amado's novels might be called misogynistic, and they project troublesome Brazilian norms in terms of their treatment of women. In the eyes of Amado's narrator, however, these characters are part of a moral environment in which virtue and vice are not opposites but are on a continuum. Amado points to another set of metaphysical realities, embodied in the African *orixás* and their human manifestations, in which ethics do not map onto behaviour in expected ways. These metaphysical realities give rise to the African practices – folk forms that overturn the norms of the Catholic Church – to prevail in *The War of the Saints*.

The hero of the Brazilian narrative is Odyssean in the sense that he is on a journey towards an existential home. In truly American or New World fashion, the Brazilian hero is constantly attempting to establish a new life in an unprecedented environment, but the pull of the past is the god that threatens to unravel things. In the case of the centaur in Scliar's novel, the hero is part of an immigrant Jewish family who escaped the pogroms in Russia only to face ghettoization in the New World because of their otherness. After 1989, the picaresque hero is still present: the protagonist of Noll's *Hotel Atlantico* wanders somewhat aimlessly throughout Brazil pursuing his career as an actor. In some regards, it might be argued that the hero of *The War of the Saints* is the African goddess Yansan, who arrives in Brazil in many forms as early as 1500. The narrator of *The Discovery of America by the Turks*, meanwhile, offers a story of exploration of America that is as yet untold: that of the arrival of 'Turks' in the early 1900s. There is a heightened sense of freedom in the post-1989 novels, but the question remains: freedom to do or to be what?

Historical Background: The Brazilian Military Dictatorship and 1989

Repressive political regimes in twentieth-century Brazil, both before the dictatorship and after, needed strong ideology to impose their rule. In *Freedoms Given, Freedoms Won*, Kim Butler characterizes the rise of Brazilian modernity and its political ideology in the following way:

> The choice of the word 'progress' in the Republican national motto reflects the roots of the Brazilian elite in the scientific ideology of the nineteenth century, steeped in the philosophical traditions of the Enlightenment, Darwinism, and Positivism. Darwinist science had also introduced the notions of biological and environmental determinism, both of which has serious negative implications for a tropical nation whose population was largely descended from what were believed to be lesser races.[9]

In place of indigenous and pre-modern cultures, Brazilian modernity would ostensibly offer the 'scientific ideology' generated by nineteenth-century industrialization and progressive thinking. Native Americans and slaves were not modern selves, as the observations of such writers as Louis Agassiz made clear in his 1895 *Journey to Brazil.* Nevertheless, Agassiz and others would impose the Enlightenment thinking, Darwinism and Positivism of the time upon them. As the stereotype went, tropical peoples might be primitive, but their quaint cultural contributions – which early twentieth-century Brazilian sociologist Gilberto Freyre, educated in America at Columbia University under Franz Boas, celebrated – added to the national culture.[10]

Butler shows the ways that this discourse, present before and after the dictatorship, helped shape Brazilian culture for former slaves. As Butler puts it, 'the poorer states and the military were not the only groups dissatisfied with the Republic. There was little opportunity for meaningful political involvement by the middle and lower classes, the illiterate, women, workers – in general, people without economic power'.[11] Various forms of repression emerged.[12] The regime repressed labour movements,[13] and the repression of cultural, political and ideological difference can be felt in Butler's poignant assertion that during the early Republic, 'the mere fact of being Afro-Brazilian was, by extension, antipatriotic'.[14] Ethnicity was accepted because it made Brazil unique, but only to the extent that the regime could tolerate it.[15] The African retentions that, by the early twenty-first century, would draw tourists from all over the world to Brazil, were heavily repressed in the period leading into the military dictatorship and during its height. Names that would come to be known worldwide as Brazilian cultural icons – Gilberto Gil, Caetano Veloso, Chico Buarque – were inimical to the regime. As the narrator puts it in *The War of the Saints*, 'they were the top names in *tropicalismo*, a musical movement to which seditious movements had been attributed by the dictatorship, stamped as degenerate, criminal, subversive art'.[16] In the novel, a staged carnival celebration that a French director films in Pelourinho, a popular historic district in Salvador, clearly echoes Marcel Camus' Oscar-winning film and the controversy surrounding it: the controversial idea of a foreigner trading on Brazilian culture; questions of what is Brazilian, given that *Orfeu Negro* might in some arguments be called a French film; and the role of artists and citizens of African descent in the movie, particularly since it was shot in the poor ghettoes or *favelas* of Brazil and capitalizes on the poverty in those neighborhoods to point up a narrative of the 'noble savage'.[17] These markers of identity were prevalent before the rise of the military dictatorship; they were secondary to a national, political and economic identity during the regime, and after 1989, they reemerge.

It is worth noting, therefore, the extent to which aspects of the repressive framework of twentieth-century Brazilian politics shifted after 1989. The first, to recapitulate, was the lack of opportunity for former slaves, for the lower classes, or even for labour, ironically, to make progress. The regime had celebrated the 'integrated theory of natural sciences',[18] which set Europe in Hegelian dialectic against its primitive counterparts: indigenous Americans, Africans and other non-European groups. In contrast, sublimated phenomena return after 1989, as can be seen in the role of the supernatural. While 'God played no role' under the scientific enlightenment,[19] gods certainly would proliferate not only in the pantheon of Yoruba culture, as in *The War of the Saints*, but also in practices that emerge from outside of Europe, such as Islam, evident in *The Discovery of America by the Turks*. The narrator of *The War of the Saints* invokes the violence, torture, and oppression of the military regime. Hundreds of people disappeared, and bodies were dismembered to hide the atrocities.[20]

Classical Myth as Allegory for Cultural Expression in Brazilian Literature before 1989: *The Centaur in the Garden*

> ...in a new society there is room for everyone, even someone with horses' hooves.
>
> Moacyr Scliar, *The Centaur in the Garden*, 45

Moacyr Scliar's *The Centaur in the Garden* is emblematic of the interaction between national identity – 'order and progress' – and its subcultures under the military dictatorship. Similar to the post-1989 works I have discussed, Scliar's novel is, on the surface, apolitical. Nevertheless, Scliar recognizes that writing is in itself essentially a political act.[21] Unlike Amado and Noll's novels, however, classical myth in *The Centaur in the Garden* predominates over other cultural forms, just as we have seen in other literary genres of the period. The anti-hero in this case is a centaur, and his adventure is a quest for normalcy despite the pressures that difference causes. The protagonist Guedali's optimism that 'in a new society there is room for everyone' is somewhat misplaced, notwithstanding what seems to be measured optimism regarding Brazil on the part of his creator.[22]

Classical myth is an opaque rather than transparent way to deal with difference, which in this case is Jewish identity. It becomes evident early on in the novel that the classical, mythological character of the centaur is analogous to Jewish – and immigrant – identity.[23] The narrator's father, Leon Tartakovsky, 'saw the Russian Jews living happily in faraway regions in South America; he saw cultivated fields, modest but comfortable homes, agricultural schools' (9). In other words, the hope of advancement in the New World, that the richness of the land sustains life, calls the family to Brazil, a place that promises a 'new society' of progress, opportunity and equal treatment under the law. Guedali's family is agricultural, but the city provides the greatest opportunities for assimilation. Differences remain, however, even in the urban centres of the New World. The myths that hound Jews in Russia follow them to Brazil:

> During the Revolution of 1923 tales were told of a mysterious creature, half man and half horse, who would invade the Legalist camps at night, grab a poor young recruit, take him to the riverbank and cut off his head.
>
> (26)

Guedali recognizes that he is implicated in all of these stories. He is a centaur, and as a Jew, he is seen as different, grotesque and other. Classical myth opaquely covers the difference and allows exploration of the implications of otherness. Guedali's Jewishness is aligned with guilt: of the stories he hears of Jews in Russia who are rumoured to be centaurs, he claims, 'It wasn't me. I wasn't born until later' (26). Yet, at the same time, his mother gave birth to him, 'an herbaceous creature' (11); at his birth, the midwife 'understands that I need green stuff, and mixes finely chopped lettuce leaves in with the milk' (11).[24]

In place of the reality of cultural difference is the cover of myth on the one hand, and the positivism of science on the other. Enlightened thinking is ostensibly everywhere a factor in the translation of the Greek myths of centaurs into the modern frame. Genetics, for example, are a feature in the narrative. Guedali's sister does not show the signs of being a centaur (that is, a Jew) because of dominant and recessive genes. While Guedali spends his early years concealing his identity as a centaur, his sister marries a 'lawyer from Curitiba' (48).[25] Later in the narrative, Guedali's son is born. There is no indication of his being a centaur: 'Nature was unkind to you, but you have struggled and won' (122). In contrast to his sister, Guedali learns early on that difference is not rewarded in the Brazil of the early twentieth century because cultural difference is thought to stand in the way of national economic progress. The Brazilian nation competes on an international front, but innovation still seems to come from outside. Guedali travels to Spain, where surgical advancements enable the removal of visible signs of his difference (93). (Spain is a curious site of otherness, given its own dictatorship, but space here will not allow for speculation.) Within this framework, remnants of Brazilian cultural lore seem shameful and backwards. The farmer Zeca Fagundes' stories of the women on his ranch having sex with sheep parallels Freyre's stories of the Portuguese and black Africans (69).[26] It is not accidental that during this period Guedali meets his first blacks, a *rara avis* in a city like Curitiba (58). These are the differences that at the beginning of the twentieth century are said to mark Brazilian identity; under the dictatorship, they will be carefully managed.

Given the apolitical nature of the narrative, the political backdrop of those years at times peeks out in curious ways.[27] How the narrator marks time is noteworthy, 'the Revolution of 1923' (above) being an example already present in the family's years in the Old World. In Brazil, Guedali uses the national narrative as a benchmark for his own experiences, but he goes no further in commenting on the political realities. Dating his time in the circus as a young man to the 1930s, he comments that 'I must have passed through São Borja about the time they were burying President Gertúlio Vargas. Of course at the time I knew nothing at all of these matters. I only galloped on' (67). This brings us to the 1950s. The narrative is told in retrospect, once the narrator has shed external signs of his difference. (Hooves remain, but special shoes that Guedali obtained in Spain allow him to 'pass' as fully human.) Thus the events told in it primarily precede the military dictatorship and take place during the period of the Republic. When the narrative does turn to the dictatorship, the incursion of politics into the cultural realm is evident: 'Everyone was discussing the political situation – it was 1964' (131). Politics intrude on the business plans of Guedali and his upwardly mobile friends, who are building a development: 'two days before the actual construction was to begin, President João Goulart was overthrown' (136). Despite the severance of culture from politics, something rings hollow with the assertion that 'in the new society there is room for everyone'. It is difficult to believe the narrator's retrospective assertion: 'Yes, I can tell everything' (5).

The mixed narrative resolution of *The Centaur in the Garden* hints at the dissatisfaction – the *saudade* or 'longing', accompanied by sadness, that becomes part of Brazilian cultural expression – with a culture primarily severed from the political realm. Guedali is able to assimilate, in the end: 'Our appearance is absolutely normal' (1). Nevertheless, psychological torment is at least in part the reason for Guedali's dalliance with the wife of one of his upwardly mobile friends, one of the young, urban leftists that they befriend (110).[28] Even though the surgery in Spain to hide his difference is successful, Guedali and his wife, Tita, cannot escape the memory of difference (107). Guedali's love for Tita cannot be normal, given that he is a centaur: 'Although she doesn't say anything, we know that deep down she considers our relationship something grotesque, even sinful' (78). Tita's pain remains: 'I'm dead, Guedali, dead' (125).[29]

His 'Jewish paranoia' persists, despite the fact that he keeps telling himself that '*Everything is all right now*' (4). The narrator ultimately juxtaposes the notion that in the new society there is room for everyone with the Marxism that fuels the neoliberal nation. Although Marx admired the Elgin Marbles and classical mythology (44), he recognized religion as the opiate of the people. The myth of the centaur reveals that *difference* (being visibly other), and not religion, is actually the opiate.

Brazilian Novels after 1989: *Hotel Atlantico* (1989)

One reviewer of J. G. Noll's *Hotel Atlantico*, Richard A. Preto-Rodas, writes of the novel that 'one can hardly imagine a less "Brazilian" work amid such alienation and solitude, where even the climate is generally presented as unbearably dank and gray'.[30] Indeed Preto-Rodas rightly juxtaposes perceptions of Brazilian culture – as full of life, joyous, hopeful – with the bleak, aimless environment of Noll's narrative. Notwithstanding the cultural repression of the military regime, Brazilians remained a hopeful and joyous people, and the image that the country projected internationally was one of joy, *alegria*. The message of the regime, moreover, was that of a racial paradise, a place of 'order and progress'. Accepted cultural forms closely monitored by the regime give a sense of pluralism, and classical myth provided an acceptable analogue for allegory and opposition, as we have seen in *The Centaur in the Garden*.

Even with the anti-hero as a persistent aspect of the Brazilian novel, Noll's protagonist is especially morbid. The nameless narrator, a washed-up actor from soap operas, whom people recognize from television but who has done nothing substantial since his younger years, meets one defeat after another. Even his unexpected trysts are horrifying and end sadly. Lisa Shaw links this narrative to the absurd reality projected in Brazil's *telenovelas*, the television serial dramas prevalent throughout Latin America.[31] The protagonist faces defeat at every turn, despite his resilience.

The narrative opens with the character checking into a hotel where someone has just been murdered; at the end of the book he is in the hotel after which the novel is named. In between, he is on trains, cars, buses and in a hospital. The prevalence of public spaces in the narrative is ironic, given the apolitical nature of the novel.[32] Whereas *The Centaur in the Garden* uses the military dictatorship as a backdrop against which the narrative takes place, time in *Hotel Atlantico* is disjointed and without contemporary markers. In one of the protagonist's attempts to flee a foe, imagined or real, his means of escape also moves the imagination out of the present: 'I picked up a book to calm myself down. It was a bestseller set during the Second World War. I read the first page, and then looked around: the man with the dark glasses had left the bookshop. I went back to my book, relieved' (21). Although he is often confused about where his wanderings are taking him, in his book he reads about a British spy, who 'begins the story by going into a church in Paris, and in this church he thanks God for the grace of living in a time when it is clear who it is that one must fight against: the enemy' (22). In contrast to the Catholic British spy, the protagonist does not know against whom he is fighting. Prior to this, he has met an American woman who, leaving behind a broken marriage, has come to Brazil in search of pre-Columbian civilizations. Although the protagonist and his new travel companion clearly connect – they hold hands on the bus as night falls after a day of conversation – he discovers that she is numbing the pain of her life with barbiturates (20). The protagonist puts his book down to see that a crowd has gathered around the bus, as the woman has overdosed and is dead. Given that he was the last person seen with her, he runs from the scene, afraid he will be suspected of her murder.

These kinds of mishaps make up the entire novel. In the opening hotel scene, the protagonist draws the desk clerk into his room and has sex with her (10), but any fantasy of pursing a fulfilling relationship falls flat because of the narrator's ongoing existential crisis (11–12). The reader later learns of the narrator's earlier marriage and his infertility, which led his wife to leave him (92–95). Some time after, he consummates a relationship with a traveling actress, Amanda ('lovable one'), a young mother whom he chooses exclusively over a potential *ménage à trois* (82–87). Amanda eventually leaves him to continue her travels. Later, Amanda's daughter Cris returns, now in her late teens (106). The potential of an inappropriate romantic relationship with Cris is a constant undercurrent (e.g. 114, 117, 132), but the narrator in fact poses as Cris' father and guides her toward a successful acting career.

If classical myth was the central trope in *The Centaur in the Garden*, classical analogues have retreated to the background in *Hotel Atlantico*. They are still present, but they are more of an integrated aspect of the environment than allegorical. It might be argued that the status of classical myth has returned to its early twentieth-century modernist form, that of organic consumption and anthropophagy. A few examples should suffice. Early in the novel, after the woman has died on the bus, the protagonist runs away from the scene and is able to hitch a ride to Santa Catarina with a man called Nelson, who is soon to marry his fiancée there. Nelson is the protagonist's 'ferryman across one more river' (27), the novel's equivalent of classical mythology's ferryman, Charon, who guides the souls of the dead across the River Styx. The reference heightens the sense of danger for the knowing reader, but even without it the narrator's 'relief' is misplaced. Indeed, it soon becomes clear that something is amiss with Nelson and his friend, although it is never revealed exactly what. The protagonist believes he overhears the men insisting that he must be killed since he has witnessed (or suspects) some crime. Once again, he takes flight from the situation.

The reference to the ferryman is consistent with other classical fixtures in the novel. They are sparse and not necessarily fixed. In a later passage, the narrator's distress at his lover Amanda's departure leads to a description that calls to mind the plague from Sophocles' *Oedipus the King*. Giving himself over to emptiness, he does little but sunbathe, and he imagines himself as a sad child in a photo. The resultant sunburn brings on an existential sickness similar to the plague:

> At first, when I came around, all burnt and cut, I had full view of a queue on a huge open stretch of ground, that's right, an enormous queue of people with a suppliant look in their eyes, in rags, some with wounds like me, wrecks of people, children were leaping about over imaginary obstacles, a shrill gibberish issuing from their mouths that none of the adults seemed to have any will to contemplate, for it was this children's activity that attracted my attention most strikingly.
>
> (88)

The narrator's description of the plague-like scene sparks the nostalgic recollection of childhood, 'the little coloured kid in the print from my childhood' who smiled and made him smile: 'I decided to give that smiling a go too, a manic smile, smiling at everything and nothing' (87). In this case as in others, classical myth figures for cultural experiences that are at once collective and personal. Oedipus the child is exposed and thus might not have experienced the childhood bliss to which the depressed protagonist hearkens back. The child suppliants in the Oedipal vignette overwhelm the narrator's psyche: 'I don't know, that nonsensical activity of the children, that running about, that fitful shouting while this grave sometimes descends upon mankind, that was what attracted me, helped me come out of my stupor' (88). The children buoy him up. The narrative in some ways rights the wrong of the Oedipus story by introducing the *Sehnsucht nach Kindheit*, the pristine moment of childhood to which all can return but Oedipus. In a different way from *The Centaur in the Garden*, *Hotel Atlantico* fragments the classical presence so that it is never whole, never overwhelms the timeless, placeless and aimless narrative.

The War of the Saints (1993)

The narrative of *Hotel Atlantico* is without many cultural markers. As Preto-Rodas indicates, the novel is not particularly 'Brazilian'; in some regards, the existential narrative could have taken place at any place or at any time. This is not the case with *The War of the Saints*, however, a narrative that depends on cultural experiences repressed in the main prior to 1989. The novel is ostensibly about Adalgisa and Manela and 'a few other descendants of the love between the Spaniard Francisco Romero Pérez y Pérez and Andreza da Anunciação'. These two characters are in fact part of a much larger ensemble of inhabitants of Salvador da Bahia, and the love between the Spaniard and the Brazilian unearths the deep cultural miscegenation – and the inherent conflicts in it – that the regime coopts under the guise of 'order and progress'. The occasion that sets in motion the story of Adalgisa and Manela – and all of the other stories in the novel – is the arrival to Brazil of a statue of Santa Barbara Yansan, herself a melange of a Yoruba *orixá* (Yansan) and Catholic saint (Barbara). Because of Yansan's link to erotic love, Amado also invokes Aphrodite as a mythic parallel. In the novel, a German monk, Dom Maximiliano, who serves as director of the Museum of Sacred Art in Salvador, has written an important book on the statue: 'He'd developed a breathtakingly daring thesis concerning the origin and the artist of this famed piece of religious sculpture' (3). Maximiliano and others await the arrival of the statue, but the plot shifts when the statue disappears right from the outset of the novel. Journalists, one of whom has a longstanding opposition to Maximiliano, feed on the fodder of the statue's disappearance, a plotline that elicits the narrator's lament about the emptiness of the news during the years of the dictatorship (already tackled in the epigraph). In truth, however, the statue is not missing; in an instance of magical realism, Santa Barbara Yansan has wandered off to spend time with her flock, the people of Salvador.

Although for Amado classical myth is a feature of the narrative, he is more interested in Yansan as a cultural artifact. The narrator weaves classical myth into his twisting tale that is 'intricate and multiple, as are the places and times where the yarn of life unrolls' (90). The yarn analogy is natural and does not have to immediately call to mind the story of Theseus and the Minotaur, where the thread that Ariadne gives the hero enables him to escape the labyrinth after slaughtering the bull. The narrator picks up on the analogy, however, on 'the day before the scheduled opening of the exhibit of religious art', when 'events began to pile up, to bump into each other, apparently disconnected, rendering the existing entanglement all the more confusing, a veritable labyrinth' (112). The story is of a collective, not of one particular individual; of a culture that emerges 'from the depths of the slave quarters' (5).

Although there are many strands to the narrative, the main plots involve the repressed Adalgisa and her niece, Manela, whom she tries to raise with similar Catholic rigidity after the girl's parents die in an accident; Dom Maximiliano, the expert on the statue, whose already precarious reputation hinges on its return; and a priest who is in love with Paulina, one of the dancers involved in the staged carnival. Adalgisa believes that her Catholicism precludes the enjoyment of certain aspects of life, whereas the worship of Yansan calls for the incorporation of all fleshly and spiritual experiences. Adalgisa's unhappy marriage is figured in classical terms as the worship of Hymen (152). The painful and unpleasant loss of her virginity parallels the near crucifixion of Dom Maximiliano because of the disappearance of the statue of Yansan. Vulgate Latin marks his imminent demise: *consummatum est*, 'it is finished', the words of Christ on the cross, which Maximiliano now applies to himself. The hybridity, syncretism and miscegenation evident in the tales run counter to at least one character's beliefs, those of Dom Rudolph, who asserts that it was most urgent 'to separate the wheat from the chaff, good from evil, and white from black, to impose limits, to draw boundaries' (67). Rudolph advances a view of cultural purity that would mean the separation of Aphrodite from Yansan, but the narrator is well aware of the overlaps between the two and the reality of cultural syncretism. Yansan is so real and present that the statue in fact comes to life. Morphing from statue to spirit, she inhabits the body of Adalgisa, who has previously been sexually cold. Through Yansan, Adalgisa learns that the all things are good even though she previously scorned the Afro-Brazilian religion of *candomblé*.

Given the parallels between the personal repression of characters and the repressiveness of the regime under which they lived, it is no wonder that the climax of the novel is figured in military terms, as a battle. As the book builds up to the clash, we learn of an array of forces on the side of cultural hybridity, with not only Adalgisa but in all 'six Yansans had appeared at the *caruru* in the market in the lower city, all of them fatally beautiful' (314). On the side of Catholicism and the moral homogeneity and rectitude that it seems to promote in the novel, the narrator hints at the failure of the Church to address the needs of the poor, the politically oppressed, and those who were emblematic of difference (blacks, women) in Brazil during the dictatorship.[33]

In the end, all parties learn their lesson. Adalgisa embraces the nature of Yansan. Dom Maximiliano is absolved with the return of the statue. And the priest learns that renouncing marriage might not necessarily mean renouncing sex and physical love – such is the *jeito* or the 'style' of Brazilian anti-heroes and their narrative resolutions. Yansan returns to her form as a statue and relieves Dom Maximiliano of certain doom. Her triumph in the *Battle of the Saints* marks the victory of hybridity over cultural nationalism, and even to some extent the real over the symbolic. At the same time, the presence of the supernatural is ever a factor in Amado's novels. Within this context, classical myth is still present, although it retreats from a dominant place to that of one of many possibilities.

The Discovery of America by the Turks (1994)

As its title makes clear, the book opens with the surprising revelation that America was discovered by the Turks. Previous accounts, it is suggested, are contentious: 'The Spaniards parry with other papers, other testimonials, so who'll ever know who's right? Certificates have been falsified; testimonials have been bought with vile metal' (18). Behind the facetious comments of the narrator is the reality that cultural narratives themselves are constructed, such that those who come after can seldom 'know who's right'. Dominant narratives of conquest, such as that of the Spanish and Portuguese, repress other stories. The tale of the Turks is one such narrative. The reader soon discovers that this is not a serious narrative of war and conquest. The pursuit of God, gold and glory, in this case, serves little national or collective function. The story is of Raduan Murad, 'a fugitive from justice for vagrancy and gambling', and Jamil Bichara, a Syrian merchant. Jamil seeks a sexual conquest, that of marrying Adma, the unattractive daughter of a successful storeowner, having been persuaded by Raduan that she will elevate his status and wealth.[34] While Jamil seeks to serve Allah and gain wealth, the Devil is at work to undo all good works:

> None of the characters gathered at the bar, at the whorehouse on the upper floor of the living quarters could have guessed that all that talking and activity was part of the scheme put together by Shaitan, the Islamic devil.
>
> (41–42)

Classical myth plays little active part in the narrative, although there are passing references throughout. Jamil, for example, knows that Allah watches over him when he 'met and gathered to his bosom the capricious Jove, a wild and lusty half-breed' (27). This woman is the lover of a colonel, Anuar Maron, who 'had set up a house for Jove'. When Jamil sleeps with the whore – who for all intents and purposes belongs to Anuar Maron – the colonel looks the other way, as it were. The analogy of a woman from the red-light district with the king of the gods conveys an irony characteristic of Brazilian literature, the profundity of which requires an astute reader. In another passage, Adma is referred to as a *virago*, which recalls the sanctified treatment of virginity in *The War of the Saints*. The Catholic Church preserves a reverence for the virgin that is paralleled in the classical context; names like Procópia recall the naming of slaves after the classical fashion. Outside of these passing references, however, there is not much that is recognizable from classical myth, yet Classics remains integrated into the narrative in the style of the modernist anthropophagy.

What is present is the sovereignty of the narrator, who like a bard is able to weave together a story from all the material available and choose its outcome. Since Raduan Murad had told the story of Adma's virginity and her wealth to both Jamil and a bartender, these men are, comically, in competition for an ugly woman, each unbeknownst to the other. As the narrator puts it, 'the rest fell to God to do, and he did it with magnificence, skill, and speed, as everyone can attest' (75). The bartender accidentally bumps into the girl and beats Jamil to the altar. Whenever Raduan Murad told the story, the 'real and the magical limits of the story of Adma's nuptials, called his listeners' attention to the well-known circumstance that God is a Brazilian' (84).

To conclude, 1989 is not an arbitrary date for a shift in the Brazilian novel, but it is also not conclusive. In some ways, Amado had been a cultural champion before 1989 and had even already gained notoriety at the margins of the Brazilian regime by 1964. Many features of his novels – the piecemeal consumption of many narrative influences, the adventure, the picaresque hero – are present in Noll's *Hotel Atlantico*. Yet these aspects were a factor even before 1989. For *The Centaur in the Garden*, culture – being a centaur – more than religion, was a counter to the regime. But for Amado, irrational aspects of culture, those seemingly running counter to positivism and progress, which he saw in Brazilian Afro-descendent practices, lessened his need for the allegories that classical myth provided Scliar. After 1989, at least in the novels surveyed here, the Classics retreat entirely to the background, consumed and incorporated along with other influences.

Bibliography

Amado, Jorge (1988 [1993]), *The War of the the Saints*. New York: Bantam Books.

Amado, Jorge (1994 [2012]), *The Discovery of America by the Turks*. New York: Penguin Books.

Bartsch, Shadi (1998), *Actors in the Audience: Theatricality and Doublespeak from Nero to Hadrian*. Cambridge, MA: Harvard University Press.

Butler, Kim D. (1998), *Freedoms Given, Freedoms Won: Afro-Brazilians in Post-Abolition São Paulo and Salvador*. New Brunswick, NJ: Rutgers University Press.

Cavalcanti, H. B. (1992), 'Political Cooperation and Religious Repression: Presbyterians under Military Rule in Brazil (1964–1974)', *Review of Religious Research*, 34: 97–116.

Cohen, Youssef (1987), 'Democracy from Above: The Political Origins of Military Dictatorship in Brazil', *World Politics*, 40: 30–54.

Eakin, Marshall (1998), *Brazil: The Once and Future Country*. Basingstoke: Palgrave Macmillan.

Flynn, Peter (1991), '*The Politics of Military Rule in Brazil 1964–85* by Thomas E. Skidmore. Review', *The History Teacher*, 24: 1991.

Freyre, Gilberto (1946), *The Masters and the Slaves: A Study in the Development of Brazilian Civilization*, trans. Samuel Putnam. New York: Knopf.

Hamilton, Russell G. (1967) 'Afro-Brazilian Cults in the Novels of Jorge Amado', *Hispania*, 50 (2): 242–252.

Lindstrom, Naomi (1984), 'Oracular Jewish Tradition in Two Works by Moacyr Scliar', *Luso-Brazilian Review*, 21: 23–33.

Namorato, Luciana Camargo (2006), 'Interview with Moacyr Scliar', *World Literature Today*, 80: 42–45.

Noll, J. G. (1989 [1993]), *Hotel Atlantico*, trans. David Treece. London: Central Books.

Nunes, Maria Luisa (1973), 'The Preservation of African Culture in Brazilian Literature: The Novels of Jorge Amado', *Luso-Brazilian Review*, 10: 86–101.

Pirott-Quintero, Laura E. (2000), 'A Centaur in the Text: Negotiating Cultural Multiplicity in Moacyr Scliar's Novel', *Hispania*, 83: 768–778.

Preto-Rodas, Richard A. (1990), 'Review of *Hotel Atlântico* by João Gilberto Noll', *World Literature Today*, 64 (2) (Spring): 285.

Rudich, Vasily (2013), *Dissidence and Literature Under Nero: The Price of Rhetoricization*. London and New York: Routledge.

Serbin, Kenneth P. (2001), '"Bowling Alone," Bishops' Biographies, and Baptism by Blood: New Views of Progressive Catholicism in Brazil', *Latin American Politics and Society*, 43: 127–141.

Shaw, Lisa (1998), '*Hotel Atlantico* by J. G. Noll; David Treece. Review', *Portuguese Studies*, 14: 294–295.

Smallman, Shawn C. (2000), 'The Professionalization of Military Terror in Brazil, 1945–1964', *Luso-Brazilian Review*, 37: 117–128.

Stam, Robert (1997), *Tropical Multiculturalism: A Comparative History of Race in Brazilian Cinema and Culture*. Durham, NC: Duke University Press.

Vieira, Nelson H. (1989), 'Testimonial Fiction and Historical Allegory: Racial and Political Repression in Jorge Amado's Brazil', *Latin American Literary Review*, 17: 6–23.

Vieira, Nelson H. (1996), '*Descoberta da América pelos Turcos* by Jorge Amado. Review', *World Literature Today* 70: 173–174.

2

Ibrahim Al-Koni's Lost Oasis as Atlantis and His Demon as Typhon

William M. Hutchins

Arab critics typically classify authors by the decade in which they first published. An equally useful classification for outsiders is by the period during which they achieved recognition. For Ibrahim al-Koni – the Tuareg writer who has become a multi-award-winning author of Arabic novels – that period began with 1989. His masterpiece, *al-Majus* (*The Fetishists*), is dated as having been written between 20 December 1989 and 28 December 1990. Alongside ancient Egyptian, Tuareg and Arab myth and folklore, his books show a consistent interest in ancient Greek myths, including those relating to Athena, Echidna, Typhon/Typhoeus, the labyrinth, Atlantis and Odysseus/Ulysses. In this chapter I enquire into the innovative ways in which he invokes these mythologies.

Al-Koni has said that he created his own desert and filled it with his own symbols, archetypes and myths; he added that myth 'is the soul of the desert. A desert without myth is absolute nonexistence. But myth is not a simple collection of symbols'. For him, it is instead the condensed cultural history of the great desert dating back 11,000 years. That ancient culture, however, has only come down to us piecemeal. So he explained: 'My project as a novelist is to actualize it and bring it to life by using myth, which best expresses the word of the desert.' One myth he mentioned in this context is the Tuareg legend of Waw – the lost oasis that appears only to those virtuous travellers not seeking it. He explained that this myth expresses the same idea as Atlantis or the Biblical lost paradise.[1]

Inspired in part by passages in Oswald Spengler's *Decline of the West*,[2] al-Koni has explored the shared cultural heritage of the Mediterranean Basin, the Sahara and the Near East through an investigation of the names of places and gods in the vocabulary of the Tuareg and of other ancient tongues in a multi-volume work.[3] In this linguistic encyclopedia he even assigned meanings to individual consonants and syllables and pondered whether the *Ur*-language for Ancient

Egyptian and Sumerian may survive in 'the language of a dead or near dead tribe like . . . the Tuareg in the Great Desert'. He asserted:

> Its isolation in a labyrinth, named the great desert, through all this time has allowed it to preserve the secret of the Egyptians as well as the secret of the primeval creed . . .[4]

He explained: 'The language of the forgotten mother religions survives in the language of the Tuareg today.'[5] Thus he wrote about 'The two halves of primitive society: the Egyptian and the Tuareg'[6] and asserted: 'The religion of the ancient Egyptians was the religion of the Tuaregs . . .'[7]

Spengler wrote that words in languages 'are more or less homeless and wander from one to another',[8] and in his encyclopedia al-Koni quoted several lines from Spengler's work with obvious enthusiasm. The passage ends with the claim:

> Everywhere we meet, and very early indeed, rigid cult-languages whose sanctity is guaranteed by their inalterability, systems long dead, or alien to life and artificially fettered, which have the strict vocabulary that the formulation of eternal truths require.[9]

Al-Koni then commented: 'The language of the Ṭuareg is this exiled, rigid, cult-language that has been paralyzed for thousands of years.'[10]

Al-Koni has recommended that critics interpreting *al-Majus* read his encyclopedia, which he described as 'the secret key to my works',[11] and called *al-Majus* 'an archaeological, mythological, and anthropological epic with a complicated structure . . .' with implicit rather than explicit meaning. [12] Some readers consider al-Koni an author of tales of youths racing across the Sahara on camel back, but his works typically have multiple layers of meaning and glazes of allusion.

Al-Koni's encyclopedia and novels contain several traditional Tuareg myths that he associates with ancient Greek and Egyptian ones. These include the goddess Tanit as Athena and Neith, Waw – a floating, lost oasis or even a continent – as Atlantis, the Sahara Desert as the Minotaur's labyrinth and Wantahet, a Tuareg demon, as Typhon (Typhoeus) and Seth (Set).

Tanit as Athena

In the third volume of his autobiography, *'Adus al-Sura*, al-Koni wrote:

> In the language of its ancient people, 'Libya' means 'possessed by the spirit of the Goddess Yit', in other words by that first beloved goddess, who bore the name

> 'Yit', which signifies unity, 'Tanit', which means possessor of unity, 'Tannes' who created in Egypt the Kingdom of the Delta, 'Tunis', and likewise Athena, as Herodotus, the father of history attested.[13]

Some of Ibrahim al-Koni's novels contain frequent references to Tanit. He has explained:

> The name 'Tanit' combines two parts: *tan*, which means 'possessor of' and *it*, which is a feminine marker. In its combined form, the word means 'possessor of the feminine'.[14]

Tanit is clearly a moon goddess, and her Greek counterpart would be Selene. In his encyclopedia, though, al-Koni said that Athena 'is the desert Tanit, as Herodotus affirms'.[15] Herodotus wrote:

> Now, it seems likely that Athena's clothing and aegis, as shown on her statues, were copied by the Greeks from Libyan women.[16]

Paul Cartledge's note for the translation by Tom Holland observes:

> Diffusionistic theories were dear to H., who tended to favour the notion of Greeks as recipients rather than donors of seemingly shared cultural practices.[17]

Similarly, al-Koni is fond of theories that highlight Tuareg culture. Herodotus apparently understood Athena, Tanit and Neith to be the same goddess, because he used 'Athena' to refer respectively to Tanit in a reference to Libyan sacrifices and to Neith with regard to one of her temples in Egypt.[18] Al-Koni holds that, in addition to being Athena, Tanit is Isis, Hathor and Anath.[19]

The apparently idiosyncratic detail in *al-Majus*, that the Dervish used boiling hot olive oil to cauterize his groin when castrating himself,[20] takes on an added level of meaning when we find that Kerényi wrote of Athena:

> When called Pandrosos ... she displayed herself under another, bright aspect, which was associated with the olive. A sacred olive grew on the Acropolis, in the temple of Pandrosos.[21]

Vincent Scully also observed of Athena: 'She brought the olive and was attended by the snake ...'[22] In short, the Dervish's self-mutilation is linked to his worship of the Goddess.

In his encyclopedia, al-Koni said the olive is a sacred cure-all, 'which all nations of the Mediterranean Basin have worshipped'.[23] In *al-Majus*, when the Dervish stole the olive oil from his foster mother, the author rhapsodized:

Olive oil – legends say it flows from majestic, age-old, pharaonic trees distributed around Jebel Nefousa like black stars – dark beads in prophets' strings of prayer beads.[24]

References to the goddess Tanit and to her symbol, the triangle, appear frequently in al-Koni's novel *The Seven Veils of Seth* (*al-Bahth 'An al-Makan al-Da'i'* or *In Search of the Lost Place*, 2003). The oasis' sage, Elelli, exclaims for example: 'I swear by the supreme goddess Tanit that this is the way prophetic messengers speak.'[25] Amghar, the chief merchant of the oasis, refers to Tanit's control over fertility when he says: 'I promised a banquet to the goddess Tanit if one of my wives became pregnant.'[26] Isan, an avatar of the Egyptian god Seth, is portrayed in a flashback as married to a woman who identifies herself as Tanit. When he says to her, 'I see you're speaking with the certainty of a priestess,' she replies,

'I am woman. I am the feminine. I am the mother. I am the earth. I am the goddess Tanit, whose soul was born from her soul and who created the entire desert from her flesh.'[27]

When Isan's wife kills their child and presents him with the baby's corpse, this infanticide may echo child sacrifices to Tanit. In any case, the ancient mythic figures Seth and Tanit exert a magnetic force on the novel's plot through their avatars.

Since Isan is Wantahet, who is both Set/Seth and Typhon, Isan's wife corresponds to Typhon's mate, Echidna, who in Greek mythology was half maiden and half serpent. Some of their offspring were monsters slain in memorable ways.[28] Kerényi described Echidna in this fashion:

She was born in a cave, the divine Echidna ... In half of her body she was a beautiful-cheeked, bright-eyed young woman; in the other half she was a terrible, huge snake, thrashing about in the hollows of the divine Earth and devouring her victims raw.[29]

Perhaps it is a coincidence, but in *al-Majus* the Fetishists' god Amnay (a natural stone formation that resembles a man), eats maidens sacrificed to him when they are thrown live into his pit. Here is another reference to a serpent-linked goddess, and it parallels al-Koni's repeated references to the hissing of Wantahet, as in *The Scarecrow*.

In al-Koni's novel *Anubis*, it is Tanit, rather than a male god or demon, who has top billing. In *New Waw*, al-Koni includes at least three references to her. In one passage the excavator, who eventually digs the well that creates the oasis, makes four triangles with pebbles of different colors in order to symbolize Tanit. White and grey pebbles are arranged around a cross formed from gold and black pebbles. These stones form a Tanit mandala.[30] In his encyclopedia, al-Koni says that a cross in the Tifinagh alphabet represents the 't' feminine marker.[31] This symbol was also used as a camel brand in Azjirr,[32] as well as the triangle. People have used the combined cross and triangle as an amulet symbolizing the goddess.[33] Al-Koni explained:

> The triangle as a sign of the goddess, then, is justified by the derivation of the three essential elements compounded as the principle of nature as *existence*, whereas the *spirit*, represented as a metaphysical concept is justified by the goddess's second symbol, which takes the form of a cross. [34]

Some of al-Koni's novels are clearly set in a mythic, ancient past and others at some period since, including the present. A reader might suppose a reference to Tanit places a novel in the pre-Islamic past, but the author has instead insisted:

> The descendants of these emigrants have not abandoned their belief in the Unitarian goddess even today – their embrace of religions with heavenly scriptures notwithstanding – and not merely because they recognized their Law and ancient Unitarian belief in these new religions, as we previously stated, but because their attachment to the Beloved Goddess became deeply embẹdded in their souls.[35]

In the same volume, but in a different passage, al-Koni affirmed: 'The people's worship of the primal goddess has not been diminished by religious or ritual distance.'[36]

In another volume of his encyclopedia, al-Koni said that the goddess is

> A spiritual value . . . a lost paradise about which primitive man in ancient Egypt sang praises to Sau or Asahu and that the Tuareg shaped into tunes of yearning called Asahag . . . metaphysical yearning for a lost homeland . . .[37]

In his encyclopedia, al-Koni dedicated a chapter to Sau and Asahu and said that Egyptologists have found a link between them and a three-star constellation that Egyptian priests believed was their ancient homeland.[38] The Tuaregs also considered these stars as their lost homeland and called their songs of longing *Asahag*.[39] In *al-Majus*, when the Dervish is castrating himself:

> He saw the stars, those white olives, hermits' companions, the guide to men eternally lost in the earth's desert and the sky's desert.[40]

In a discussion of Tanit, al-Koni said that an individual Tuareg tribesman:

> Always strove upward toward the sky ... from which he derived a spiritual existence more precious than his bodily, physical, terrestrial existence, which he never considered anything but a real exile in contrast to his original paradise.[41]

In *Marathi Ulis* (*The Elegies of Ulysses*) the hero finds solace in gazing at the stars of the Pleiades.[42]

Finally, one of Tanit's avatars in Tuareg folklore is Tannes. Al-Koni has said that comparison of the legend of Tannes and Wannes with that of Isis and Osiris shows that:

> Tannes is Isis, as scholars have agreed and Wannes, which means ascent, is Osiris, whose name means descent – because ascending to the sky, speaking mythologically, is equivalent to descending to the netherworld.

Both legends feature 'the feverish love of the sister for her mischievous brother and her death-defying struggle to rescue this love ...'.[43] In Tuareg folklore the molla-molla bird offered the mother of the evil co-wife of Tannes to tell her a secret if she would share some of her food, but she refused and so ate her own daughter's flesh.[44] In *al-Majus*, the dervish alludes to this legend when Udad is about to eat the flesh of his totemic bird, which taught him to sing.[45] The legend of Tannes is told in al-Koni's early novel *al-Bi'r* (*The Well*),[46] and she appears with her brother, Atlantis, in the quartet *al-Khusuf* (*The Eclipse*) of which *al-Bi'r* is the first volume.[47] In *Marathi Ulis*, Atlantis and Wannes are mentioned as alternative names for the brother for whom Tannes sacrifices her life.[48]

Waw as Atlantis

Al-Koni wrote:

> The people of the Great Desert ... still today talk in Tuareg legends about the existence of the ill-fated land that disappeared from existence at some point in time. Generations have continued to dream of discovering a way to it.[49]

Al-Koni included in his encyclopedia a chapter called 'Atlantis: Immortal Dream of Generations', in which he discussed Plato's accounts of Atlantis in his *Timaeus* and *Critias*. Al-Koni traced 'atlantis' with emphatic 't' ('t' with a sub-dot) to 'atlantis' with plain 't' (both being voiceless dental plosives) to 'atlant'. He wrote that Plato mentioned that Poseidon possessed a continent he named 'Tlnt' in honor of his first-born son. Next al-Koni suggested that, given typical consonant shifts, 'Tlnt' became 'Trnt', which is used in the culture of the great desert as a compound word meaning: 'Star of Yit'. Herodotus mentioned a desert tribe that called itself 'Atrant' as a generic name for all the tribe's members – who refused to take an individual name – as a demonstration of their devotion to the divine name. The full name of the tribe (and its individuals) was 'Stars of the Goddess Yit'.[50] The passage in Herodotus is:

> A further ten days' on from the Garamantes there is another hill of salt, complete with water and a ring of human settlements. The people who live there are called the Atarantians, and they are unique in the world, so far as I know, in having no personal names. Instead ... they are all known by the one collective name 'Atarantians'.[51]

In short, al-Koni is comfortable with locating ancient Atlantis in the great Tuareg homeland, and his claim that Waw corresponds to Plato's Atlantis is more than a metaphor.

Al-Koni included, in 'Terrestrial Waw and Celestial Waw' in *al-Majus*, two relatively long accounts of fortunate if desperate travellers for whom Waw opened its portals.[52] In the first telling, a traveller who is lost in the desert's labyrinth becomes so thirsty that he strips off his clothes. Al-Koni's explained that the Tuaregs' Lost Law (Anhi) said:

> Heaven deliberately delays mercy till thirst has purified the wayfarer's body of pride and stripped his awe-inspiring veil from that shameful orifice ... the mouth.
>
> Anhi says that proud, obstinate people, whose arrogance does not allow them to remove their veil and clothes and to kiss the earth, find the portals of Waw closed in their faces. Angels patrolling the desert lose their way when searching for them.[53]

In addition to searching in the labyrinth of the desert for a perfect Lost Oasis, the Tuareg people treasure their Lost Law's dicta that address the concerns of both the physical and spiritual worlds. Al-Koni explained:

> Their legends say it was lost – whether it was a book carved on slabs of rock or recorded on sheets of leather – when torrents swept it away so long ago that no one remembers when.[54]

Waw is described in the first narrative as having lights that twinkle playfully on and off.[55] It is like a shadow that 'flees from those who search for it but chases those who have despaired of finding it'.[56] When the first traveller regains consciousness, he finds himself lying on a feather bed and surrounded by: 'walls that were translucent and coated with a gleaming glaze ...' They 'emitted a calm, silver glow like moonlight'.[57] The description continues: 'Outside celestial birds began singing their delightful ballads again in the labyrinth (*mataha*) of the orchards.'[58] The second narrative's desperate wayfarer, a merchant, hears water purling while he visits Waw. The first version explains that the desire to return to Waw after visiting: 'is sinful, because bashful Waw must travel to the Unknown to purify itself after sheltering a human being.'[59]

Finally, Waw is also the name of a letter in the Arabic alphabet comparable to 'w'. In his encyclopedia, in a discussion of Plutarch's treatise *On the 'E' at Delphi*, al-Koni identified the Arabic letter و (waw) with the Greek letter E (epsilon)[60] and pointed out:

> Plutarch deliberately held back the truth about this sacred letter until the end of the text. Then he proclaimed the same truth that the Tuareg tongue has announced and that is still latent in the concept of Existence, namely that this sacred letter refers to God.[61]

'Waw' then may refer not only to the Lost Oasis, the Lost Paradise and the Lost Law, but also to a Lost God (or Goddess).

The Sahara as a Labyrinth

Al-Koni repeatedly uses the Arabic word *mataha* in his novels to refer to the desert and the related verb *taha* (*yatihu*) to refer to travelling through it. A standard Arabic–English dictionary starts its definition of *mataha* with: 'maze, labyrinth; a trackless, desolate region. . .' and provides a similar definition for *tih*, an alternative form of the word.[62] Al-Koni has said that primitive man 'found himself defenceless, isolated, and alone as a traveler through the labyrinth (*mataha*) of this world . . .'.[63] In his encyclopedia he wrote that the Tuareg repeat the saying:

> 'Imuhak Amihakan', or, in other words, 'The Tuareg are lost or dispossessed', to express their profound sense of having gone astray – not merely in the labyrinth represented by the Great Desert – but their tragic sense of having lost their way in human existence.[64]

The flipside of a life spent yearning for a lost paradise, then, can be a sense of being lost in a labyrinth.

In the novel *Anubis*, the eponymous hero becomes lost in the labyrinth of the desert after he makes the strategic error of following a hare,[65] an ill-omened creature. This hero, who later morphs into a gazelle, is – as his name implies – an avatar both of the Egyptian god and of the Tuareg folk hero Anubi. Moreover, in his introduction, al-Koni described his research for the novel – collecting ancient Tuareg tales and consulting manuscripts.[66]

When discussing Stone Age and Bronze Age Greece, Vincent Scully described the use of caves by Stone Age people:

> Movement through the labyrinthine passages which led to the caverns seems also to have formed an essential part of the ritual, and schematized representations of the labyrinth itself can be found in some caves.[67]

This linkage between caves and labyrinths places the Minotaur myth in a larger context and opens up interesting possibilities for the interpretation of al-Koni's novels, which include repeated scenes in labyrinthine caves with ancient, ritual paintings. Such caves often serve to inspire or console heroes but also can become the scene of a death – as in *al-Majus*, when warriors are trapped in a cave in the sacred mountain by Bambara warriors,[68] or in *New Waw*, when the well-digger sacrifices his life [to the goddess?] in the labyrinthine passageway that he has dug deep into the earth to find water for the tribe.[69]

Labyrinths occur naturally in caves in mountains like sacred Mount Idinen, which looms over the action of *al-Majus* and is crowned with a natural rock fortress.[70] Al-Koni's portrayal of Mount Idinen recalls Scully's description of the ancient Greek ceremonial 'horned' mountain.[71] In *al-Majus*, the character Idikran, who is a diviner linked to a pre-Islamic Berber faith (and therefore an avatar of Wantahet), lives in caves in sacred Mount Idinen while visiting the plain.[72] A reader who ignores ancient Greek myths and the relationships that al-Koni sees between them and Tuareg folklore thinks that a pathetic advocate of pagan human sacrifice to the wind god Amnay is holed up in a cave – end of story. With the varnishes that Greek myths supply to the Arabic text, a reader finds a priest, who worships the Goddess Tanit/Athena and who is also a minotaur in a labyrinth in a mountain sacred to the Goddess, seeking to subdue Typhon with an appropriate human sacrifice, and so forth.

Wantahet as Typhon

Ibrahim al-Koni considers Tuareg Wantahet, Egyptian Seth, Greek Typhon, German Mephistopheles and Iblis (the Islamic Devil) to be manifestations of the same demon.[73] When asked – at the 2011 Georgetown University Colloquium on his works ('Tents in the Desert') – for further details from Tuareg folklore about Wantahet, Ibrahim al-Koni replied that he uses fragments of folklore as a starting point for his creations.

Hesiod said that Typhoeus (Typhon) has 'a hundred snaky heads –/Those of a dreadful serpent . . .'. Not surprisingly therefore, 'when they hissed the echoing sound beneath the hills was heard'.[74] Kerényi described Typhoeus in the following manner:

> Above the hips he was shaped like a man . . . From the hips downwards he was shaped like two wrestling serpents, which towered up to the height of his head and yelled hissingly.[75]

In al-Koni's *The Scarecrow* and many other novels, hissing is a sign of Wantahet. *The Puppet* includes repeated references to serpents – Aghulli, the sage and leader of the oasis community, has a nightmare about a serpent – while in *The Seven Veils of Seth*, Isan, the Seth/Wantahet character, 'hissed hoarsely: "You didn't know that Serpent is one of my names"'.[76]

In Islamic terms, Wantahet is presumably one of the *jinn* – beings who occupy a status below the angels and above human beings. In his encyclopedia, al-Koni associated the word *jinn* with *al-hayya*, the word for serpent, and said 'In the mythology of the ancient world, the serpent is synonymous with the spirit (*al-ruh*) guarding water sources' and 'The water that the serpent guards is the physical counterpart of the mysterious principle called the spirit (*al-ruh*)'.[77] In his encyclopedia he wrote:

> The serpent in the mythology of the ancient world is synonymous with the spirit (*al-ruh*) that guards springs and wells.[78]

Al-Koni's encyclopedia entry for 'Iblis' – the proper name corresponding in Islam to Satan – pairs Iblis with his predecessor, the ancient Egyptian god Set (Seth) as both 'standing opposite the concept of divine lordship'. [79] Seth famously killed Osiris and fought Horus. Richard Wilkinson summarized Seth's status:

> Seth seems to have been originally a desert deity who early came to represent the forces of disturbance and confusion in the world.[80]

Hesiod in his *Theogony* mentioned the similar rebellion against Zeus by Typhoeus:

> . . . he, Typhoeus, would have been the ruler of gods and men,
> If not for the keen reckoning of the wise father then . . .[81]

Hesiod also attributed gales to Typhoeus, especially damp ones, and said:

> And on the boundless, blooming land all these [winds] can equally
> Destroy the lovely husbandry, the works of earthborn men,
> Filling them full of dust through roaring dust storms that cause pain.[82]

In al-Koni's *al-Majus*, a wind called the Qibli blows sand so hard for so long that the community's well and survival are threatened.

Al-Koni wrote in his encyclopedia:

> Iblis in the primeval language of the Tuareg means anger and was derived from *yblys*, which means to become extremely angry. It expresses its negative reality in angry outbursts that religions perceive as evil . . . The Arabic word *bls* refers to black hair suits the ancients prescribed for people sentenced to death.

Al-Koni thought this use was derived from the sovereignty of Iblis over the dark recesses or 'darknesses' (*al-zulamat*).[83]

In an email al-Koni stated that 'In the Tuareg language the word *tyfon* means black or dark recesses. . .' and can also refer to black Africans. 'The devil (*al-shaytan*) . . . is the lord of the dark recesses.'[84] The Arabic title of his masterpiece is *al-Majus*, which literally means the Magi or Magians, in other words, the Zoroastrians. From a Muslim and especially a Sufi point of view, Zoroastrians are the Other. Throughout *al-Majus*, this term is also used to refer to the Other, but now the Other refers not to Zoroastrians but to Bambara and other Bantu adherents of traditional African folk religions – because they are polytheists or 'animists' (rather than monotheists), because they practise settled agriculture, and because they trade in gold. The word here has also a second, neo-Marxist use, derived from Marx's discussion of 'commodity fetishism'.[85] In *al-Majus*, Idikran, a devotee of the pre-Islamic Tuareg religion, has a long conversation with Adda, the tribe's leader about who is a Fetishist. They agree he is not the person who bows before a stone god, but a man who replaces concern for God in his heart with a lust for gold.[86]

The chapter entitled 'Wantahet' in *The Scarecrow* includes a version of the famous banquet served on a carpet spread over an abyss – in a tale about a contest between proponents respectively of anger, envy, hatred and revenge. [87] The Chief Vassal later remarks to the demonic ruler that by repaying good with evil he has demonstrated he is a human being and not a demon.[88]

In *The Seven Veils of Seth*, the chief of the oasis community teases his visitor:

> How can you expect our elders not to think ill of you when you arrive on the back of a jenny, as if you were the accursed Wantahet, who has been the butt of jokes for generations?[89]

There is a more complete version of this accusation later in the novel:

> The master of the jenny at the end of time would approach villages to entice tribes to a banquet only to pull the banquet carpet out from under them, allowing them to fall into a bottomless abyss.[90]

'Wantahet' means 'Master of the Jenny', and al-Koni has stated, 'The donkey is the literal embodiment of the spirit of Sheth.'[91] Isan in *The Seven Veils of Seth* is called the Jenny Master because he rides a she-ass, and the novel includes a vivid account of how he learned to hate camels and love a wild she-ass.[92] Similarly, the demonic hero of *Lawn al-La'na* is said to have travelled south to Africa's forestlands on a camel but to have returned on a she-ass.[93]

H. Te Velde includes in *Seth, God of Confusion* a chapter about the 'Seth-animal', which has been connected with various mammals, real and imaginary, including the wild ass.[94] E. A. Wallis Budge in *The Gods of the Egyptians* says that 'The Ass, like many animals, was regarded by Egyptians both as a god and a devil.'[95]

In Islamic history there is a famous Donkey Master or Sahib al-Himar: Abu Yazid Mukallad ibn Kayrad al-Nukkari (d. 947 CE) who was a Berber rebel against Fatimid rule in what is today Tunisia.[96] From a Tuareg point of view, this possible counterexample presents no problem, because a Berber rebelling against Shi'i Arab rule in North Africa channels Wantahet, the Jenny Master.

In his encyclopedia, al-Koni devoted more than half a volume to Seth and then included a separate discussion of the Seth animal. He pointed out that Plutarch in *Isis and Osiris* associated Seth (called Typhon by Plutarch) with the ass and that in his *Table Talk* Plutarch discussed the resemblance between the Seth beast and 'that detestable animal . . . the hare.'[97] Jan Assman repeats the story that Typhon 'erected a statue of his sacred animal, the ass, in the temple at Jerusalem.'[98] Al-Koni explained that the Tuareg 'consider nothing else in the world of the desert as ill-omened as the hare.'[99] It was entrusted with a mandate that would have brought mankind glad tidings of immortality but changed this into a death knell.[100] Al-Koni continued that Tuareg culture forbids any mention of donkey or hare before sunrise.[101]

For its part, the ass, al-Koni wrote (according to *Isis and Osiris* by Plutarch):

> Became hated and ill-omened in the primitive mind once it rescued the Beloved Seth, who fled on its back, escaping from punishment by Horus by traveling to Jerusalem as king.[102]

Both paraphrasing Plutarch and reflecting Tuareg culture, al-Koni added: 'The factor that the donkey and Seth have in common is their red colour.' For the donkey, this is simply its natural color, but, 'For Seth it is fire, substance, knowledge, and evil'.[103] Plutarch in *Isis and Osiris* did say more than once that Typhon has a red complexion.[104]

A potion that al-Koni's Isan (in *The Seven Veils of Seth*) slips into the pool causes women in the oasis to miscarry, but he can also cure their fertility problems. In his encyclopedia al-Koni wrote:

> Since the phallus plants life in a woman's womb to assure the human genus, it is comparable to divinity that brings creatures to life with the spirit's miracle . . .

Both perform the same creative role. Nature, then, must be paired with the spirit.[105]

Te Velde said of Seth that he is 'the god who brings about abortion'.[106] In *The Seven Veils of Seth*, Seth cures infertility by judicious use of his phallus. Te Velde also said of Seth: 'Seth is a god of sexuality which is not canalized into fertility'.[107] In short, in al-Koni's depiction of his Typhon/Seth archetype, whom he usually calls Wantahet, there is a dialectic between good and evil. He has stated, 'Our world would not exist if evil did not'. He added that the word 'veils' in the title *The Seven Veils of Seth* refers to this profound view.[108]

In al-Koni's encyclopedia, the first chapter of Part II ('Set (Sheth, Zed, Shaz, Shat') is entitled: 'Set: Dialectic of Sanctity and Baseness.'[109] Then in Chapter 6 of Part II, he states:

> The balanced dialectic of the primitive intellect, however, suggests a solution that is simpler than we might expect. Seth is truly a god, and Seth is also a demon. As a luminous essence, Seth is a principle of goodness, and for this reason is a Beloved Lord. As a fiery essence, Seth is also an evil principle, and for this reason is an outcast Beloved. God and Satan are two contradictory halves but derive from a single root, which is the letter 's'. In the primitive language it stands for two opposites: light and fire.[110]

He later added:

> Light is divine so long as it remains light but becomes an enemy of the divine when it turns into fire. A river's water is likewise divine and good (Osiris) while flowing between its banks but evil when it floods and becomes a sea (Seth).[111]

Ibrahim al-Koni as Odysseus/Ulysses

Perhaps the single clearest use of Greek literary myth by Ibrahim al-Koni is his sketch for an autobiography *Marathi Ulis* ('Elegies of Ulysses'), in which he presented, in third-person narration, the protagonist, who at one point is abandoned to float on a 'plank' in the Mediterranean, as Odysseus.[112] The book's third chapter is 'Remembrance of the Valley', which is a full rendition of the expulsion of mankind from the valley of Paradise, thanks in part to Wantahet.[113] The section about al-Koni's education in the Soviet Union is set in 'Daylam', and a mythic section about a couple's murder-suicide is cut into the narration of al-Koni's marriage to a Russian woman.[114] The book ends with the sentence: 'Only idiots don't realize that obtaining Truth (*al-haqiqa*) . . . can be achieved only by someone granted to courage to kill himself [or: kill his self].'[115] That follows a description of his failed suicide attempt.[116] *Marathi Ulis* has been supplemented by a multivolume work called *'Adus al-Sura* (*The Night Wanderer*).[117] This is a more conventional memoir, but in the third volume al-Koni again refers to himself as Ulysses.[118]

Conclusion

The twentieth-century Egyptian playwright and novelist Tawfiq al-Hakim sought direct inspiration from ancient Greek myth and classical Greek literature. He wrote an 'Isis' play, a 'Pygmalion' play, and spent several years perfecting his Arabic-language, Islamic version of *Oedipus the King* by Sophocles.[119] The contemporary Tuareg Saharan author Ibrahim al-Koni, has turned upside down al-Hakim's paradigm of seeking inspiration from Greek culture. Instead he has claimed for Tuareg folklore a primacy coeval with ancient Greek and Egyptian cultures by incorporating ancient archetypes and myths into his novels. He has, moreover, created his own Saharan archetypes and myths and implemented an equal-opportunity policy for myths of whatever origin. Tawfiq al-Hakim typically used a modernizing strategy with the myths he adapted – asking, for example, 'How would I feel if I were Pygmalion or Oedipus?' By contrast, Ibrahim al-Koni's novels often read like myths or epics. Since al-Koni is an author who systematically creates archetypes for his fictional world, when he mentions Atlantis, Athena, Typhon or the labyrinth, these references are adoptions rather than experiments like al-Hakim's.

Whether or not a reader chooses to follow al-Koni through all his linguistic analyses of ancient languages, the affinities he sees between ancient Greek and Egyptian myths and Tuareg folklore and myths provide a guide for interpreting his novels, which – far from seeming antiquated or obscurantist – constitute an innovative approach in contemporary Arabic literature. Thus the use of Greek myth as spectacles for viewing the novels of Ibrahim al-Koni provides interesting, unexpected insights into his work.

In religious studies jargon, 'myth' refers to a narrative so sacred that people can guide their lives by it. Perhaps, then, it is hardly surprising that the ancient myths and deities that al-Koni has used in his novels converge around the guiding concepts of a lost paradise, a lost Law, and the magnetic pull of positive and negative divinities.

Bibliography

Almrtdi, Mustafa (2014), *La Notion de temps dans la quadrilogie d'Ibrahim Al Koni.* Saarbrücken: Éditions Universitaires Européennes.

Assman, Jan (2008), *Of God and Gods: Egypt, Israel, and the Rise of Monotheism.* Madison, WI: The University of Wisconsin Press.

Babbitt, Frank Cole, trans. (1936), *Plutarch's Moralia*, vol. 5 (Loeb Classical Library). London and Cambridge, MA: Heinemann and Harvard University Press.

Budge, E. A. Wallis (1904 [1969]), *The Gods of the Egyptians*. New York: Dover Publications.

Bury, R. G., trans. (1942), *Plato, with an English translation*, vol. 7, *Timaeus: Critias; Cleitophon; Menexenus; Epistles*. Rev. ed. Loeb. London: Heinemann.

Deheuvels, Luc-Willy (2002), 'Le Lieu de l'utopie dans l'oeuvre d'Ibrahim al-Kawni', in Boutros Hallaq, Robin Ostle and Stefan Wild (eds), *Le Poétique de l'espace dans la littérature arabe modern*, 25–42. Paris: Presses Sorbonne Nouvelle.

Fähndrich, Hartmut, trans. (2002), *Ibrahim al-Koni, Die Magier: Das Epos der Tuareg.* Basel: Lenos Verlag.

Holland, Tom, trans. (2014), *Herodotus: The Histories*, with Introduction & notes by Paul Cartledge. London and New York: Penguin.

Hutchins, William Maynard (2003), *Tawfiq al-Hakim: A Reader's Guide*. London and Boulder: Lynne Rienner Publishers.

Kerényi, C. [Károly] (1951), *The Gods of the Greeks*. London and New York: Thames and Hudson.

Kern, Otto, ed. (1922), *Orphicorum Fragmenta*. Berlin: Weidmann.

al-Kawni, Ibrahim (2002), 'Le "Discours" du desert: Témoignage', in Boutros Hallaq, Robin Ostle and Stefan Wild (eds), *Le Poétique de l'espace dans la littérature arabe modern*. Paris: Presses Sorbonne Nouvelle.

al-Koni, Ibrahim (2005), *Anubis: A Desert Novel*, trans. William M. Hutchins. Cairo: The American University in Cairo Press.

al-Koni, Ibrahim (2008), *The Seven Veils of Seth*, trans. William M. Hutchins. Reading: Garnet Publishing.

al-Koni, Ibrahim (2014), *New Waw, Saharan Oasis,* trans. William M. Hutchins. Austin, TX: The Center for Middle Eastern Studies: The University of Texas at Austin.

al-Kuni, Ibrahim (1998), *al-Fazza'a*. Beirut: al-Mu'assasa al-'Arabiya li-l-Dirasat wa-l-Nashr.

al-Kuni, Ibrahim (2001), *al-Majus*. 4th ed. Limassol and Beirut: al-Multaka Publishing.

al-Kuni, Ibrahim (2001 and 2008), *Bayan fi Lughat al-Lahut: Lughz al-Tawariq Yakshifu Lughzay al-Fara'inah wa Sumar* (*An Investigation of the Vocabulary for the Divine: The Riddle of the Tuaregs Sheds Light on the Riddles of the Pharoahs and Sumer*, Beirut and Limassol: Dar al-Multaqa

al-Kuni, Ibrahim (2004a), *al-Suhuf al-Ula: Asatir wa Mutun*. Beirut: al-Mu'assasa al-'Arabiya li-l-Dirasat wa-l-Nashr.

al-Kuni, Ibrahim (2004b), *Marathi Ulis: Murid*. Beirut: al-Mu'assasa al-'Arabiya lil-Dirasat wa-al-Nashr.

al-Kuni, Ibrahim (2004, 2005, 2006), *Malhamat al-Mafahim: Lughz al-Tawariq Yakshifu Lughzay al-Fara'inah wa Sumar*. Beirut: al-Mu'assasa al-'Arabiyah li-l-Dirasat wa-l-Nashr.

al-Kuni, Ibrahim (2005), *Lawn al-La'na*. Beirut: al-Mu'assasa al-'Arabiya lil-Dirasat wa-l-Nashr.

al-Kuni, Ibrahim (2012, 2013, 2014), *'Adus al-Sura*. Beirut: al-Mu'assasa al-'Arabiya lil-Dirasat wa-l-Nashr.

al-Musbahi, Hasuna (2012), *Yatim al-Dahr*. Beirut: Jadawel S.A.R.L.

Prasse, Karl-G., Alojaly Ghoubeïd and Mohamed Ghabdouane (2003), *Dictionnaire Tuareg–Français (Niger)*. Copenhagen: Museum Tusculanum Press.

Scully, Vincent (1962 [2013]), *The Earth, the Temple, and the Gods*. San Antonio, TX: Trinity University Press.

Schlegel, Catherine M. and Henry Weinfield, trans. (2006), *Hesiod, Theogony and Works and Days*. Ann Arbor, MI: The University of Michigan Press.

Spengler, Oswald (1932), *The Decline of the West*, trans. C.F.A. New York: Alfred A. Knopf.

Te Velde, H. (1967), *Seth, God of Confusion*. Leiden: E. J. Brill.

Wehr, Hans (1994), *A Dictionary of Modern Written Arabic (Arabic-English)*, ed. J. Milton Cowan. 4th ed. Urbana, IL: Spoken Language Services, Inc.

Wilkinson, Richard H. (2003) *The Complete Gods and Goddesses of Ancient Egypt*. New York: Thames & Hudson.

3

Greek Myth and Mythmaking in Witi Ihimaera's *The Matriarch* (1986) and *The Dream Swimmer* (1997)

Simon Perris

Scholars of classical reception tend to ignore New Zealand.[1] Perhaps too few have sufficient motivation and expertise. Africa and the Caribbean, not to mention Europe and the Americas, furnish plenty of material. Perhaps this is a dead end. The classical idea(l) has never flourished in New Zealand, and engagement with antiquity tends to be unsystematic, much less systemic. Few high schools offer Latin; none Greek. One cannot assume the same brand of cultural literacy which one tends to expect of readers and writers in other parts of the former British Empire. In short, New Zealand cultural soil is not so fertile for cultivating the classics as, say, Derek Walcott's St Lucia, with its 'Greek manure'.

Still, there is work to be done. This chapter concerns the only New Zealand novel known to me which models itself on a classical text: Witi Ihimaera's *The Dream Swimmer* (1997), the sequel to *The Matriarch* (1986; revised 2009). In particular, I argue that: first, *The Dream Swimmer* presents itself as an adaptation of Aeschylus' *Oresteia*; and second, this differs markedly from Ihimaera's treatment of classical material in *The Matriarch*.

As the first indigenous (Maori) New Zealander to publish a novel and also the first to publish a collection of short fiction, Witi Ihimaera is a living icon in the full sense of that phrase. He is also the postcolonial author *par excellence*: a Maori New Zealander from provincial Poverty Bay with genealogical links to tribes still fighting for the return of land stolen by the government; a father of two by a Pakeha wife, living 'out' as a gay man; a former diplomat turned writer, professor and now national treasure. At the centre of Ihimaera's canon stands a diptych: *The Matriarch* and *The Dream Swimmer*.[2] The first novel won both the Wattie Book of the Year Award and the lion's share of attention; *The Dream Swimmer* went the way of all sequels. By rereading the novels' mythical substrate, I aim to rehabilitate *The Dream Swimmer* (even if only a little) and reinstate it in New Zealand literary history where it belongs. I aim also to reinstate the South Pacific (even if only a little) in classical reception studies where it, too, belongs.

The protagonist-narrator Tama Mahana, a Maori diplomat from the east coast village of Waituhi, has two daughters by his Pakeha wife. (Like many of Ihimaera's protagonists, Tama bears a striking resemblance to his creator.) In the mid-1970s, Tama begins researching his dead grandmother Riripeti 'Artemis' Mahana. He recounts her pivotal role in a 1949 delegation to Wellington to campaign for the return of tribal lands lost in the 1800s; he remembers Riripeti teaching him Maori myth and history. The story contains three main 'threads', as Tama himself calls them: Tama's investigation; his childhood with Riripeti, especially the 1949 delegation; and the mythico-historical past. The great revelation to which the novel builds is that Riripeti, leader of the Mahana clan, once appointed Tama to be her successor and receive her *mana* (spiritual authority). The climax involves a flashback in which Riripeti uses her *mana* to intervene in the delegation, by way of magic (realism). *The Dream Swimmer*, by contrast, highlights the relationship between Tama and his mother, Tiana. Once again, we read three main threads. Following on from *The Matriarch*, Tama investigates a curse on the Mahana clan, suspecting it to be Tiana's doing. In the process, he learns about *her* past and recollects his own troubled upbringing. The climactic event here is another flashback: Tama returns home from boarding school and almost kills Tiana to avenge her abuse of his sisters. A law-court scene presents the major revelation of *The Dream Swimmer*: Riripeti's will named Tama her legal heir; he was dispossessed of this legacy not by his mother, but by his father; this breaking of succession caused the curse. An epilogue reveals that a new generation, including Tama's recently born cousin Eretra, is campaigning for the land to be returned.[3]

I have catalogued elsewhere more than one hundred classical references in Ihimaera's *oeuvre*.[4] Of these, more than twenty occur in *The Matriarch* (including the 2009 revised edition) and more than thirty in *The Dream Swimmer*.[5] Most obviously, the Matriarch, Riripeti 'Artemis' Mahana, bears the name of the Greek goddess. Tama's mother, who challenges Riripeti, is Tiana (= Diana). Each novel thus depicts Tama investigating a female ancestor named Diana/Artemis. Tama's aunt, who challenges the succession, is named Circe. While *The Matriarch* does not systematize its classical allusions, *The Dream Swimmer* does, particularly within the wider context of the House of Atreus. Note that *The Dream Swimmer* introduces Tama's cousin, Eretra, that is, 'Electra'.

Two passages from *The Matriarch* do refer directly to classical literature. The first concerns the sacred canoe, *Takitimu*:

> I must tell you now of the holy ark of the iwi Maori, the *Takitimu*, and the two taniwha [magical beasts, monsters] who escorted the sacred canoe from Hawaiki to Aotearoa. I will tell it as it was told to me by the matriarch . . . But to understand all, you must know all, from the very beginning of *Takitimu*'s making. So draw near and listen to the story of the holy ark.
>
> . . .
>
> In the Hesiodic fable, Cronus separated the heavenly pair by mutilating his oppressive father Uranus. Remember this context as I tell you about *Takitimu*.
>
> (*M* 252)

Although Tama forgets Hesiod by the time of *The Dream Swimmer*, he draws a pointed analogy here between early Greek epic and Maori storytelling. Tama's *Takitimu* story is to rank alongside the *Theogony* as an oral epic.[6] Ihimaera thus presents this Pacific odyssey along the lines of a classical *epyllion* (mini-epic) embedded in a larger whole, like something from Ovid's *Metamorphoses*. He marks it as *oral* epic in an *oral* performance tradition: 'I must tell you now', 'as it was told to me', 'listen to the story'. He performs 'the saga of the voyage of the *Takitimu*' (263), including aetiologies for New Zealand settlements and parallels to other epic voyages, Viking and Arthurian (275–276). The discourse on cosmogonic myth functions as a formal epic proem ('Remember this context'), after which Tama divides his narrative into distinct, formally marked phases:

> 'The story begins in faraway Hawaiki at the settlement of Pikopiko i whiti.'
>
> (*M* 252)
>
> . . .
>
> 'So we come to the journeying of the holy ark, *Takitimu*, from Hawaiki to the land that Kupe had found, far to the south.'
>
> (*M* 259)
>
> . . .
>
> *'Behold,' the matriarch said. 'Ara.' And in that place where the pillars met the sky she told me of the* Takitimu *and the mauri* [spirit] *it brought to make the new land sacred.*
>
> (*M* 271)

Tama's miniature maritime epic includes an elaborate account of the canoe's origins in Hawaiki, the mythical home of the Polynesian diaspora (252–258); the long voyage across the Pacific (259–265); and the journey around New Zealand to the canoe's resting place (271–277). Indeed, *The Matriarch* as a whole presents itself as an epic novel:

> [The characters' experiences are] meant to be representative of the whole Maori experience. It tells, in Kipling's phrase, 'the tale of the tribe' and by extension the tale of the race . . . it is also an epic in the sense that it attempts to dramatise the memory of a time before the worlds of subject and object became separate.[7]

Contrast Tama's one lapidary reference to Greek drama in *The Matriarch*: 'Tiana and my sisters, Teria, Erina, Vanessa and Meri, were waiting like a Greek chorus, silent and eternal' (*M* 377). Greek tragedy is not a major force in *The Matriarch*. As we shall see, the reverse is true of the sequel.

Previous scholarship downplays or misrepresents classical allusions in the diptych.[8] For example, Calvert reads references to the *Oresteia* as a parable about dispossession of land. Greek myth thus offers 'another angle through which the machinations of the Mahana whānau [clan, family] may be understood by the European reader . . . The Mahana clan is heavily based on Ihimaera's own family so by extension Ihimaera elevates his private family history to the level of public myth.'[9] Calvert elides any problems we might – should – have with rereading the *Oresteia* as an archetype for postcolonial conflict, and privileges 'the European reader' (whoever that is). Thomson misses the point altogether: 'This story of grandmother, mother and son is much closer to the legends of, say, the labours of Hercules, than to those of Clytemnestra and Orestes.'[10] On the whole, I agree with Fox: 'the Greek myths enshrined in the *Orestaia* [*sic*] . . . provide the conceptual framework of the whole novel.'[11]

In arguing my case, I rely on four types of evidence. First: isolated allusions to various classical myths. Second: references to Clytemnestra, Orestes and the Furies. Third: plot parallels between *The Dream Swimmer* and the myth of Orestes. Fourth: extended passages in which characters themselves explicitly discuss classical material. It would appear that Ihimaera sometimes worked not from the Aeschylean trilogy per se but from an intermediary. A list of sources which prefaces the published text of *The Dream Swimmer* includes A. S. Murray's *Who's Who in Mythology* (1874 [1988]). A 1990 typescript of the novel bears a handwritten instruction appended to a summary of the *Oresteia*: 'See p.302, Alexander S. Murray.'[12] Murray's 'Orestes' entry begins on that very page. Moreover, *The Dream Swimmer* repeats idiosyncratic details from the *Who's Who*. For example, each places Iphigenia in 'Tauros' (that is, in the mountain range in southern Asia Minor) rather than 'among the Taurians' (that is, in the Crimea in the land of the Tauri).[13] Finally, the *Who's Who* never mentions the

Oresteia. Otherwise, one imagines that neither Ihimaera nor Fox would have misspelled it 'Orestaia' [*sic*]. That said, my thesis remains: *The Dream Swimmer* presents itself as an adaptation of the *Oresteia.*

We have seen already that character names in the diptych create certain expectations left unexplored in *The Matriarch.* More broadly, scattered classical references create a mythological patina.[14] This patina at least suggests some kind of equivalence between classical and Maori myth, and Ihimaera often draws an explicit, syncretistic parallel. For example:

> [Uncle Alexis]: "Someone's stuck pins in my eyes."
>
> (*DS* 23 ≈ *M* 12)

> Alas, Uncle Alexis.
>
> He was Tiresias, the Blind Man in Greek mythology, the one who waits at the crossroads near the feet of the sphinx in the hot noon sun. He was the oracle of Apollo, waiting for Orestes to come, to direct him to his destiny at Mycenae. He was the seer, the divinator, the matakite.
>
> (*DS* 24)

My second category of evidence groups together Orestes, Apollo, Clytemnestra, the House of Atreus and the Furies. References to these specific figures cumulatively bolster the analogy with the *Oresteia*, and at significant junctures they assume programmatic force. For example, the very first classical reference in *The Dream Swimmer* – aside from the character names – comes at the start of 'Act One', when the narrator decides to continue his narrative. Even in the framing story, Tama casts himself as an(other) Orestes:

> Back in Athens, I decided to go up to Delphi to consult the oracle of Apollo. There are some places in the world where the boundaries between the past and future, living and dead, are so fine that you can read the patterns of destiny. Waituhi is one such place; Venice is another; and so is Delphi. Why else would it be so associated with divinations?
>
> (*DS* 22)

Tama ≈ Orestes. This is *the* fundamental analogy which structures *The Dream Swimmer* as a whole, and it functions locally and globally. For instance, the novel comprises a prologue, an epilogue and six acts divided into named sections, two of which have titles relevant to the *Oresteia*: 'House of Atreus', in which Tama returns home to plan another delegation; and 'The Furies', in which Tama almost kills his mother. That is, a *nostos* to reclaim a birthright and an interrupted matricide, each given a programmatic title.

The connections accumulate. For example, the 'House of Atreus' section concludes Act Four with the novel's first reference to the Furies (Greek *Erinyes*, Latin *Furiae*), foreshadowing the 'Furies' section to come:

> Then I thought of Tiana. Her memory conjured up the sounds of the rustling pursuit of the Eryinnes [*sic*]. I looked out the window of the plane. Somehow I felt the Furies were not far behind me.
>
> *You've always had the power to take it off, Son.*
>
> What I did not know was that the Furies weren't behind me at all. They were ahead, waiting with their net of memories, to trap me in Wellington.
>
> (*DS* 196)

This is a significant juncture. Henceforth, references to the death of Clytemnestra proliferate, moving beyond Orestes to the *Oresteia* with a rare reference to Aeschylus' *Agamemnon*:

> The spirit of Clytemnestra had invaded the soul of Riripeti. The House of Atreus was in its decline and fall.
>
> (*DS* 273)

> [Artemis to Tama] E mokopuna, my grandson, you must be careful as you walk in the world. Beware, particularly, of the way of the Pakeha for it will be like unto a red carpet so comforting to your feet … it is a carpet of blood which your ancestors have trod before you into the House of the European …
>
> (*DS* 276)[15]

During and after Tama's violent confrontation with Tiana, references to the Furies proliferate:

> The waves stormed across the concrete wall. As they flung their spray toward the moon I saw three dark shapes advancing and knew –
>
> The Furies were coming.
>
> (*DS* 284)

> Of course I should have known that the Furies would take judgement against me. I had forgotten that matricide, the murder of a mother, was the highest of all homicides.
>
> (*DS* 302)

And on the penultimate pages:

> In my darkest moments I have even called upon the Furies to put me out of my misery. Come daughters of Kronos and Eurynome. Come, Tisiphone, Alekto, Megaera; take me now, avengers of a son who murdered his mother.

> The Furies are merciless. They know only too well that to live with the memory of my guilt is the worst punishment of all.
>
> (*DS* 421–422)[16]

Classical references in *The Dream Swimmer* thus establish a structural analogy. Tama ≈ Orestes; Tiana ≈ Clytemnestra; *The Dream Swimmer* ≈ *Oresteia*. Hence, my third category of evidence: plot parallels which play out this analogy. The basic correspondences are not at all subtle. Agamemnon, the chief whose death interrupts succession: at Riripeti's death, Tama does not inherit. Clytemnestra, the abusive mother: Tiana abuses her children. Orestes, the son who returns to kill his mother: Tama returns from boarding school to kill Tiana. The Areopagos, setting for the conclusive courtroom scene: in an extended flashback, Tama is deprived of his birthright, in court, by his father. Athena and the Erinyes' settlement: Tama's narrative ends with the hope that his cousin, Eretra, and other youngsters will eventually mount a successful legal campaign for the tribe's land. In short: *Libation Bearers* with a pinch of *Agamemnon* and a liberal dash of *Eumenides*.

In the final two chapters, Tama reflects:

> Although I have forgiven my clan, I have yet to find forgiveness for myself.
>
> I have been like Orestes. I have deservedly been pursued by the Furies, permitting no peace to my throbbing heart. But as Orestes did, so have I tried to make restitution to Artemis. Although the Furies continue to persecute me, I shall proceed to Athens and there call for a trial in the Areopagus.
>
> With their help, I pray Apollo and the great goddess Athene will secure my acquittal. May the Furies end their persecution.
>
> (*DS* 420)

> Once, when we were children, my sister Erina asked, 'If we were ever lost, do you think Mum would find us?' . . . And our mother will kiss us all and say, 'Let's go home, my children.'
>
> And as heavy as we are, we will not be a burden to her because our mother, Tiana, has always loved us.
>
> Always.
>
> (*DS* 422–423)

Thus, my own reading of *The Dream Swimmer*: a tendentious mythopoeic adaptation of the *Oresteia* into a story of maternal love against the odds. General classical references encourage this reading; isolated references to specific figures signpost it; and the plot, shaped by the narrator, performs it.

Now to my final category of evidence: metafictional, intertextual passages in which Ihimaera *directs* our reading of the adaptation. That is, extended, didactic, overt discussions of specific classical phenomena, embedded as dialogue, which guide the reader towards architectonic parallels.

Three such passages concern the matricide in the *Oresteia*. In the first, Regan (Tama's wife) compares at length the cursed Mahana clan to the House of Atreus.[17] Her garbled summary of the 'Orestaia' [*sic*] (*DS* 92–95) establishes the main conceit of the novel. She puts it bluntly, just in case we miss the point; repetition of 'like', as in a Homeric simile, emphasizes the basic analogy:

> 'Do you know the Orestaia? Your family's like that.'
>
> (*DS* 92)
>
> . . .
>
> 'You're like Orestes,' she said. 'The Orestaia tells us that at the murder of Agamemnon and the banishment of Orestes, things fall apart . . . . Order will not be restored until Orestes returns to rescue the sisters and—'
>
> 'And?'
>
> Regan's voice drifted in the night.
>
> 'He kills his mother.'
>
> (*DS* 93)

Tama later asks Sylvia, a classicist no less, whether Orestes acts justly. Sylvia then discusses justice and theodicy in the *Oresteia*. 'Your question may be simple but the answer is not so simple. Which has the greater argument for rightness? Where do you think a son's devotion lies?' Tama replies, 'I love my father' (*DS* 150). Ihimaera thus supplements Regan's earlier précis with an interpretative crux; we are to read *The Dream Swimmer* with one eye on justice in the *Oresteia*. Later still, Ihimaera answers Sylvia's question for (and with reference to) himself: 'I had answered wrongly and had been punished. I now know that the answer should have been: "With my mother, Tiana."' (*DS* 410).

These passages reinterpret the *Oresteia* as follows: first, the *Oresteia* is *the* archetypal narrative of mother–son antagonism; second, although the question of justification resists simple analysis, the predominant claims on our affection, sympathy and loyalty are those of the *mother*, with the corollary that matriarchy trumps patriarchy; third, matricide is the worst crime; fourth, internecine violence in the royal household causes cosmic and earthly disorder. Indeed, it is only *after* the two major didactic passages that Tama makes much of the Orestes myth. Those passages, therefore, collectively dramatize Tama's acceptance of the tragic paradigm which Regan suggests: he subordinates other intertexts to it and, most importantly, structures his narrative around it.

I add a fourth passage in which Ihimaera plays fast and loose with tragedy. In the middle of a basketball game while away at boarding school, Tama witnesses a vision of his abusive mother Tiana:

> There is a moment in the great Greek drama, *Medea*, which is similar to this. Princess of Colchis, Medea has married Jason of the Argonauts and borne him three children. Tiring of her charms, however, Jason has gone to Corinth where he has fallen in love with Glauce. Black with rage, Medea arrives at Corinth. 'Is this the place where the vile gain protection?' she asks. 'Is it here the traitor finds joy?'
>
> Medea pleads with Jason to return to her. He does not. Medea burnishes Glauce's crown with poisonous barbs so that when she puts it on she falls down dead. She then murders the three children she had with Jason. While flames shoot out of the temple, she appears at the door with the Three Furies beside her. Jason asks Medea, 'Why did you kill them, Medea?' She answers, 'Why? They were your sons.'
>
> (*DS* 294)

This bears little resemblance to Euripides' *Medea*. As it happens, Tama describes not 'the great Greek drama' but the great Italian opera, Cherubini's *Médée* of 1797.[18]

Despite a fuzzy grasp of the sources, Tama draws a crystal-clear analogy: Medea/Tiana/Clytemnestra hurts her children to punish Jason/Tama by proxy. The Erinyes' bizarre appearance – are they following Jason or Medea? – cements this triangulation between Medea, Tiana and Clytemnestra.[19] Note also the emphasis, however misdirected, on staging: the narrator's mini-lecture on a surprise theatrical epiphany punctuates a surprise epiphany in his own narrative.

The Dream Swimmer would be a self-consciously theatrical novel even without its classical intertexts. Aside from the hidden Cherubini reference, Verdi quotations constitute 'a symbolic subtext that, in combination with elements drawn from Greek myth, helps to shape and intensify the whole fictive representation'.[20] Yet these quotations remain unexplained in *The Dream Swimmer*, whereas Ihimaera includes notionally authoritative, explicit discussions of Greek tragedy. Over the course of the novel, that is, Regan, Sylvia and Tama ostensibly teach the reader the basics, broadly construed, of the *Oresteia* and *Medea*. The recurring didactic thread, absent from the original version of *The Matriarch*, thus dramatizes the incursion of classical material into the Mahana saga, mediated by Murray's *Who's Who*. The revised edition of *The Matriarch* demonstrates this best of all. That edition interpolates a shorter version of Regan and Tama's very first expository conversation about the *Oresteia* from *The Dream Swimmer*, even situating it in a different place and time.[21] As I have put it elsewhere: '*The Matriarch* [revised] now prefigures, loud and clear, Ihimaera's wholesale adaptation of the *Oresteia* in *The Dream Swimmer*: the intertextual makeup of the sequel has intruded on the rewritten original.'[22]

Intertextuality with the *Oresteia* thus turns the (epic) story of the grandmother into the (tragic) story of the mother, moving our gaze from the matriarch Artemis Riripeti to the 'woman of no account', her near-namesake Tiana. In light of the onomastic connection and real-world rivalry between these avatars of Artemis/Diana, it is therefore no surprise that *The Dream Swimmer* also includes a didactic passage about the goddess. Tama discovers, vicariously, that Riripeti once visited a temple of Artemis in Venice. Signor Nucci, a librarian, describes this particular manifestation of Artemis in a conversation related second-hand:

> 'She [Artemis] became the Great Mother and was throughout looked upon as a goddess of the female reproductive power in nature. She had at least a dozen other names, and was, of course, Diana to the Romans . . . here it was the Ephesian Artemis who was worshipped. She had divine power over wild beasts, fertility, childbirth, the moon and hunting . . . As the mother of wild beasts she suckles all Nature . . . This image tells us that in this house was practised the religion of the original Artemis of Ephesus, not the Artemis of the Greeks or Romans. This sect has been here hundreds of years . . .'[23]
>
> (*DS* 237–238)

On the one hand, this odd sequence retrospectively ties in to the confusing ending of *The Matriarch* later clarified in the 2009 revision (Riripeti promised Tama to Artemis and took with her a sacred sword; Tiana offers herself as a substitute; her death pays the price; Tama returns the sword to the temple in Venice). On the other hand, Riripeti's Venetian backstory also ties *The Dream Swimmer* more tightly to the *Oresteia*: a tribal leader offers her descendant to Artemis in return for helping the tribe fight for something which was stolen; the boy's mother resists; a sacrificial substitution is made. (That is: Agamemnon, Artemis, Helen, Clytemnestra, and Iphigenia.)

With this sacrificial substitution in mind, I mention one final parallel by means of which Ihimaera has his cake and also eats it. That is, the sequence in which Tama mutilates Tiana's corpse (*DS* 388–393). Tiana dies, leaving Tama specific instructions as to the manner of her burial. Still angry, he follows these instructions faithfully: he exhumes the body in Gisborne and takes it to a cave halfway up the sacred mountain, Hikurangi; he sews his mother's eyelids together, breaks her wrists and ankles, binds her legs and places a piece of wood in her mouth. She had written, '*I wish my own powers to be returned to the earth.*

I must be the last of my kind' (*DS* 392). Sometimes a cigar may well be just a cigar, but in this instance the symbolism is clear, heavy-handed even: mutilation of the corpse, already well thematized in Greek epic (the *Iliad*) and tragedy (*Antigone*), stands in for matricide. Thus ends Tiana, and thus ends the curse on the Mahana clan. Of course, the mother–son antagonism persists, for Ihimaera plots the mutilation of the corpse *before* the final revelation of Te Ariki's guilt and Tiana's innocence. 'Tiana must have known that I would be so compelled by my anger of her that I would not deny what she wanted' (*DS* 392). Nevertheless, Tama's final act of violence towards his mother ultimately becomes an act of filial piety. To the very end, then, *The Dream Swimmer* positions itself with respect to Aeschylus' *Libation Bearers* and the violence at the heart of that play, all the while eschewing an actual matricide. (The *Iliad*, likewise, eschews actual mutilation of corpses.) In the face of various inconsistencies, loopholes and oddities, the fidelity of Tama's story to that of the *Oresteia* is quite remarkable.

In turn, this mutual entwining (re)configures the *Oresteia* as the ideal hypotext for a tragic novel about family conflict. During Regan's programmatic discussion of the *Oresteia*, Tama attempts to explain his mother's abuse: 'She was born out of violence. I know it's not an excuse, but it's a reason that I can understand. Violence begets violence' (*DS* 93). This figures the tragic trilogy as a parable not of armed resistance or postcolonial dispossession, nor even of state-mandated judicial solutions to blood-vengeance, but of reconciliation between *philoi* – between family members. Compare Aristotle: 'these days the best tragedies are composed about a few families ... who have suffered terribly or done terrible things' (*Poetics* 1453a17–22).[24] Ihimaera plans to write the third novel, *Eretra*, but admits to having no real idea about where the story will (could?) go.[25] *The Dream Swimmer* has already lifted a courtroom scene from *Eumenides*; Tama's dalliance with his cousin Tepora parallels Orestes' marriage to Hermione (as in *Orestes* and *Andromache*). Only melodrama remains: Electra's marriage to Pylades and Orestes' death by snake-bite.

So, then, *The Dream Swimmer* takes up elements already present in (the original version of) *The Matriarch* and maps those elements onto the *Oresteia*. Ihimaera's preface declares, '[S]ome scenes from *The Dream Swimmer* have been directly referenced from *The Matriarch* ... The purpose of such intersections, whenever they occur, is to tighten the two stories of both novels on to one frame and to enable the reading of *The Dream Swimmer* without having to refer to *The Matriarch*' (*DS* 8). The revision of *The Matriarch* continues in this vein by clarifying the narrative 'threads' of *The Dream Swimmer*, by explaining its own sequel so to speak (!).[26] Tama picks up his narrative after a long break:

> Eleven years have passed since that winter of 1986 when I put down my pen on the story of the woman who wore pearls in her hair, my grandmother the matriarch, Riripeti Mahana née Pere, whom some called Artemis, ruler of the Mahana family for three generations.
>
> (*DS* 21)

He also accepts that Riripeti's heroism is no longer possible. 'The days of the charismatic leader with supernatural powers to aid him or her have gone' (*DS* 418). That is, the kind of national epic on display in *The Matriarch* in 1986 no longer really works.

Ihimaera has been 'writing New Zealand' for over forty years.[27] His early stories and novels worked 'to establish and describe the emotional landscape of the Maori people'.[28] Dissatisfied with the positivist, pastoral and 'tragically out of date' vision of his early works,[29] Ihimaera (like Tama) put down his pen for a decade. Upon his return, *The Matriarch* became a statement of intent. In that novel, a newly radicalized Ihimaera undertook the postcolonial project of 'writing back', not only against colonial oppression but against his own earlier (mis)representations of the Maori people. *The Matriarch* is soaked in radical politics. Williams puts it well: *The Matriarch* is 'a historical novel which attempts to record the whole response to colonisation, political, military, and psychological, of the Maori people during 150 years of Pakeha occupation.'[30] As Riripeti enjoins young Tama, 'Always fight. Never give up. Your *mana* will help you. Fight fair if you can. But if you must, use whatever devices are at hand. Remember' (*M* 31). Also in this radical period, Ihimaera rewrote Katherine Mansfield in *Dear Miss Mansfield* (1989) and wrote a quasi-autobiographical coming-out novel, *Nights in the Gardens of Spain* (1995).[31]

By contrast, Ihimaera's 'late' works from the new millennium map out a turn to the global.[32] In a telling scene from *The Uncle's Story* (2000), at an indigenous peoples' gathering in Canada, Michael Mahana uses the Rangi–Papa creation myth as an image of indigenous LGBT people coming out the world over. 'I am a gay man. Of all the children of the gods, my kind – gay, lesbian, transvestite and transsexual – inhabited the lowest and darkest cracks between the Primal Parents. We, now, also wish to walk upright upon this bright strand.'[33] And in *The Rope of Man*: 'All Maori and all New Zealanders jointly bring an example of what can be achieved in terms of excellence, equity and justice to all mankind . . . . We bow only to the highest mountain.'[34] Ihimaera had earlier described *Nights* as 'keeping faith with his gay audience' much as he had kept faith with his Maori audience.[35] In these late works, two of Ihimaera's audiences – Maori and GLBT people – take their place, and fight against injustice, on a world stage.

As I see it, *The Dream Swimmer* straddles Ihimaera's middle (political) and late (global) periods. Observe, principally, an unprecedented optimism concentrated in the epilogue. 'The entire fabric of New Zealand governance has reached warp speed as Maori men and women connect into the power sources of the Pakeha and, thus empowered, establish a different set of systems for the nation' (*DS* 417). Second, a note of reconciliation, resonating with *Eumenides*: 'With great forbearance, I have forgiven my father and the Mahana clan' (*DS* 418). Third, a universalized postcolonialism: 'So I wander from one international crisis to the next, absorbing man's inhumanity to man, always being busy, always trying to make a difference . . . When she [Riripeti] spoke so passionately on the *marae* [meeting house] in Wellington in 1949, she was talking about the Pharaoh not just in New Zealand but throughout the world' (*DS* 419). Finally, a global role for Maori, later fleshed out in *The Rope of Man*: 'Indeed, there is so much that the Maori spirit can offer to the world' (*DS* 419). In sum, optimism, reconciliation, internationalism and local actors working globally. Ultimately, however, what trumps all this, right at the very end of the novel, is not myth, history, or revolution or whatever, but love. '[W]e will not be a burden to her because our mother, Tiana, has always loved us. Always' (*DS* 422–423). I find it extraordinary that Ihimaera uses Greek tragedy to make this move.

And so to conclude. First, *The Dream Swimmer* contains more, and more frequent, classical references than any other of Ihimaera's novels or indeed any other New Zealand novel known to me. Second, specific references to Clytemnestra, Orestes and the Furies proliferate as the novel progresses. Third, the narrator models his plot on that of the *Oresteia*. Fourth, didactic passages direct the reader to interpret the story as a version of the *Oresteia*. Cumulatively, this conditions the reader to expect that Tama will kill his mother, and sets up the not-exactly-a-surprise ending foreshadowed in *The Matriarch*: his mother loved him all along. What *is* surprising is that this bona fide postcolonial novel appropriates classical material in such a positivist fashion. Walcott's *Omeros* this is not. Regan may gesture briefly at Achebe by saying that 'things fall apart' in the *Oresteia*, but it is the Pakeha interlocutors – Regan herself and the classicist, Sylvia – who introduce the Maori narrator to Greek tragedy. Tama well nigh reveres Greek tragedy with nary a thought for the colonial baggage which it might bring.[36] Throughout, then, the classical source material goes hand in glove with a melodramatic plot and a new political agenda, destabilizing any simple picture of Ihimaera qua radical Maori writer.

As a result, *The Dream Swimmer* has much to offer classical reception studies and New Zealand letters. On the one hand, it adapts a classical text wholesale.

On the other hand, it marks an important transition in the *oeuvre* of our pre-eminent Maori novelist. As in *The Matriarch*, postcolonial conflict is still prominent, but accommodated to broader concerns: love, family, the world and of course Greek tragedy. All told, therefore, I hope to prompt a reassessment of sorts, both of classical reception in New Zealand culture and also of Ihimaera's politics and poetics. At the very least, I hope to have illuminated (even if only a little) *The Dream Swimmer* as a work of fiction.

Bibliography

Belfiore, E. (2000), *Murder Among Friends: Violation of* Philia *in Greek Tragedy*. New York and Oxford: Oxford University Press.

Calvert, J. (2002), 'Contextualising Maori writing : a study of prose fiction written in English by Witi Ihimaera, Patricia Grace, Keri Hulme and Alan Duff', PhD thesis: University of Waikato.

Crawford, J. M. (2004), 'The Thematic Development of the Magical Child in Fifteen Recent New Zealand Novels', PhD thesis: University of Wollongong.

Ewans, M. (2007), *Opera from the Greek: Studies in the Poetics of Appropriation*. Aldershot: Ashgate.

Fox, A. (2006), 'The Symbolic Function of the Operatic Allusions in Witi Ihimaera's *The Dream Swimmer*', *Journal of Postcolonial Writing*, 42 (1): 4–17.

Fox, A. (2008), *The Ship of Dreams: Masculinity in Contemporary New Zealand Fiction*. Dunedin: Otago University Press.

Harrison, S., ed. (2009a), *Living Classics: Greece and Rome in Contemporary Poetry in English*. Oxford: Oxford University Press

Harrison, S. (2009b), 'Catullus in New Zealand: Baxter and Stead', in S. Harrison (ed.), *Living Classics*, 295–323. Oxford: Oxford University Press.

Heim, O. (2007), 'The Interplay of the Local and the Global in Witi Ihimaera's Revisions', *Journal of Postcolonial Writing*, 43 (3): 310–322 <DOI: 10.1080/17449850701669641>

Ihimaera, W. (1986), *The Matriarch*. Auckland: Heinemann.

Ihimaera, W. (1989), *Dear Miss Mansfield: A Tribute to Kathleen Mansfield Beauchamp*. Auckland: Viking.

Ihimaera, W. (1994), *Bulibasha*. Auckland: Penguin.

Ihimaera, W. (1995), *Nights in the Gardens of Spain*. Auckland: Secker and Warburg.

Ihimaera, W. (1997), *The Dream Swimmer*. Auckland: Penguin.

Ihimaera, W. (2000), *The Uncle's Story*. Auckland: Penguin.

Ihimaera, W. (2005), *The Rope of Man*. Auckland: Reed.

Ihimaera, W. (2009), *The Matriarch*. Revised edition. Auckland: Penguin.

Jackson, A. (2003), *Catullus for Children*. Auckland: Auckland University Press.

Jackson, A. (2009), 'Catullus in the Playground', in S. Harrison (ed.), *Living Classics*, 82–96. Oxford: Oxford University Press.

Jackson, A. (2014), *I, Clodia, and Other Portraits*. Auckland: Auckland University Press.

Jannetta, A. E. (1990), 'Textual strategies of identity formation in Witi Ihimaera's fiction', *Commonwealth*, 12 (2): 17–28.

Love, H. (2011), *Hūrai*. Wellington: Steele Roberts.

Mastronarde, D. J., ed. (2002), *Euripides: Medea*. Cambridge: Cambridge University Press.

Miles, G., J. Davidson and P. Millar (2011), *The Snake-Haired Muse: James K. Baxter and Classical Myth*. Wellington: Victoria University Press.

Millar, P. (1998), 'Witi Ihimaera', in R. Robinson and N. Wattie (eds), *The Oxford Companion to New Zealand Literature*, 254–256. Melbourne and Auckland: Oxford University Press.

Murray, A. S. (1874 [1988]), *Who's Who in Mythology: A Classic Guide to the Ancient World*. 2nd ed. Bracken Books.

Perris, S. (2013), 'Classical References in the Work of Witi Ihimaera: An Annotated Commentary', *Journal of New Zealand Studies*, 16: 19–51.

Perris, S. (2015), 'Witi Ihimaera and the Dread Goddess', *Journal of New Zealand Literature*, 33: 85–109.

Thomson, J. (1998), 'New Zealand (with the South Pacific Islands)', *The Journal of Commonwealth Literature*, 33: 75–98.

Thornton, A. (1999), *Māori Oral Literature: As Seen by a Classicist*. 2nd ed. Wellington: Huia.

Vigier, S. (2008), 'La fiction face au passé: Histoire, mémoire et espace-temps dans la fiction littéraire océanienne contemporaine', PhD thesis: University of Auckland.

Wedde, I. (2001), *The Commonplace Odes*. Auckland: Auckland University Press.

West, M. L., ed. (1966), *Hesiod: Theogony*. Oxford: Clarendon Press.

Williams, M. (1990), *Leaving the Highway: Six Contemporary New Zealand Novelists*. Auckland: Auckland University Press.

4

War, Religion and Tragedy: The Revolt of the Muckers in Luiz Antonio de Assis Brasil's *Videiras de Cristal*

Sofia Frade

Published for the first time in 1990, Luiz Antonio de Assis Brasil's *Videiras de Cristal* (*Crystal Vines*), subtitled *o Romance dos muckers* (*The Novel of the Muckers*), is a novel set in the Brazilian province of Rio Grande do Sul during the reign of Dom Pedro II (1872–1874), the second and final Emperor of Brazil. It tells the true story of a group of immigrants from Germany who, under the leadership of Jacobina Maurer, fought the imperial forces in defence of their messianic Protestant faith. Jacobina Maurer's husband used to cure immigrants with plants and herbal remedies, while his wife gave spiritual support to the sick. Over the course of time this woman became the spiritual leader of a small community of Germans and Brazilians, both Protestant and Catholic. Jacobina Maurer called herself the new Christ and, like Christ, chose her own apostles.

In this chapter I set the novel in the contexts of Brazilian history and the ways in which Brazilian novelists, including Assis Brasil, have portrayed that history, before analyzing the role played in the text by classical literature, especially Euripides' *Medea*. I argue that while there are strong parallels between Jacobina and Medea, the novel portrays classical authors as the cultural property of the elite class who oppress the Muckers. Through the figure of the military officer who eventually suppresses the revolt, San Tiago Dantas, the novel explores the dichotomy between the classical literature consumed by the rich, and the truly tragic experience of the poor, taking place in reality.

Most of the German immigrants to Brazil were given some land by the government and left to their own devices; without any kind of support from the Emperor, they had to build their own houses and make a living for themselves. Most of these immigrants' villages lacked access to proper healthcare, spiritual guidance or even food. As a result, the Muckers became quite popular as a movement. Yet it went on to prompt a violent reaction from both Catholics and Protestants, from the families of the newly converted, and finally from the authorities. Not long after, a real war started in the Morro do Ferrabrás. *Videiras de Cristal* gives us the perspective of the opposing forces on both sides of the conflict and exploits the deep social challenges that underpin the Mucker movement. The first attack against the Muckers by Brazilian troops took place on 28 June 1874, with the troops losing to the Muckers hiding out in the forest. A few subsequent attacks were again disastrous for the troops, but on 2 August they managed to overcome the last of the Muckers.

As Jacobina becomes increasingly important, her husband, who used to be the centre of the community, becomes less significant and ends up assisting his wife. Jacobina becomes the main character in the book and is integrated into the religious narrative created by herself as both subject and object, which simultaneously brings her closer, and distances her from, both her community and us as readers. This religiosity renders most of her dramatic appeal. She is the centre of the plot and the main character, yet we are given no indication of how she thinks or feels. All we have are her words and the interpretation thereof by those around her.

Assis Brasil, an author from Rio Grande do Sul, published his first novel in 1976. He studied in a Jesuit school and received a solid classical education that enabled him to use and develop references to the classics in his novels, although to varying degrees.[1] For example, in 1985, he published *As virtudes da casa (The Virtues of the House)*, a novel set against the background of the war with Artigas, which took place on the Brazil–Uruguay border between 1816 and 1820. The book is inspired by Aeschylus' *Oresteia*, with the colonel Baltazar Antão Rodrigues de Serpa coming back home from war to find his wife Micaela in love with the French Félicien de Clavière.

Videiras de Cristal is Assis Brasil's eighth novel. Several of his previous works focus on his native region. His first novel, *Um quarto de légua em quadro* (*A Quarter of a Mile in Painting*, 1976), is centred on Portuguese immigration from the Azores to Santa Catarina and Rio Grande do Sul. His 1978 work, *A Prole do Corvo (The Raven's Offspring)*, is a historical novel set during the *Revolução Farroupilha*, a republican revolt against the imperial government of Brazil between 1835 and 1845. In 1982 he returns to Rio Grande do Sul with *Manhã transfigurada (Transfigured Morning)*, which narrates the story of Camila, a woman fighting against the restrictions of patriarchal society in the eighteenth century. Then came *As virtudes da casa* (1985), and finally, two years later, *Cães da Província (Dogs of the County)*. Again set in the south of Brazil, the novel focuses on an historical character named José Joaquim de Campos Leão (nicknamed Qorpo-Santo), who lived between 1829 and 1883. He was a journalist, poet and playwright, who was accused of being insane and whose own family had him declared legally unfit to manage his affairs. His personal life was quite dramatic and his works only came to be fully appreciated in the second half of the twentieth century. *Videiras de Cristal*, therefore, shares several themes with previous novels: the location of Rio Grande do Sul, home of the author; the war; the social problems experienced by immigrants; the tensions between city and rural areas; the tension between the immigrants and the Brazilians; the fine line between sanity and madness; the role of women in patriarchal societies; and the overtones of Greek tragedy.

After *Videiras de Cristal*, Assis Brasil wrote a trilogy, once more set in Rio Grande do Sul, but since then his most recent texts share neither the location nor historical basis of his previous novels. His historical works correspond chronologically mainly to the dictatorship period and slightly after. This is not an unusual feature in Brazilian literature; in fact, historical novels seemed to flourish during that time.

Brazil was under a dictatorial regime between 1964 and 1985.[2] The military revolution happened, supposedly, in order to protect national safety in times of crisis and was born of a fear that the then-president João Goulart, with his policies of left-wing agrarian reforms, nationalizations and some expropriations, would turn Brazil into a new Cuba. A new constitution was approved in 1967; censorship and persecution of those suspected to be against the regime was instituted. In the 1980s, the regime lost its appeal and in 1984 the first proper presidential elections in twenty years brought democracy back to Brazil. During these years, the relationship of writers with the power changed a lot, as Valente has argued:

> It is important, however, to bear in mind that whereas most nineteenth-century historical novels participated in the process of myth-formation sponsored by the elites (yielding what Franco calls 'blueprints of national formation'), these recent historical novels express open scepticism about the modernization project embraced by the elites in the twentieth century. Unquestionably, the attitude of writers toward the established powers has changed drastically from that of partner to that of critic, from collaboration to contestation. Readers have noticed a conscious attempt on the part of Brazilian writers of the 1970s and 1980s to distance themselves from anything 'official'. Looking back into the past was a way to try to understand the present. More than that, looking into the past was a way to talk about the present. If fiction started as part of a program

> to define Brazil's identity and to create a nation, united and coherent, during the second half of the twentieth century it turned into a way to address the social problems of the present and still be able to pass through the rigors of censorship.[3]

The themes of historical Brazilian novels are mainly divided between rural and urban, the main source of social differentiation in Brazil.[4] In recent years, the popularity of the rural novel has declined, while the urban novel is still attractive for a more urban and 'Europeanized' audience. Yet, during the dictatorship, historical novels blossomed as, for some reason, they suffered much less from the repressions of censorship than did other forms of literature, such as drama. The novels became popular within relatively restricted circles, and even though they were not encouraged, the authors had relative freedom.

Malcolm Silverman has pointed out that, historically, this genre was very important at two moments in Brazil's history. Since there is a chronological coincidence between romanticism and the independence of Brazil in 1822, the historical novel became a way of defining identity.[5] The novel used autochthonic myths in order to better explain this identity, but, European and classical myths were not completely ignored: indeed they became mixed with indigenous stories and folklore. Fiction has been one of the principal ways to deal with these ambiguities and these unique realities.[6]

Returning to *Videiras de Cristal*, one of the main themes of this novel is the social tension in the colonies of immigrants. This occurs both between the immigrants and the Brazilians, and even among the immigrants themselves. The first generation was able to settle without many problems, achieving a certain degree of wealth and power. Thereafter, however, and as noted above, the incoming Germans were awarded land and left to make their own way. In this novel we find at least three different worlds: the world of politics, with its traditional divisions between liberals and conservatives; the world of religion, with a division between Catholics and Protestants; and finally the world of the poor immigrants, and within this, the community of the Muckers. As in a tragedy with different characters and episodes, we are offered a variety of views from these different worlds and are able to understand that at no point whatsoever are they able to communicate with each other. Each lives their own tragedy, unable to comprehend the others.

The novel presents us with a world that is changing, a world where modernity is just starting, a world where the modern conveniences of Europe are arriving at this increasingly less exotic and distant land. The uncle of Dr Fischer – a stereotyped German living in a German town that resembles a gothic illustration – receives a box from his Brazil-based nephew, who has sent cacti for his uncle's ever-growing collection. When the uncle finds some German newspapers with his plants, he is shocked: 'Quem diria que naquele parte remota do mundo se imprimiam jornais alemães?' ('Who would have known that German newspapers were printed in that remote area of the world?') (412). Yet this modernity does nothing to help the livelihoods of the immigrants. They remain poor, without any proper healthcare, without any kind of support; even their priests are often not properly ordained. In this context, they turn to what is given to them, and that is Jacobina's spiritual guidance.

The lawyer Fogaça is one of the few to understand the social problems that run through this religious movement:

> De quem é a culpa? Por certo não será dessa gente fanática e inculta, posta à margem desse capitalismo perverso que impera aqui.
>
> [And whose fault is it? Certainly this is not the fault of this fanatical and uneducated people, left aside by the perverted capitalism that rules over this land.]
>
> (213)

But even this recognition is used by the liberal Fogaça to attack the conservatives rather than to help the immigrants. In fact, Fogaça is represented in a particularly ironic way: just after saying those words, he is described as fat and bald, barely able to balance himself on top of a box. At no point do the authorities do anything to change the situation for the better. The principal tensions and problems of the characters in the text are those experienced by contemporary Brazilian society at the time that Assis Brasil is writing.

So what is the importance of classical elements in this text? In what ways does Greek myth add to the readings and the relationship between past and present? There are various tragic themes in this novel:[7] the way the characters are self-involved; the way that we are shown each character's thoughts and feelings, giving us, the readers, a view of the diverse lines of thought, just as a Greek tragedy's audience would have had, even giving us an equal account of both parties at war, making us see what the characters just cannot see. As the tragic overtones become stronger and the rhythm of the novel speeds up, there is one tragedy in particular that seems to be invoked by the author: Euripides' *Medea*.

In the last few pages, the children of Jacobina become especially important, particularly Leidard:

> Esta criança, gerada e nacida em nossa fé, ela será o sinal. O seu destino será o nosso destino ... Leidard, com sua saúde e sua beleza, é a imagem da nossa inocência e nossa verdade, o leite que ela suga dos meus peitos é a bênção que que derramo sobre vocês todos, meus filhos pelo poder do Espírito.
>
> [This child, born and bred in our faith, will be the sign. Her destiny will be our destiny ... Leidard, with her health and beauty, is the image of our innocence and our truth, the milk she suckles from my breasts is the blessing I extend on all of you, my children by the power of the Spirit.]
>
> (295)

The destiny of Leidard and the community is one and the same. And it will remain so, as the destiny of the Muckers and the baby will be sealed within the space of a few minutes. As the last survivors fight hopelessly, Jacobina makes a final decision about herself and her younger daughter:

> – Não. Não a cobrirão de vergonha. – E, fitando Ana Maria com um olhar que já é do outro mundo, diz: – Faça o que seu coração tanto quer. Você já sabe. – E entrega-lhe a criança.
>
> Ana Maria aconchega Leidard nos braços e, sob as vistas de todos, pede ao avô Maurer que lhe dê a faca ... Quando ela sai da choupana carregando Leidard, Jacobina põe-se de joelhos.
>
> – Leidard era o último elo que nos unia ao mundo. Nada mais nos resta a não ser a misericórdia de Deus ...
>
> ['No. They won't cover her with shame. – And looking upon Ana Maria, with a gaze that was already from another world, she says: – Do what your heart longs to do. You know it. – And gives her the child.
>
> Ana Maria holds the child in her arms and, in front of everybody, asks grandfather Maurer for his knife ... when she leaves the hovel carrying Leidard, Jacobina falls to her knees. – Leidard was the last link binding us to the world. Nothing is left for us except God's mercy ...']
>
> (407)

Leidard's death is the death of the community, her life is the symbol of the Muckers, and their tragedy is the same. There are a few differences between Jacobina and Medea, perhaps the most important of all being the fact that she does not kill her child with her own hands. Yet there are other points that bring them together and can make us look at the novel in a new way. Both women are foreigners in a land that does not give them what they expected; both are in desperate situations, and for both – to a greater or lesser degree – it is their own fault. However, while Jacobina dies, Medea does not.

It has been argued that the text, despite having many connections with Greek tragedy, cannot be viewed as such, because of the Christian context underlying it: there is always hope.[8] I would like to go back to the phrase: 'O seu destino será o nosso destino.' ('Her destiny will be our destiny.') This phase has no connections with Euripides' *Medea*, yet it does echo a Brazilian adaptation of the play:

> JOANA — Jasão, é importante pra mim. Eu vou mandar as crianças sim, porque meu destino depende disso. Pode deixar . . .
>
> [Jasão, it is important to me. I will indeed send the children because my destiny depends on that. Leave it be . . .]
>
> (Chico Buarque and Paulo Pontes, *Gota d'Água*)

Gota d'Água is a 1975 musical written by Chico Buarque and Paulo Pontes. Joana is the contemporary Medea, destroyed by the capitalist dreams of Jason, who wants to marry the daughter of a rich businessman. The play is set in a *favela* in Rio de Janeiro, and the socio-economic aspects of the slums in Brazil are strongly highlighted during the play.

Joana's destiny, like Jacobina's, is closely related to her children. Joana, like Jacobina, dies in the end, killing her children and then herself. In *Gota d'Água* the tragedy is there, despite the Christian background, or maybe even because of it. The final scene takes place on a stage dominated by an altar. The chorus sings multiple songs with the refrain, 'Deus dará, Deus dará' ('God shall give, God shall give'). However, in complete contrast to the original Medea, there is no god to save Joana, no divinity to intervene. In *Gota d' Água*, as in *Videiras de Cristal*, the women and their communities, left behind by the strong economic powers, turn to God. Jacobina does so to a much greater extent than Joana, and yet God or the gods seem to be absolutely absent. The last hope is no hope at all. These women are driven to tragic acts by their social and political context, and bring their children with them, or in Jacobina's case, their larger community. They die. And the social, economic and political context that drove them to that point does not alter.[9] By filtering the story of Jacobina through Medea's myth, the novel gives us a new tragic framework and opens up fresh perspectives on the text. First of all, both women are foreigners and both have some mystical power and charisma, yet these qualities are rendered almost useless. In fact, it is that difference that both creates the characters and, at the same time, renders their destruction.

This myth of Medea, especially when filtered by another Brazilian text, and a highly political one at that, brings this historical novel into the present. As we have seen, one of the main topics of the novel is the social tension in, and fragile situation of, rural communities. That was a painful reality in Brazil by the end of the dictatorship and the beginning of the democracy. For all the economic progress that the leaders of the country boasted about during the 1970s, none but a small elite had experienced real improvements in their everyday wellbeing. The life of those in remote rural areas, or those in urban slums, was still miserable. The country was assailed by social and economic issues that politics could not and would not address. As in the novel, the movements that threatened the established order were dealt with, but the real problems underneath were not.

It is interesting to see how the classics are used in the text: we have Jacobina as the new Medea, a tragic character and not at all innocent, although her misfortune is far greater than her misdeeds. Not once, however, does the character make reference to herself as a tragic heroine; not once does she make reference to any tragic myth; not once are such references made in relation to her by the other characters. Yet the connections are still there, to be found by the reader, adding a new layer of complexity and a new meaning to the plot. On the other hand, the authorities – and most notably the lawyer Fogaça – make classical references all the time: they love to say things in Latin, to compare themselves to the phoenix, to allude to classical history. But their classical references are just that: references, words, verbal nods to an erudite culture or the appearance of it. Yet they are empty, as are all the discourses that Fogaça provides us with to explore the deep problems of that community; they serve their own interests and their own ideology. The true classics, the real tragic action, is happening silently elsewhere, where no one recognizes it as classic or tragic, where erudition is completely absent; but there, only there, do the myths come to life again, in the misery, in the despair, in the poverty.

I believe that this very fragile contradiction would have been destroyed had the references to Medea been made more explicit, since it is precisely the fact that the main characters do not recognize themselves as 'classical' or 'tragic' that gives them their truly tragic dimension. Jacobina does not recognize herself as a Medea; that would imply a cultural superiority over the rest of the characters that she does not have, and would bring a rationalization to her actions that does not exist in the text. If the authorities recognized her as a Medea-type figure, that would mean they understood the Muckers' tragedy, and they patently do not. The authorities, the elites, see themselves as the 'heirs' of classical culture with their Latin quotes and general mythological references, yet the true heirs of classical paradigms are the ones that have nothing, the ones that live in poverty and do not know enough to recognize their heritage. In this text we clearly have two ideas of classical culture: a rhetorical, empty one; and that present in the tragedy of the quotidian. These two positions are irreconcilable, for the ones owning the first cannot understand the meaning of the second, while the ones living the second cannot distance themselves enough to understand it. Only the reader can understand them, but for that s/he has to let go of the empty formulas, of the 'elite' version of myth, and be able to recognize them in the actions and the suffering of the people.

Finally, in a character that has been noted to be a sort of alter ego of the author, at the end of *Videiras de Cristal* there are a few remarks that help us understand another meaning of the text. They startle us into realizing we are not just facing words, or plots or characters, but also the present, the reality, the pain and the misery of real people, who may be our neighbours today. San Tiago Dantas is the captain who will eventually gain the military victory over Jacobina and her followers. But he is also objective and can view what is happening through the author's eyes. There are at least three moments in the text where this becomes very evident. In the first of these moments we see this character using the military expedition as a basis for his literary endeavours:

> – A propósito, Capitão, vi que você escrevia numa caderneta quando cheguei ao cemitério.
>
> – São anotações.
>
> – Que anotações?
>
> – Anotações para um livro que desejo publicar depois desta campanha.
>
> (...) – Faça como achar melhor. Só lhe digo uma coisa: estamos numa operação militar. Isto não é uma página de literatura.
>
> – Mas um dia poderá ser, Coronel. Quando os fatos desaparecem, fica apenas a literatura.
>
> ['By the way, Captain, I saw you writing on a notepad when I arrived at the cemetery.
>
> 'I'm taking notes.
>
> 'What kind of notes?
>
> 'Notes for a book I want to publish after this campaign.
>
> 'Do as you wish. I just want to tell you something: we are in the midst of a military operation. This is not a page of literature.
>
> 'But one day it could be, Colonel. When the facts disappear, only literature remains.']
>
> (456)

In this first conversation between Captain Dantas and Colonel Genuíno, it is the latter who reminds the former that what is happening around them is not just a basis for literature. Dantas' initial reaction to the Mucker crisis is to see it as material for literature to be written after the event. Obviously, with his affirmation that 'But one day it could be, Colonel', there is a break in the narrative. The readers know that the events they are reading about *will* be turned into literature; they are reading an account of them in the form of a work of fiction. This is the first stage for the reading of this novel: this is literature. Yet, there is still some way to go before the literature is created. And not much later, we have a shift of perspective from Dantas:

> San Tiago Dantas relê o que escreveu. Excesso de adjetivos, excesso de advérbios, muitos "quês" dançando na página, vírgulas errantes. Mas como descrever uma tragédia sem ser excessivo?
>
> [San Tiago Dantas reads what he wrote. Too many adjectives, too many adverbs, too many 'whats' dancing on the page, wandering commas. But how to describe a tragedy without being excessive?]
>
> (531)

In this second episode, we see Dantas both recognizing what is happening around him as a tragedy and at the same time being uncomfortable with his own literary style. There is a problem in his text; it is excessive, heavy and full of adjectives and adverbs. The notes turned into a tragedy, a literary text exploding with emotions. The disengaged captain, who was previously just sketching down observations, is now beginning to relate them to what surrounds him and as he does so, he is faced with a literary problem: how to write about such a tragedy?

Finally, in a third passage, reality imposes itself on the literature. There is a complete shift of perspective; reality is no longer just the backdrop, but instead it forces itself centre-stage. The gunpowder leaves a stronger odour than any writing could:

> San Tiago Dantas fecha a caderneta de anotações, guarda-a no alforje de couro e bafeja as mãos. Será mesmo que de toda a tragédia ficarão apenas aquelas frases ornamentais, lidas pelos Barões da Corte do Rio de Janeiro entre um arroto e um palitar de dentes? Sente o cheiro acre da pólvora ainda pegado aos dedos: isto não é literatura.
>
> [San Tiago Dantas closes his notepad, puts it in his leather saddlebag, and warms up his hand with his breath. Is it possible that out of all this tragedy all that will remain are these overly decorated sentences, read by the Barons in the Rio de Janeiro court while burping and picking their teeth? He feels the bitter smell of gunpowder still clinging to his fingers: this is not literature.]
>
> (503)

There is a kind of evolution in Dantas; he wants to write a book, so he begins by saying that once things are over, all that is left is literature. But as he becomes increasingly engaged with what is happening before his eyes, he is presented with much more than literature: he is presented with a tragedy, but not a staged one.

In the last passage there is a clear appeal to the reader. There are two ways of reading this novel: either, like the aristocrats, looking at it as a book, as words to entertain them while they eat and enjoy themselves; or alternatively, to look at one's *reality*, to look at one's own hands and understand that what you see is not literature, not a fictional plot, a literary tragedy. This is reality; it is happening right here and now. And the realization that this tragedy is happening at this very minute should move the reader to do something, or else to remain forever like the burping Baron, listening to a story while picking his teeth.

Bibliography

Barreto, Eneida Weigner. (2001), *Demônios e Santos no Ferrabrás, Uma leitura de.* Videiras de Cristal: Porto Alegre.

Hall, Edith (2014), 'Divine and human in Euripides' Medea', in D. Stuttard (ed.), *Looking at Medea*, 139–155. London:, Bloomsbury.

Masina, Léa (1992), 'O trágico em videiras de cristal', *Travessia*, 25: 129–138.

Silverman, Malcolm (1998), *Protesto e o Novo Romance brasileiro*. Rio de Janeiro: Civilização Brasileira.

Valente, Luiz Fernando (1993), 'Fiction as History: The Case of Joao Ubaldo Ribeiro', *Latin American Research Review*, 28 (1): 41–60.

5

Translating Myths, Translating Fictions

Lorna Hardwick

'Why is it so hard for nations and for people to remember what they have done?'[1]

'Vergangenheitsbewältigung [the process of getting over the past] is a German word: I don't know whether it can be translated into another language.'[2]

Translation is a key aspect in the creation, recognition and dissemination of world literature. This chapter examines some of the tensions involved when there are multiple phases of translocation. These take myth and its variations temporally and spatially away from its versions in antiquity to those reworked in subsequent traditions and crises. Mythical narratives, and the figures and practices that they translocate, provide histories of shifts in sensibility, understanding and memory.

Some myths and figures lend themselves particularly well to the interface between ancient myth and modern fiction, especially in fiction that moves across national and cultural boundaries to become 'world' literature. Ngũgĩ wa Thiong'o claimed that translation 'opens the gates of national and linguistic prisons. It is thus one of the most important allies of world literature and global consciousness',[3] and the same might be said for myth. However, such claims have to be nuanced. There are tensions between the spiky particularity of some modern fictional receptions of Greek myth and the smoothing out of difference between ancient and modern, and between different examples of the modern that are sometimes evident in the preparation and marketing of material for international readers and audiences for whom translation and translocation can signal an anodyne global cultural vernacular.[4]

Here, I want to explore some of the nuances. The discussion that follows assumes that the concept of translation is not confined to the desire to produce some kind of verbal equivalence but rather to a relationship of exchange, resistance and interpenetration between different languages and cultures. It involves what Sherry Simon has called 'creative interference'.[5] I also draw on recent scholarship that explores the pliability of myth, including that of mythical figures and the traditions associated with them.[6] This fluidity brings into the equation the differing ways in which myths are articulated, both within a particular writer's aesthetic and in the wider context of their (re)generation and circulation.

The main part of this chapter selects and examines two examples of how changes in the ideological climate since 1989 have interacted with this aesthetic. One example has been drawn from a European context: Christa Wolf's *Medea: Stimmen* (1996), originally written in German but translated into many languages and therefore in its iterations an example of the importance of 'double translation'.[7] The second is from a non-European context: Zakes Mda's *Ways of Dying* (1995), originally written in English, which is one of the eleven official languages of the 'new' South Africa. These two works differ greatly in their genesis, temporal and spatial locations, forms, tonal and modal qualities but they also have affinities, not only because of their overt and/or incidental relationships with classical material but also, and most importantly, because of their central role in transition literature. By 'transition literature' I mean literature that emerges in contexts of extensive social, political, institutional and ideological change and which also shapes subsequent conceptions of and attitudes to those changes. Because the transitional force is embodied in the language and formal structures, it also provides markers for shifts in literary aesthetics.

In both works, their contributions to the stages and phases of the development of cultural memory and its transmission are important both as agents in the shaping of their own cultural and political contexts of understanding and for their contribution to mapping the development of world fiction. They demonstrate the multiplicity of fictional techniques open to writers and the consequent demands on readers. My aim in this discussion is to probe the distinctive contribution of ancient myth to these specific examples of creative processes and then to draw some provisional conclusions about the contribution of ancient myth to fictional transition literature more broadly.

Crisis, Critical Distance and Transition Literature

In an essay that examined Christa Wolf's selection of fiction, articles, essays, speeches and interviews for publication, Christopher Colton focused on the importance of recognizing moments of crisis and stress, both in the writer's own life and experience and in the course of history:

> The understanding of these crucial moments of decision or transition in historical and individual experience, beset with fear and insecurity, is the key to maintaining the necessary dynamic of development and the constant expansion of the individual and the collective.[8]

This presents one particular – and author-centred – perspective on crisis literature.[9] Crisis literature can have a sharp generative energy but it is only one element in transition. Transition may be a process as well as a series of watersheds and it may be constructed retrospectively from a position of aspiration for progress and understanding as well as dread of crises. Christa Wolf has commented as follows:

> Sometimes it helps to venture far away in space and time, to travel into a past known only through myths and legends and see what you can find there. You know full well that you are carrying baggage you'll never get rid of: your own individual self.[10]

Wolf has also indicated how she used this tool:

> When I first discovered myth – this was in the early 1980s – I realised the advantage of what I had found . . . you enter what looks like an open market of materials and motives, but you contemplate only what touches you, you reach out only for what fits your hand.[11]

In the writing of individual authors, the deployment of Greek myth offers the opportunity to insert a 'safe' distance that enables them to write back to their own experiences, inner uncertainties and the constraints of their own environment and its cultural politics. As Wolf saw it: 'Myth provides a model that's open enough to incorporate our own present experiences while giving us a distance from our subject that usually only time can make possible.'[12] However, the potential of myth in fiction goes far beyond the light shed on the author's own state of mind. It also provides a vehicle for reaching out metaphorically to sensibilities that may be raw because of the consanguinity of readers' own experiences with those animated in the ancient and the modern works. Equally, readers' sensibilities may be conditioned by apparently different experiences that need to be brought into a relationship with those in the mythical and fictional narratives. Ancient myth is both distant and personal. It provides a conduit between crisis and transition that is both explanatory and challenging to authors and readers alike.[13]

Zakes Mda, *Ways of Dying* (1995)

Transition literature can, therefore, take many forms. Here, I want to focus briefly on one recent example of transition literature that also raises significant questions about how ancient and modern works can be read against and with one another. The work in question is the novel *Ways of Dying* (1995) by Zakes Mda. Mda is a South African playwright, poet and novelist, whose best-known work – besides *Ways of Dying* – is his 2000 novel, *Heart of Redness*. In *Ways of Dying* the conflict and violence of shanty-town life, set against the background of the social and political tensions of post-apartheid South Africa, are observed by the novel's principal character, Toloki. He is a professional mourner who travels between shanty towns to perform at funerals. He sets up home with Noria, a woman of his own village whom he knew when they were children, when he is hired to mourn at the funeral of her son Vuthu, and their different perspectives and approaches to life and death crystallize the challenges of nation-building after the trauma of apartheid.

Mda was born in 1948, the son of a nurse and a teacher, and grew up in the Eastern Cape of South Africa and in the Gauteng black African township of Soweto, iconic for resistance to the oppression of the apartheid regime in South Africa. In his account of his early work in community theatre – *When People Play People* (1993) – Mda describes his experiences of travelling through Lesotho using theatre as a way to increase popular participation in development processes and consciousness-raising in remote communities. He argues that difficulties can be mitigated by a carefully thought-out methodology that combines participation and intervention and revitalizes people's own forms of cultural expression.

His work makes a distinctive contribution to this discussion because it uses fiction as an aesthetic mode that creates links between past and present through the representation of social rituals. Mda's novel is also a work of translation in that it uses traditional oral performance techniques to transpose experiences that might also be communicated through any of the official languages of modern South Africa. It therefore has an added intra-cultural dimension. Yet at the same time that an aesthetic that is long-established in South Africa can be turned to focus on its present (i.e. the new society that emerged in the 1990s), it can also be used to focus backwards in time to the narratives, the societies, customs and values represented in Homer's *Iliad*. In a comparative study of the two works, Elke Steinmeyer has demonstrated how both exploit the motifs of threnody and its place in rites of mourning in order to illuminate societies that are in the process of change. Steinmeyer comments on how the 'striking similarities [sc. of the place of mourning and funeral scenes in oral traditions] ... invite one to read Mda not only in his South African context but also in relation to an ancient classical tradition'.[14] In Mda's novel, the professional mourner Toloki has a dual role. His task is not only to lament the departed but also to take on the role of the Nurse who tells the mourners how the dead person died and reports their last words. In fulfilling this role, the professional mourner becomes the commentator who shapes how the dead person is remembered by the community. This discursive blending within the novel also replicates the role of the author who is both part of the society in transition and also the creator of its image in the public imagination. This blending of internal structure and authorial intervention is a feature common to Mda's novel and to Wolf's.

In an article on *Ways of Dying*, Johan van Wyk identifies its key features as characteristics of transitional literature.[15] These include the persisting catastrophic effects of violence and death, repression of the past and its re-birth, the use of dreams, images of apocalypse and carnival and loss of a sense of 'reality'. The carnivalesque is an important feature in transition literature because it symbolizes the suspension of traditional rules and ways of seeing the world. This can operate as an episode or layer of tonality in a narrative or can be structured into the whole to make this disruption the centre of the work (disruption is also a feature of Wolf's creative practice).

Mda's novel moves his aesthetic and his political purpose from participative theatre into a fictional mode in which the readers view the performative aspects of mourning rituals and their social contexts. This implies continuity as well as disruption. Myth facilitates this paradox in a generic way because of its associations with ritual and performance. The role of myth as a transhistorical and transcultural carrier of memory also allows it to act as a conduit between constructions of the past and their implications for the present. Steinmeyer's analysis of this process through comparison with mourning in Homer sets up a comparative model for correspondences in human psychology and behaviour across cultures while locating Mda's treatment of these within the new South Africa.[16] In Mda, however, the relationship between the narratives of Greek myth and those of the modern context is neither narrative nor intertextual. The links are those of affiliation, mediated through understanding of human behaviour and activated by readers. The contribution of Affiliation Studies as a field of cultural enquiry may have much to offer classical reception research at a time when direct knowledge of, and engagement with, Greek and Latin texts, myths and material culture cannot be automatically assumed in any modern social and educational sphere. Affiliation scholars seek to identify and map buried connections between writers and artists through two, three or even four degrees of separation.[17] Such separations need not be temporal but can also involve mediation through genre, and through idiom and register.

Affiliation analysis raises important questions about repression, loss and transformation of perceptions about antiquity as well as about the cultural agencies involved. Mda's exploitation of the commonalities of mourning provides a bridge between the powerful oral tradition of indigenous African languages and the European-language narrative of his novel. The enterprise marks a step forward from the polarized position taken up by Ngũgĩ wa Thiong'o in his work on the politics of language in African literature. Ngũgĩ argued for the use of vernaculars in order to avoid the suppression of culture signalled by the adoption of hegemonic colonial languages.[18] However, in *Ways of Dying*, Mda both recognizes the status of English as a South African language and also uses it to make central the anthropological and mythical aspects of oral traditions. The affinities with Homer analyzed by Steinmeyer bring a hermeneutic triangularity to ways of reading Mda's text, emphasizing cross-cultural affiliation rather than aetiology and authority in any one language system.

Christa Wolf, *Medea: Stimmen* (1986)

Wolf's work example involves much closer links to specific myths that have been textually and formally transmitted by ancient authors and subsequent poets, painters and novelists. Wolf herself has commented publicly on those aspects of her work.[19] So, to the analysis of text and context must be added the documentary evidence of her own self-reflections. This raises further questions about agency. Are texts in themselves the only source of energy in the encounter between one or more pieces of writing? In what sense can the text be said to be an autonomous interlocutor and a deliberative discussant – or indeed a resister? If we give a role to readers in understanding and creating meaning, can we exclude the perspective that the author may articulate once he or she stands outside the text? What is the role of form in facilitating the dialogues identified by the scholar or created by the new writer?[20] Or is the agency of the text primarily identified and generated by the scholar (or the creative writer or artist or thinker or rhetorician)? The status and modus operandi of the text as a partner in dialogue has become more problematic since literary theory, most notably Roland Barthes, posited the 'death of the author', assuming that meaning is not stable/fixed and that intentionality is not a defining criterion for meaning. Scholars who wish to re-inscribe the concepts and agencies associated with literary humanism also need to resuscitate the author.[21] An additional aspect of the value of Wolf for the study of the relationship between myth and modern fiction is that the evidence is not confined to her published texts, her life experiences and the analyses presented by scholars, but also includes her own perspectives on her ways of working and the intentions and modifications that underlie her work.

When investigating 'connectivities' and 'agencies' – the when, where, how, by whom and to whom, why and with what effects of the relationships between ancient texts and their subsequent migrations, rewritings/re-drawings and re-thinkings – it is also helpful to delete the 're' and to recognize that there may be mutation via creativities of various kinds into 'new'. Some aspects of the ancient text may be disrupted or discarded or reappear in different guises; connections are not always constant or consistent. It is usually necessary to think on several planes simultaneously.[22] Furthermore, it is important to distinguish between the creator of the reception cultural artefact (poem, performance, film, painting, speech) and the activities of the scholar who has a different frame for analyzing and situating these. The creative practitioner, from Dryden to Picasso to Anne Carson, provides (in addition to the aesthetic value of his or her work) a conduit of communication between antiquity and subsequent spectators, viewers and readers (including scholars) that unsettles fixed interpretations.

Wolf's Engagement with Greek Myth – from *Cassandra* to *Medea*

In May 1982, Christa Wolf gave a series of five 'Lectures on Poetics' at the University of Frankfurt. These were based on her Greek travel and studies. The first four lectures provided a detailed background ('Conditions of a Narrative') to the fifth, which was a draft of Wolf's novel *Cassandra*. She subsequently revised and expanded these for publication (in German, 1983; in English translation, 1984).[23] In her introductory remarks to the first lecture, Wolf commented on the provisionality of the aesthetic fabric with which she was working:

> This fabric that I want to display to you now did not turn out completely tidy, is not surveyable at one glance ... There are wefts which stand out like foreign bodies, repetitions, material that has not been worked out to its conclusions.[24]

With hindsight, the observation stands as a metaphor for the relationship between *Cassandra* and her later work *Medea: Stimmen* (1996) and is reinforced by this observation a few sentences later:

> There is and there can be no poetics which prevents the living experience of countless perceiving subjects from being killed and buried in art objects.[25]

Cassandra asked questions about the historical reality of a figure from myth and literature within the framework of the situation of women writers. In *Medea: Stimmen* Wolf shifted her approach, adapting the form of the novel to create a fictional exploration that disinterred the living experience of the mythical figure of Medea, producing a counter-text that challenged the ways in which she had subsequently been portrayed in literature and in the public imagination. In so doing, Wolf also explored through a creative medium the anxieties and epistemological issues that she had identified in the lectures in which *Cassandra* was embedded, with the result that the 'she' that I referred to in my previous sentence also stands for Wolf herself and the complexities of her experiences and public responses to them in the intervening period after the collapse of the GDR in 1989.

There are several significant passages in the 'Conditions of a Narrative' lectures that foreshadow the substance and techniques used in *Medea: Stimmen*. In a substantial sequence (176–180) she discusses the figure of Clytemnestra and the ambiguity of the ancient Greek language that is so difficult to render in translation (for example, in conveying Aeschylus' irony in the tapestry scene in the *Agamemnon* (line 913) when Dike, the goddess of justice, is invoked by Clytemnestra as Agamemnon is being enticed into the house and to his death). Wolf's interlocutor makes the point that various generations of translator not only render the lines according to their own moral views and interpretations but that the task is complicated because the ancient irony of the passage depends on the notion of double standards of morality. While modern readers also have double standards, these differ from the ancient ones.[26]

In her *Medea: Stimmen*, Wolf interrogates double standards that are transhistorical as well as historical and to do that she has to find forms that match the times. In the third lecture, Wolf drew on the fiction of Virginia Woolf and posed this question:

> Why should the brain be able to 'retain' a linear narrative better than a narrative network, given that the brain itself is often compared with a network? What other way is there for an author to tackle the custom (which no longer meets the needs of our time) or remembering history as the story of heroes?[27]

This anticipates and justifies the structure she was to develop for her *Medea* in order to bridge the gap in comprehension of what 'really' happened and its presence in memory and recollection. The final piece in the jigsaw of her embryonic aesthetic is found in the fourth lecture, in which she alludes to the influence of Schiller's poem 'Kassandra' (1802) in encouraging her to probe beneath the surface of Greek literature (in that case, the *Iliad*) to retrieve other traditions and variations of a narrative.[28] Nevertheless, the mythical figure of Medea, and Wolf's underlying concerns in adapting it, result in a shift from the monologue form of *Cassandra* to a polyphony of voices (*Stimmen*) in *Medea: Stimmen*. This in turn reflects unease with the inherited traditions surrounding Medea and with the implications for the relationship between individuals and the events that consume them.[29]

Text, Myth and Variation in Antiquity and in Wolf

In antiquity the Medea myth was both pervasive and pliable.[30] Wolf's variations, both on the myth and its textual forms, offer significant illumination of the development of her insights and strategies from *Cassandra* to *Medea: Stimmen*. What Wolf does and does not pick up from the Euripides text, and what she picks up but changes, also provokes examination of how Euripides' treatment of the myth relates to other examples from antiquity. In his Introduction and Commentary to his scholarly edition of Euripides' text, Donald Mastronarde starts with observation that 'In terms of story-pattern, Eur.'s *Medea* may be analysed as a revenge play'.[31] Pointing to the extensive scholarship on this aspect, he adds that 'A revenge play commonly features such elements as grievance, overcoming of obstacles, deception, murder, and celebration of success, and these may easily be identified in Eur.'s play'. At first reading, Wolf appears not to present her rewriting of the myth as a revenge play, or at least not in terms of the internal structure and tonality of the work. However, when placed in its fuller context, *Medea: Stimmen* can still be read as a variation on the model of the revenge story and I shall return to that aspect in the concluding section of this chapter.

The first level of analysis of comparison between Euripides and Wolf reveals that Wolf has peeled back Euripides' presentation of Medea's emotional behaviour, 'otherness' and violence, a triangulation that shapes the association with infanticide that was so eagerly seized on by subsequent artists and commentators.[32] Margaret Atwood, who herself later produced a novella retelling the story of the *Odyssey* from the perspective of Penelope and the maids in her 2005 *Penelopiad*, commented that, 'Her [sc. Wolf's] attack is head-on and original. Christa Wolf's Medea flatly denies that she committed any of these crimes at all' (i.e. fratricide, infanticide, murder of Glauce by means of the toxic frock), and went on to assert that 'This tale is about Medea but also about us'. According to Atwood, Wolf's *Medea: Stimmen* stirs up uneasy questions about the decisions we would make when confronted with the imperatives of saving one's own skin and staying close to the sources of power that might bring this about.[33] These are examples of 'affiliation', of dilemmas that are recognizable in most times and places. Wolf herself recognized the potential of myth in retrieving and exploring such issues:

> Myth provides a model that's open enough to incorporate our own present experiences while giving us a distance from our subject that usually only time can make possible. In this sense – as a kind of model – myth seems to me a useful tool for any fiction written today.[34]

Wolf's exposure to myth also involved reflection on its effects on her sensibility:

> Myth presents you with a character and a framework to which you must adhere, but within that framework, if you only let yourself go deep enough, undreamt of vistas open before you, and you're free to select, to interpret, to look at the ancient story with a contemporary eye, to let yourself be stared at and touched by figures from the depths of the past ... My methods – fantasy and imagination – were literary rather than scientific.[35]

Nevertheless, Wolf also commented that her writing was informed by as much knowledge as she could gain: 'many people believe that the less you know, the "freer" you are to invent – not so.'[36] She specifically said that she 'found the multitude of sources in this prehistoric field especially stimulating, even exciting, instructive, delightful', especially when they revealed 'the multitudes of a story's possible variants'.

What, then, did Wolf discover and what did she do with the multiple possibilities?[37] The ancient evidence about the variations on the myth reveals that plot-makers (then and subsequently) had a wide choice. The outlines of the myths associated with Medea were well known, both in antiquity and subsequently, and this gives extra point to the variations that are introduced, especially when they problematize alternative strategies that are smoothed out in the summary versions.[38] For example, Euripides is thought to have introduced the infanticide; in other versions the children were killed by the Corinthians in revenge for the killing of their princess or of Creon, or Medea killed them by accident.[39] Scholiasts suggest that the children were honoured by a cult.[40] In antiquity the themes of Medea's relationship with Corinth and the killing of the children were opaque and Wolf exploited this pliability, as did Euripides. Euripides' play begins with the Nurse and the Tutor expressing their concerns about Medea's state of mind (1–95) and there is emphasis throughout the play on her roots in Colchis and her 'otherness'. Wolf refines this to present Medea as alienated in every respect, including from Colchis. She also disrupts Euripides' sequential narrative to present a polyphonic tapestry of accounts by different characters from different perspectives.

Wolf structured her work in eleven sections, each presented by a distinctive voice – Medea (1, 4, 8 and 11); Jason (2 and 9); Agmeda (3), a Colchian former pupil of Medea (his testimony is not to be equated with 'truth'; he recognizes that he is not an objective witness but 'playing a part' (61)); Akamas (5), a Corinthian, Creon's First Astronomer. He comments on the effects of 'internal discord' (94) and how 'normal people don't risk their lives for a phantom' (99). There is also Leukon (7 and 10), another Corinthian, Creon's Second Astronomer and an observer, rather like the watchman in Aeschylus *Agamemnon*, whom he echoes in referring to 'the roof terrace of my tower' (125) and in his capacity to 'see through everything and to be able to do nothing as though I had no hands'. He also uses the ancient and modern vocabulary of physical crises and civic plague, resonating across the centuries between Thucydides and Camus (136–8). Glauce (6), Creon's daughter, is there too, and poses the agonizing question as to what 'known' means (120); and there are seventeen other characters. Each Voice is prefaced by an epigraph quoting an ancient or modern writer (Seneca, Plato, Euripides, Cato, Bachmann, Girard, Kamper, Cavarero). Medea's final sequence (11) brings the Corinthians' actions and the death of the children together with the historic effects:

> '***Dead.*** They murdered them. Stoned them, Arinna says. And I had thought their vindictiveness would pass if I went away. I didn't know them . . . Where can I go? It is impossible to imagine a world, a time, where I would have a place.'[41]

This pessimistic ending raises questions about the extent to which Wolf's treatment of the Medea myth can be read as a comment on her own situation. In a speech 'Thoughts about September 1st 1939' delivered at the Academy of Arts, West Berlin on 31 August 1989, Wolf reflected on the difficulties of addressing the recent past and the problems of finding a new German identity that neither denied the Nazi past nor imported it into present patterns of thinking.[42] In this and other speeches shaped by the events of 1989, dominant themes emerge: the difficulty of working out new structures of feeling and thinking; the role of literature in filling these 'vague empty spaces' and in investigating the 'blind spots in our own past'; the language associated with turning points; the unpalatable truth that 'it hurts to know' (Wolf 1998, 319). These serve as a sub-text to the revelation in 1993 that Wolf had been an informant to the Stasi (the secret police in the German Democratic Republic, the Soviet-dominated East Germany that emerged in the aftermath of the Second World War). Widespread disgust and accusations of hypocrisy ensued.[43] For the topic of this chapter, the most interesting point to emerge is that Wolf said that she had simply forgotten the details of the episode (which covered the years 1959–1962). She recalled meetings with the Stasi but not the details of the information she had passed to them. She claimed to have repressed the memories.[44] Whatever the facts of the matter, it provides an additional and compelling lens through which to read *Medea: Stimmen*, not just for the urgency that it adds to the perspectives of the various Voices on how to live with the fears of insecurity under a repressive regime,[45] but also to the whole work's concern with the process of constructing history and the reputations of the individuals who live it.

Coda

Much has been said about how temporal and cultural translation and transposition are practised by Mda and Wolf. It is a truism of classical reception studies that distance affords critique, but less frequently recognized that distance also permits repression. Both writers in different ways demonstrate awareness of this aspect and develop an aesthetic that tackles it. However, in Wolf's case the problematics of repression involve the personal as well as the socio-political. Is Wolf's Medea an *apologia pro vita sua* as well as an aesthetic exploration of the agency of contradictory voices in changing the trajectory and status of testimony in transitional literature? I hope that this chapter has shown that differing interpretations of her creative practice can be kept on the same agenda. It is less a question of either/or than of both/and, and the respective balances between the alternatives depend not just on the contexts of reading and interpretation but also on keeping tabs on the whole sweep of evidence in the debate. The 'hot spots' in the intersections between myth and fiction enable us to get a feel for the layering and shifting of the myths and of the writing practices that communicate them.

A second key question is: what do these two examples of very different kinds of relationship between modern fiction and Greek myth add to our understanding of transition literature? Here I would argue that both add to understanding of the relationship between the 'umbrella' concept of transition literature and the associated areas of crisis literature and trauma studies. There are, too, wider questions about the contribution of both writer's work to the burgeoning fields of memory studies and of cultural and political amnesia and repression. Both writers are, in different ways, editors: they discover and interrogate oral and literary sources and cultural practices associated with conflict and death. They both look behind the 'given' evidence and experiences. In the case of *Medea: Stimmen*, this includes the multiple manifestations of the myth. The tasks of the reader and the scholar are to be alert to what the author/editor is doing with the material and how he or she achieves the effects that seep into the readers' consciousness. Wolf's self-reflexive engagement with the intersection between the mythical narratives and the modern fiction that she creates challenges the histories of the myth's reception and the judgements made by her critics as well as her self-perception as human being and as author.

The 'distancing' characteristics of classical myth provide a field for contests but also for avoidance. Although it does not follow the same narrative trajectory of Euripides' play nor of any one of the many versions of the myth, Wolf's *Medea: Stimmen* nevertheless includes the raw material of a revenge tragedy.[46] However, while constituent elements such as grievance, deception, killing and celebration of success occur in the Medea myth and in Euripides' reworking of it, in Wolf these elements are re-articulated in a meta-narrative. Wolf's narrative is distanced from the 'events' in the myth and is structured through her adaptation of form, especially in the creation of multiple perspectives. So a better way of characterizing her work might be to think of *Medea: Stimmen* not as a 'revenge' story but as 'writing back' – 'writing back' on behalf of the Medea of myth but shaped by Wolf to embrace the additional dimension of 'writing back' to her own society, her experiences and to her inner self.[47] This is not 'writing back' in the postcolonial sense but on a number of cultural and political planes: the histories involved include personal life story; the narratives associated with the GDR (both at its time of power and when perspectives on that power were revised); and the transhistorical and transcultural recreations of the story of Medea. The result is a work that not only refictionalizes the myth but also extends its metaphorical range to embrace allusion to twentieth-century events and Wolf's own life-experiences.

Seamus Heaney, in *The Redress of Poetry* (1995), discussed how the struggle of an individual consciousness towards affirmation merges with a collective straining for self-definition. This may be true of Heaney but Wolf's personal and political-historical struggle is less easily resolved by 'merging'; the jagged edges persist, the definitions resist closure. The plasticity of the Medea story and its associated discomforts have been actualized through the interplay of the ancient myth and the aesthetic of modern fiction. Paradoxically, although the temporal and cultural 'distance' provided by the exploitation of ancient myth does facilitate sharper sensibilities and critique of the modern contexts, that distance also preserves the possibility of denial and avoidance of unwelcome aspects of the present. These can simply be shifted away from their contemporary grounding to the 'safer' realms of the more abstract 'transhistorical' plane. Both Mda and Wolf in their different ways provide variations on the question posed by Jacqueline Rose: *Why is it so hard for nations and people to remember what they have done?*[48] Myth in fiction recalls raw material but also enables the difficult questions surrounding its shattering and re-assembly to resist certainty; it leaves the possibility of a succession of open-ended readings and especially underlies the claim of Mohammad Shaheen that 'The redeeming feature of any new translation is that it forms an open invitation for a further different translation advanced to the reader'.[49]

Bibliography

Atwood, Margaret (1998), 'Medea' (https://www.randomhouse.com/boldtype/0498/Wolf/notebook.html accessed 03/03/2015).

Atwood, Margaret (2005), *The Penelopiad*. London: Canongate.

Bassnett, Susan (2014), *Translation*. London and New York: Routledge.

Clauss, James L. and Sarah Iles Johnston, eds (1997), *Medea: Essays on Medea in Myth, Literature, Philosophy, and Art*. Princeton, N.J.: Princeton University Press.

Colton, C. (1994), 'Was bleibt – eine neue Sprache?', in Ian Wallace (ed.), *Christa Wolf in Perspective*: *German Monitor*, 30: 207–226. Amsterdam and Atlanta, GA: Rodopi.

Cook, Elizabeth (2001), *Achilles*. London: Methuen.

Craig, David and Michael Egan (1979), *Extreme Situations: Literature and Crisis from the Great War to the Atom Bomb*. London: Macmillan.

Darwish, Mahmoud (2014), Translation and introduction to M. Shaheen, *Why Did You Leave the Horse Alone?* London: Hesperus Press (first published in Arabic, 1995).

Easterling, Pat (1977), 'The infanticide in Euripides' *Medea*', *Yale Classical Studies* 25: 177–192.

Frank, Joseph (1963), *The Widening Gyre: Crisis and Mastery in Modern Literature*. New Brunswick, NJ: Rutgers University Press.

Gaskin, Richard (2013), *Language, Truth and Literature.* Oxford: Oxford University Press.

Geertsema, J. (2008), 'Between Homage and Critique: Coetzee, Translation and the Classic', in Alexandra Lianeri and Vanda Zajko (eds), *Translation and the Classic: Identity as Change in the History of Culture*, 110–127. Oxford: Oxford University Press.

Graves, Peter (1994), 'The Treachery of St. Joan: Christa Wolf and the Stasi', in I. Wallace (ed.), *Christa Wolf in Perspective: German Monitor,* 30: 1–24. Amsterdam and Atlanta, GA: Rodopi.

Hall, Edith (2004), 'Introduction: Why Greek Tragedy in the Late Twentieth Century?', in Edith Hall., Fiona Macintosh and Amanda Wrigley (eds), *Dionysus Since 69: Greek Tragedy at the Dawn of the Third Millennium*, 1–46. Oxford: Oxford University Press.

Hall, Edith (2007), 'Subjects, selves and survivors', *Helios,* 34: 125–159.

Hall, Edith (2009) 'Greek tragedy and the politics of subjectivity in recent fiction', *Classical Receptions Journal,* 1: 1–17.

Hall, Edith (2014) 'Divine & human in Euripides' *Medea*', in D. Stuttard (ed.), *Looking at Medea*, 139–155. London: Bloomsbury.

Hardwick, Lorna (2010), 'Negotiating Translation for the Stage', in E. Hall and S. Harrop (eds), *Theorising Performance: Greek Drama, Cultural History and Critical Practice*, 192–207. London: Duckworth.

Hardwick, Lorna (2015), 'Audiences Across the Pond: Oceans Apart or Shared Experiences?', in Kathryn Bosher, Fiona Macintosh, Justine McConnell and Patrice Rankine (eds), *The Oxford Handbook of Greek Drama in the Americas*, 819–840. Oxford: Oxford University Press.

Hardwick, Lorna and Carol Gillespie, eds (2007), *Classics in Post-colonial Worlds.* Oxford: Oxford University Press.

Heaney, Seamus (1995), *The Redress of Poetry*. London: Faber.

Hopman, Marianne Govers (2012), *Scylla: Myth, Metaphor, Paradox.* Cambridge: Cambridge University Press.

Johnston, Kenneth R. (2013), *Unusual Suspects*. Oxford: Oxford University Press.

Lu, Yixu (2004), 'Germany: Myth and Apologia in Christa Wolf's Novel *Medea. Voices*', *Portal,* 1 (1): 1–19.

Mastronarde, Donald J., ed. (2002), *Euripides' Medea*. Cambridge: Cambridge University Press.

McCullum-Barry, Carmel (2014), 'Medea Before and (a little) After Euripides', in D. Stuttard (ed.), *Looking at Medea*, 23–34. London: Bloomsbury.

Mda, Zakes (1993), *When People Play People: Development Communication through Theatre*. London: Zed Books.

Mda, Zakes (1995), *Ways of Dying.* Oxford: Oxford University Press.

Ngũgĩ wa Thiong'o (1986), *Decolonising the Mind: the Politics of Language in African Literature.* London: James Currey.

Ngũgĩ wa Thiong'o (2012), *Globalectics: Theory and the Politics of Knowing*. New York: Columbia University Press.

Parker, Jan and Timothy Mathews, eds (2011), *Tradition, Translation, Trauma: The Classics and the Modern*. Oxford: Oxford University Press.

Pozorski, Aimee (2014), *Falling after 9/11: Crisis in American Art and Literature*. New York: Bloomsbury Academic.

Rose, Jacqueline (2011), *Proust Among the Nations: from Dreyfus to the Middle East* [Carpenter Lectures 2008]. Chicago and London: Chicago University Press.

Schiller, Friedrich (1983), *Schillers Werke: Nationalausgabe* vol. 2.1, *Gedichte*, ed. Norbert Öllers. Weimar: Böhlaus.

Steinmeyer, E. (2003) 'Chanting the Song of Sorrow: Threnody in Homer and Zakes Mda', *Current Writing: Text and Reception in Southern Africa*, Volume, 15 (2): 156–172.

Wolf, Christa (1984), *Cassandra, A Novel and Four Essays*, trans. J. Van Heurck. London: Virago (first published in German 1983).

Wolf, Christa (1993), *The Writer's Dimension: Selected Essays*, ed. A. Stephan, trans. J. Van Heurck. London: Virago.

Wolf, Christa (1996), *Medea: Stimmen*, Munich: Luchterhand Verlag.

Wolf, Christa (1998a), *Medea: A Modern Retelling*, trans. J. Cullen. London: Virago.

Wolf, Christa (1998b), 'From Cassandra to Medea: Impulses and Motives behind my work on two mythical figures', trans. J. Cullen, (https://www.randomhouse.com/boldtype/0498/Wolf/notebook.html accessed 28/02/2015)

Van Wyk, Johan (1997), 'Catastrophe and Beauty: *Ways of Dying*, Zakes Mda's Novel of Transition', *Literator* 18 (3): 79–90.

Van Zyl Smit, Betine (2010), 'Orestes and the Truth and Reconciliation Commission', *Classical Receptions Journal*, 2 (1): 114–135.

6

Echoes of Ancient Greek Myths in Murakami Haruki's novels and in Other Works of Contemporary Japanese Literature

Giorgio Amitrano

Japan may seem to offer an evident example of great cultural distance from ancient Greece. But when Japan, in the second half of the nineteenth century – and after more than two centuries of almost complete isolation – opened up to foreigners, the Greek world, hitherto virtually unknown, began quickly to be seen as a model of civilization, one almost as influential as the contemporary cultures of England, Germany, France and other western countries.

Right at the dawn of the Japanese process of modernization (and of the absorption of western models) called *Bunmei kaika* ('civilization and enlightenment'), we find an example of such admiration in the novel *Keikoku bidan* (*Inspiring Instances of Good Statesmanship*, 1883–1834) by Yano Ryūkei,[1] also known as Yano Fumio (1850–1931). Written at the height of the Freedom and People's Rights Movement and set in fourth-century Thebes, the novel was published more or less in the same years when Gilbert and Sullivan were creating and staging their comic opera *The Mikado* (1885), which was set in a picturesque and fictional Japan.[2] Both works, seen through our modern disenchanted eyes, appear quite amusing as examples of irredeemable kitsch, but the intentions of their authors were entirely different. *Keikoku bidan* is a genuine, albeit naïf, idealization of the Greek world, whereas The *Mikado* is really a satire of British institutions. Its authors, under the influence of the Japanese vogue very much in fashion at the time, chose an exotic setting without any notion of respect for the country portrayed. The opera was actually a rather fantastic representation of an Asian country, and devoid of any realistic pretence.[3]

Keikoku bidan belonged to the genre of the so-called 'political novel', then very popular in Japan. Yano Ryūkei was a bureaucrat, a politician – he was one of the organizers of the Constitutional Reform Party – a journalist and a writer. His aim in writing *Keikoku bidan* was to create a novel which would encourage young Japanese men to build a constitutional government. The remote Greek setting helped to avoid censorship, but the choice was also determined by the author's desire to project Japan's democratic ambitions onto a foreign mirror. Not just any western mirror, but the mirror that could represent to Japanese people the very cradle of western civilization. The book chronicles the struggle of Thebes and other city-states to overthrow Sparta's rule in the Peloponnesian war. The author acknowledges ancient sources and mentions both Xenophon and Plutarch, whose works he supposedly read in English translation.[4]

I mentioned the cultural distance that separates modern Japan from ancient Greece, but the cultural distance of contemporary Japan from what Japan was at the dawn of modernity is, after more than a century and a half, no less significant. Following the Meiji Restoration (1868), which in itself marked a social revolution, Japan underwent a series of changes of unprecedented intensity. Few countries have experienced such a traumatic encounter with modernity. And this was just a prelude to a much more dramatic string of painful events and traumas, which culminated in the tragic results of the Second World War. It is not my intention to summarize in a few sentences a long and complicated history, but it may be useful to remember that the Japanese population suffered shocks much greater than seeing the dream of the power of the Japanese Empire turning into a nightmare of impotence. They saw the aftermath of two atomic bombs which, besides killing so many, left a trail of ailing people for decades; they lived through the trauma of hearing the Emperor, direct descendant of the gods, publicly deny his divinity. The symbolic impact of this event was devastating and implied a dramatic crisis of identity. They experienced poverty, hunger and humiliation, then slowly recovered, and eventually became protagonists of one of the most amazing phenomena of economic growth in the twentieth century, becoming the world's second largest economy after the United States.

One might wonder whether the Greek world, after having been used as a sort of founding myth for the establishment of democracy in Japan, would remain resonant during the turmoil of the twentieth century and retain its significance for Japanese culture. Surprisingly enough, it did. So many references to Greek history, art, philosophy and literature can be found throughout the twentieth century in most fields of Japanese culture that it would be right to say that ancient Greece made a significant contribution to the construction of modern Japanese identity.

Traces of this influence are still so conspicuous that one of the most celebrated recent novels from a world-famous Japanese author – *Kafka on the Shore* (*Umibe no Kafuka,* 2002) by Murakami Haruki – draws inspiration from the Oedipus myth, of which it offers a new and original reinvention. In the interval between Yano Ryūkei's Confucian approach to Greek history and Murakami's sophisticated version of Greek myths, there have been innumerable references to ancient Greek culture in Japan, and to Greek myths in particular, by far too many writers to be presented here. Nonetheless, providing a few more relevant examples of the Greek heritage in modern Japanese culture could be useful for a better contextualization of Murakami's work.

I will begin with Mishima Yukio (1925–1970), an internationally recognized author who, in pre-global Japan, anticipated some aspects of the post-modern world (i.e. the emphasis on images, a singular capacity for using the media as a means of expression and self-promotion etc.). Ancient Greece plays a very important role in Mishima's work. Even though he meant, particularly in his later years, to enhance the value of traditional Japanese culture, his passion for Greek myths was incomparably stronger than his interest in Japanese mythology. He uses themes taken from classical Greece in various forms, as sources of inspiration for creating stories, and as instruments for plunging into the unconscious and exploring its depths. On each occasion, Mishima shows a deep affinity with the Greek world, and even his vision of suicide as a noble and beautiful death, fostered by the samurai tradition, is influenced by Greek suggestions. A few days before he committed suicide, Mishima mentioned in a letter to a friend that Plato's *Phaedo*, where suicide is considered to be an honourable choice under the right circumstances, was one of his recent readings.[5] He must have been impressed by observations like the following:

> Then, perhaps, from this point of view, it is not unreasonable to say that a man must not kill himself until God sends some necessity upon him, such as has now come upon me.[6]

Probably Mishima perceived what Sylvia Plath in her poem 'Edge', probably the last poem she wrote before she committed suicide, called 'the illusion of a Greek necessity'.[7] It may not be by chance that Plath's poem evokes the figure of the same Medea from whom Mishima drew inspiration for his short story 'Shishi' ('The Lioness', 1948).[8]

The story, declaredly based on Euripides' *Medea*, is set in post-war Japan. The heroine, Shigeko, daughter of a wealthy family, has married a man who neglects her and who has affairs with other women. They met in Mukden, in the Manchuria occupied by the Japanese army in 1931, where the young woman's father had tried to build a business. Memories of the Japanese retreat from

Manchuria and its horrors linger in Shigeko's memory. But the tragedies of war do not make her individual drama less intense, nor her feeling of having been betrayed less painful. On the contrary, human passions such as jealousy and hatred seem to relegate history to the background. Shigeko, after having heard from her husband that he has betrayed her for another woman, makes her decision. She poisons her rival and her father and then, in order to complete her vengeance and give her husband the cruellest punishment, she kills their child by strangling him.

A less sombre reinvention of Greek classics by Mishima is his novel *Shiosai* (*The Sound of the Waves*, 1954), a love story set in a fishing village of a Japanese island, between a young fisherman and the beautiful daughter of a rich islander. The novel, inspired by Longus' novel *Daphnis and Chloe*, was written a few years after Mishima's visit to Greece in 1951. To judge from his travel diary *Aporo no sakazuki* (*The Cup of Apollo*, 1952), in Greece he experienced absolute bliss. He wrote: 'Greece is the land of my dreams . . . Now I am in Greece. I am drunk on supreme happiness.'[9] He visited the Acropolis, the Parthenon, the Temple of Zeus and watched Greek tragedies performed at the theatre of Dionysus. He loved everything about Greece. When he returned to Japan, he enrolled in a course in Greek at Tokyo University and, although he did not pursue the study of the language for long, he continued to cultivate his passion for the country. Several works are homages to Greek mythology, among them a tragedy called *Nettaijū* (*The Tropical Tree*, 1960), whose story is inspired by the myth of Electra, and a comedy, *Niobe* (1949), published in a literary magazine and never produced on stage.[10]

Mishima, who was considered by many the epitome of narcissism, dedicated great attention to this theme. In his essay 'On Narcissism', he maintains that narcissism (and self-consciousness) cannot exist in a woman, because she is protected by nature – more precisely by 'the gravitational pull of the womb' – from seeing her true face in a mirror.

> Narcissus, obsessed by the beauty of his own self-reflection seen in water, plunged into that water and drowned. That he was a man, and not a woman, is evidence of the wisdom of the Ancient Greeks. For Narcissus must, of necessity, be a man.[11]

Mishima's provocative exclusion of woman from the experience of the utterly masculine process of self-consciousness could be read as an attempt to give a philosophical justification to what is basically a homoerotic fantasy.[12]

One of the most interesting literary experiments based on reinvention of Greek myths is by a woman writer, Kurahashi Yumiko (1935–2005). Her

Anti-Tragedies (Hangeki, 1971) is a group of five short novels, based on themes from Greek tragedy. The book appeared just a year after Mishima's death and showed some similarities to his approach in the way Kurahashi borrowed characters and stories from the Greek world and transplanted them in contemporary Japanese settings. The most famous among these five novels is *To Die at the Estuary* (*Kakō ni shisu,* 1971), a bizarre and eccentric version of Sophocles' *Oedipus at Colonus.*

Takayanagi, an old man, returns to his old hometown, where he has bought a house by the estuary of a river. When the old man sees the house for the first time – it was bought by a friend on his behalf – he is shocked to see the landscape of his childhood turned into a bleak industrial area. Nature has been destroyed and where the summer grasses grew, an oil refinery and chemical plant have been built. Takayanagi is accompanied by his daughter, Asako. She is so young that she looks more like his granddaughter and although everybody, including the girl herself, ignores it, she actually *is* his granddaughter, her real father being Takayanagi's son. Her mother, Takayanagi's wife, hanged herself when Asako was a little child. That is not his only secret. After his father remarried, he slept with his stepmother. 'He had been driven by the idea that it was something he had to do in order to fulfil the prophecy made about him . . .'[13] The prophecy that he would couple with his mother had been made by a blind beggar who, in his turn, had received the same prophecy. This man, who had been unable to escape from his fate, had blinded himself after killing his father and taking his mother as his wife.

It is not easy for the reader to find a way through such a narrative labyrinth. But what matters is not shedding light on the plot or understanding the complicated relations among the characters. The real interest of the story lies in the sense of an ominous prophecy lurking in an ordinary environment. The ancient myth of Oedipus has come a long way from the world of Greek tragedy to settle in a desolate industrial landscape of contemporary Japan, merging into people's daily life, being completely absorbed in Japanese culture. Kurahashi Yumiko's choice of *Anti-Tragedies* as title for her book could not be more appropriate.[14]

Also in Murakami Haruki's *Kafka on the Shore (Umibe no Kafuka,* 2002) a prophecy hangs over the young hero, the fifteen-year-old Tamura Kafka ('Kafka' is the name he gave himself as homage to the writer he admires).

> At times like that I always feel an omen calling out to me, like a dark, omnipresent pool of water.[15]
>
> (8)

It is the same Oedipal prophecy echoed through *To Die at the Estuary*, this time told to Tamura by his father: he will commit patricide and sleep with his mother and – there is a variation here – his sister. Trying to escape the prophecy, Tamura leaves his Tokyo home and goes to Takamatsu, on the island of Shikoku, where he finds shelter in a private library run by a middle-aged-woman, Miss Saeki, and a friendly young transgendered gay man, Ōshima (he describes himself as a female with a male mind). Tamura, who fled from the prophecy as well as from a cruel, malevolent father, feels at home in the library. He likes both Ōshima, who takes him under his wing, and the elusive, attractive Miss Saeki. He is a voracious reader and enjoys choosing books that he reads and discusses with Ōshima. But this idyllic situation is shattered when one night Tamura wakes up in the grounds of a Shintō shrine with his T-shirt soaked in blood, a pain in his shoulder and no memory of what has happened. When he learns from a newspaper that his father (the reader discovers for the first time that he was a famous sculptor) has been brutally killed, he fears that he himself could be the murderer. Although he could not realistically have gone to Tokyo and back in a few hours, he is aware that in a separate reality all sorts of things can happen. And they do. Miss Saeki's spirit as a girl of his own age manifests in his room every night. In a forest Tamura meets two soldiers who stepped out of time during the Second World War and live in a parallel dimension.

The existence of parallel worlds is reflected in the structure of the book. As in other Murakami novels, the story is split into two distinct but gradually converging stories, told in alternating chapters. Tamura Kafka is the hero of the odd-numbered chapters, whereas the even-numbered chapters tell the story of an elderly man, Nakata, who – despite being illiterate and having suffered some brain damage – has the ability to talk with cats. His brain damage was caused by a mysterious incident at the end of the Second World War, when a group of schoolchildren lost consciousness during a school trip in the local woods. The other children recovered and he was the only one permanently affected. Nakata, in spite of his innocent and trusting nature, is forced to commit a murder. But his purity remains unpolluted by this episode and his disarming simplicity wins him the respect of Hoshino, a young truck driver, who transports and takes care of Nakata on his trip to Takamatsu. The man Nakata killed is no other than Tamura Kōichi, the sculptor, Kafka's father, who introduced himself to Nakata under the name of Johnnie Walker.

This fact does not, however, resolves the riddle of the boy's involvement in the murder. He knows that responsibilities do not exist only in the domain of reality. As Yeats pointed out, 'In dreams begin responsibilities'.[16] The sentence is quoted in a note written by Ōshima which Kafka found in a book about Adolf Eichmann.

> I shut the book, lay it on my lap, and think about my own responsibility. I can't help it. My white T-shirt was soaked in fresh blood. I washed the blood away with these hands, so much blood the sink turned red. I imagine I'll be held responsible for all that blood. I try to picture myself being tried in a court, my accusers doggedly trying to pin the blame on me, angrily pointing fingers and glaring at me. I insist that you can't be held responsible for something you can't remember. I don't have any idea what really took place, I tell them. But they counter with this: 'It doesn't matter whose dream it started out as, you have the same dream. So you're responsible for whatever happens in the dream. That dream crept inside you, right down the dark corridor of your soul.' Just like Adolf Eichmann, caught up – whether he liked it or not – in the twisted dreams of a man named Hitler.
>
> (141–142)

So, even though Kafka tried to escape from the prophecy, he was fated to fulfil it – just like Oedipus. Whether he sleeps with his mother and his sister is not clear. Miss Saeki, with whom he has sex, might be his mother, and Sakura, a young woman he meets during his trip to Takamatsu, might be his sister, but Murakami leaves this mystery, as he does many others, unsolved. Kafka discusses the prophecy with his mentor, Ōshima, who is familiar with the Greek world and is keen on introducing it to Kafka.

> 'If I had to say anything it'd be this: Whatever it is you're seeking won't come in the form you're expecting.'
>
> 'Kind of an ominous prophecy.'
>
> 'Like Cassandra.'
>
> 'Cassandra?' I ask.
>
> 'The Greek tragedy. Cassandra was the princess of Troy who prophesied. She was a temple priestess, and Apollo gave her the power to predict fate. In return he tried to force her to sleep with him, but she refused and he put a curse on her. Greek gods are more mythological than religious figures. By that I mean they have the same character flaws humans do. They fly off the handle, get horny, jealous, forgetful. You name it.' . . .
>
> 'What kind of curse was it?'
>
> 'The curse on Cassandra?'
>
> I nod.
>
> 'The curse Apollo laid on her was that all her prophecies would be true, but nobody would ever believe them. On top of that, her prophecies would all be unlucky ones--predictions of betrayals, accidents, deaths, the country falling into ruin. That sort of thing. People not only didn't believe her, they began to despise her. If you haven't read them yet, I really recommend the plays by

> Euripides or Aeschylus. They show a lot of the essential problems we struggle with even today . . .'
>
> (164)

A reviewer of *Kafka on the Shore* writes: 'Kafka's guilt is biblical, linked to sexual maturity and the sins of the fathers.'[17] I am not completely sure if his guilt is really biblical, but certainly Tamura is dominated by it, like one of Natsume Sōseki's heroes. Sōseki, whose work is discussed in the novel by Kafka and Ōshima, excelled in portraying male heroes whose lives were ruined by a sense of culpability that was not entirely justified by the gravity of their errors.

In another dialogue between Ōshima and Kafka, the assistant librarian uses examples from Greek wisdom to lecture his young protégé.

> Ōshima gazes deep into my eyes. 'Listen, Kafka. What you're experiencing now is the motif of many Greek tragedies. Man doesn't choose fate. Fate chooses man. That's the basic worldview of Greek drama. And the sense of tragedy – according to Aristotle – comes, ironically enough, not from the protagonist's weak points but from his good qualities. Do you know what I'm getting at? People are drawn deeper into tragedy not by their defects but by their virtues. Sophocles' *Oedipus Rex* being a great example. Oedipus is drawn into tragedy not because of laziness or stupidity, but because of his courage and honesty. So an inevitable irony results.'
>
> 'But it's a hopeless situation.'
>
> 'That depends,' Ōshima says. 'Sometimes it is. But irony deepens a person, helps them mature. It's the entrance to salvation on a higher plane, to a place where you can find a more universal kind of hope. That's why people enjoy reading Greek tragedies even now, why they're considered prototypical classics. I'm repeating myself, but everything in life is metaphor. People don't usually kill their father and sleep with their mother, right? In other words, we accept irony through a device called metaphor. And through that we grow and become deeper human beings.'
>
> (218)

Ōshima feels the need to invoke Greek myths, which he brandishes as a sarcastic weapon when he argues with two feminists who visit the library and criticize harshly some aspects of the organization as sexist.

> 'That's the way every sensible woman feels,' the tall one adds, her face expressionless.
>
> 'How could any woman of generous spirit behave otherwise, given the torments that I face,' Ōshima says.
>
> The two women stand there as silent as icebergs.

> '*Electra*, by Sophocles. A wonderful play. I've read it many times, again and again.'
>
> (192)

One of the many subplots of this novel tells the story of Miss Saeki's youth. She was a singer, author of the hit song 'Kafka on the Shore' and she had a sweetheart, the eldest son of the Komura family, the owners of the library. They loved each other deeply, but he was killed at twenty, during the university riots at the end of the 1960s, by students who had mistaken him for a leader of an opposing faction. After his death, Miss Saeki had never sung again and had lived in limbo. In Kafka's room, the one which is visited by the living spirit of the young Miss Saeki, there is a painting on the wall, portraying a young boy. And even in this painting there is a reminder for Tamura of the Oedipal prophecy he seems unable to escape.

> I stand up, go over to the wall, and examine the painting up close. The young man is looking off in the distance, his eyes full of a mysterious depth. In one corner of the sky there are some sharply outlined clouds, and the largest sort of looks like a crouching Sphinx.
>
> I search my memory. The Sphinx was the enemy Oedipus defeated by solving the riddle, and once the monster knew it had lost, it leaped off a cliff and killed itself. Thanks to this exploit, Oedipus got to be king of Thebes and ended up marrying his own mother.
>
> (246–247)

Tamura Kafka has an alter ego, a boy named Crow ('Kafka' means 'jackdaw', a bird similar to a crow, in Czech), probably a projection of his own self, who scolds and encourages him like an older brother. He knows, even more assuredly than Kafka himself, that one is responsible for his actions, even if they only happened in dreams, and there is no way to escape their consequences.

> 'Even if it's in a dream, you shouldn't have done that,' the boy named Crow calls out. He's right behind me, walking in the forest. 'I tried my best to stop you. I wanted you to understand. You heard, but you didn't listen. You just forged on ahead.'
>
> I don't respond or turn around, just silently keep on trudging.
>
> 'You thought that's how you could overcome the curse, right? But was it?' Crow asks.
>
> But was it? You killed the person who's your father, violated your mother, and now your sister. You thought that would put an end to the curse your father laid on you, so you did everything that was prophesied about you. But nothing's

really over. You didn't overcome anything. That curse is branded on your soul even deeper than before. You should realize that by now. That curse is part of your DNA. You breathe out the curse, the wind carries it to the four corners of the Earth, but the dark confusion inside you remains. Your fear, anger, unease – nothing's disappeared. They're all still inside you, still torturing you.

'Listen up – there's no war that will end all wars,' Crow tells me. 'War breeds war. Lapping up the blood shed by violence, feeding on wounded flesh. War is a perfect, self-contained being. You need to know that.'

'Sakura – my sister,' I say. I shouldn't have raped her. Even if it was in a dream. 'What should I do?' I ask, staring at the ground in front of me.

(424–425)

The Japanese scholar Komori Yōichi examined meticulously the relation between *Kafka on the Shore* and the Oedipus myth in an essay on the novel. He even established a relatively elaborate chart of correspondences between Murakami's dramatis personae and the characters of the original myth. According to his interpretation, Oedipus is both Tamura Kafka and Nakata; Laius is Tamura Kōichi (Kafka's father) and Johnnie Walker (his double); Jocasta is both Tamura Kafka's real mother, who left him as a child, and Miss Saeki; the Sphinx is Ōshima and Johnny Walker; Antigone is both Sakura and Hoshino, and Apollo is Colonel Sanders, another fantastic character in the novel. The symmetry is slightly altered by Johnnie Walker's 'double casting' and by Apollo's identification with only one character, but by and large Komori's chart is well reasoned and the scholar offers valid motivations for his choice of correspondences.[18]

However, my reading differs from Komori's. In my opinion Murakami's approach is less analytical and more intuitive. His references to Oedipus and to the myths connected to him, in spite of their being based on his thorough knowledge of Greek myths, seem to surface directly from the unconscious, the undomesticated. Had Murakami consciously built an architecture in which each element comes in pairs with its mythical match, the mystery pervading the whole novel would have quickly melted into thin air. What is really attractive about Murakami's use of Greek myths is the way they linger ominously within the narrative space, instruments of revelation but also obscure agents of fate, inexplicable until the end to the reader and – it would seem – to the writer himself.

In an interview published in the Italian daily newspaper *Corriere della sera*, with a journalist who asked him repeatedly for explanations of his narrative choices in *Kafka on the Shore*, Murakami, after numerous attempts to explain to the journalist that he did not know why he had written certain things, eventually came up with the following answer:

> To me writing a novel is like riding a runaway horse, climbing desperately to his neck not to end up on the gravel. It's a fight that goes on for one, two years. Needless to say, to hang on you need physical strength and cold blood. Sometimes I can see nothing of what goes on around me. That's why when you ask a person who rides a runaway horse 'Why did you take this or that way?', he is at a loss at what to answer. The only thing he can say, albeit with regret, is: 'Ask the horse.'[19]

This answer seems to suggest that Murakami, in spite of his skill in building elaborate visions, as fantastic and carefully constructed as Calvino's invisible cities, creates riddles that he himself is unable to solve. In this sense, he shares the enigmatic quality of the Sphinx, but not her clairvoyance and certainly none of her violence.

The world Murakami creates, drawing lifeblood from Greek myths, is by no means chaos. It is a space controlled by an intrinsic order, whose rules man suffers but is not able to know nor understand. Like a player involved in an incomprehensible game, he is fatally bound to trespass limits, violate taboos, hurt people. As in Sōseki's novels, it is impossible to go through life without causing suffering to others, and not knowing the game's rules does not make guilt less strong. But, even if the consciousness of one's guilt does not amount to redemption, it can be the beginning of awareness. So a sense of justice gets in unexpectedly, like light that filters through a crack. The experience of being cursed by a prophecy – Murakami seems to suggest – is, among other things, a lesson in ethics. Tamura Kafka is guilty of raping the person who may be his sister, even though the episode took place in a dimension where he had no control over his actions. Fate, more than a supernatural or metaphysical force, is temptation. Kafka, in yielding to it, did not manage to get rid of the violence that dominates his life. And yet, when he acknowledges his possible crimes, there might be the possibility of a new life for him. At the end of the novel, and of his journey, young Tamura Kafka is ready to go back to the beginning. But nothing is going to be the same.

> 'You'd better get some sleep,' the boy named Crow says. 'When you wake up, you'll be part of a brand new world.'
>
> Eventually you fall asleep. And when you wake up, it's true.
>
> You are part of a brand new world.
>
> (505)

So even if *Kafka on the Shore* is in many ways a veritable *Bildungsroman*, when it closes we are left with the impression that the young hero's education is yet to begin.

References to Greek myths pop up throughout *Kafka on the Shore*, like brand names, references to music and books and all the other recurrent elements that Murakami's readers expect to find in his novels. It is not certainly the first time he shows such an interest. Allusions to Greece can be found in several of his works: *Norwegian Wood*, *The Sputnik Sweetheart*, and *The Wind-Up Bird Chronicle*, just to name a few. He is not an isolated case. Japanese writers, as I tried to show through the examples of Yano Ryūkei, Mishima Yukio and Kurahashi Yumiko, have since the dawn of modernity and throughout the twentieth century felt a strong attraction for the Greek world. But in my opinion Murakami's reinvention of Greek myths is the most strikingly original.

Following the metamorphosis of Greek myths through different times and cultures provides an unending source of wonder: the range of variations with which writers, artists and performers reinvent classical figures and stories is virtually unlimited. In some cases the interpretation subverts the original nucleus so radically that it is hard to recognize its features. In other cases there is an attempt to keep the new version as close as possible to its primary form. Murakami does not conform to either attitude. He is both faithful and subversive. He does not alter the features of Greek myths so much as to make them unrecognizable, and yet he projects them in an utterly new dimension. He produces a sort of hybridization, as if absorbing from myths their life and giving it back in renewed forms. They are to him like focal points where imagination, ethics and aesthetics converge. In his reinvention of Greek myths, the balance between a timeless quality and an urgency rooted in time, strongly linked to the present, can sometimes appear mysteriously perfect.

Bibliography

Cardi, Luciana (2014), 'Edipo nelle opera di Murakami Haruki e Kurahashi Yumiko', in M. Mastrangelo, L. Milasi and S. Romagnoli (eds), *Riflessioni sul Giappone antico e moderno*, 419–441. Rome: Aracne.

Fowler, Harold North (1914), *Plato with an English translation. Euthyphro; Apology; Crito; Phaedo; Phaedrus*, with an introduction by W. R. M. Lamb. London: Heinemann.

Ghidini, Chiara (2013), 'A "Confucian" Epaminondas in Meiji Japan', *ANABASES*, 18: 47–58.

Inose, Naoki with H. Sato (2012), *Persona. A Biography of Yukio Mishima*, Berkeley, California: Stone Bridge Press.

Kawabata, Yasunari (1981), *Kawabata Yasunari zenshū*, vol. 4. Tokyo: Shinchōsha.

Komori, Yōichi (2006), *Murakami Haruki ron.* Umibe no Kafuka *wo seidoku suru.* Tokyo: Heibonsha.

Kurahashi, Yumiko (1984), '*To Die at the Estuary*', in Howard Hibbett (ed.), *Contemporary Japanese Literature: An Anthology of Fiction, Film and Other Writing Since 1945.* Tokyo: Cheng & Tsui.

Lichtig, Toby (2005), 'Cats, omelettes and underwear', *Times Literary Supplement*, 19, 7 January.

Matsumoto T., Satō H. and Inoue T. (eds.) (2000), *Mishima Yukio jiten.* Tokyo: Bensei shuppan.

Miner, Earl (1966), *The Japanese Tradition in British and American Literature.* Princeton, NJ: Princeton University Press.

Mishima, Yukio (2006), 'On Narcissism', trans. Tomoko Aoyama and Barbara Hartley, in Rebecca L. Copeland (ed.), *Woman Critiqued: Translated Essays on Japanese's Women's Writing*, 83–87. Honolulu: University of Hawaii Press.

Mishima, Yukio (1982a), *Junkyō (Martyrdom).* Tokyo: Shinchōsha.

Mishima, Yukio (1982b), *Aporo no sakazuki (The Cup of Apollo).* Tokyo: Shinchōsha.

Murakami, Haruki (2005), *Kafka on the Shore*, trans. Philip Gabriel. London: Harvill.

Plath, Sylvia (1965), *Ariel.* London: Faber and Faber.

Polese, Ranieri (2008), 'Murakami: il critico letterario è l'interprete del mio romanzo.' *Corriere della sera*, 5 April 2008.

Starrs, Roy (1998), *Soundings in Time: The Fictive Art of Yasunari Kawabata.* London: Routledge.

Yeats, W. B. (1914), *Responsibilities: Poems and a Play.* Churchtown, Dundrum: Cuala Press.

7

'It's All in the Game': Greek Myth and *The Wire*

Adam Ganz

David Simon, creator of American television series *The Wire*, which was broadcast by the cable company HBO in sixty episodes between 2002 and 2008, has consistently cited Greek myth and drama as a key point of reference in the making of the series. The fashioned historical events at the heart of the show are portrayed with hyper-realism, and it draws on a whole range of representational modes and styles, which reach from the crime fiction of Richard Price and George Pelecanos, to the Polish and Czech New Wave cinema which shaped director Agnieska Holland, to Eton and the Guildhall School of Speech and Drama where Dominic West, who plays McNulty, was educated. In this chapter I want to look at why Greek myth, epic and tragedy have been so significant in Simon's process of dramatizing the conflict between the forces of law and order and the American drug subculture in Baltimore. I also want to look at *The Wire* itself as a modern *Iliad* in which the characters have undergone a process of mythologization through endless retelling as both fact and fiction.

After briefly considering some comments from David Simon, I reappraise that relationship in more detail from six different but overlapping perspectives, and argue that the dialogue between the ancient texts and modern television series is more nuanced, and more complicated, than has previously been understood. These perspectives include the importance of the classical heritage to the history of the United States and its constitution; the structural parallels with Greek theatre performance; the centrality of the local civic community; the configuration of *The Wire*'s central figure Omar Little as epic hero; the cognitive task facing the audience of either ancient epic or tragedy on the one hand or the viewer of *The Wire* on the other; and, finally, the claim that both ancient Greek literature and *The Wire* make to granting their heroes a quasi-metaphysical status by setting them up against societal forces equivalent to the implacable ancient gods, but also by immortalizing them in cultural artefacts.

It is not difficult to make a case for the influence of Greek drama on *The Wire*. On the contrary, David Simon has repeatedly proclaimed the connection, for example in an interview he gave about the series with novelist and screenwriter Nick Hornby:

> *The Sopranos* and *Deadwood* . . . offer a good deal of *Macbeth* or *Richard III* or *Hamlet*. We're stealing instead from an earlier, less-traveled construct – the Greeks – lifting our thematic stance wholesale from Aeschylus, Sophocles, Euripides to create doomed and fated protagonists who confront a rigged game and their own mortality. The modern mind – particularly those of us in the West – finds such fatalism ancient and discomfiting, I think.[1]

This, he says, explicitly distinguishes *The Wire* from other TV dramas.

> . . . instead of the old gods, *The Wire* is a Greek tragedy in which the postmodern institutions are the Olympian forces. It's the police department, or the drug economy, or the political structures, or the school administration, or the macroeconomic forces that are throwing the lightning bolts and hitting people in the ass for no decent reason. In much of television . . . individuals are often portrayed as rising above institutions to achieve catharsis. In this drama, the institutions always prove larger, and those characters with hubris enough to challenge the postmodern construct of American empire are invariably mocked, marginalized, or crushed. Greek tragedy for the new millennium, so to speak.[2]

His interest, as expressed here, focuses mainly on the metaphysical aspects of Greek tragedy – the relationship between the human and the divine, and the idea of doomed protagonists meeting their fates – and how they resonate when transplanted to a modern American social, political and economic context. This is a point to which I will return at the end of the essay.

But first, let us put the classicism of *The Wire* into a broader historical perspective. If Simon's aim was indeed 'to make statements about the nature of the American city and the national culture', then it made a great deal of sense to use the Greeks as a reference point. Ancient Greek and Roman history, philosophy, law, myth and literature were all crucial in the founding narratives of the United States.[3] The founding fathers had mostly experienced a classical education, and saw 'ancient Greek and Roman statesmen as models to be emulated in their own careers as lawmakers, civic-minded leaders, public figures of responsibility'.[4] James Madison drew heavily on Spartan lawgivers Solon and Lycurgus in framing the constitution. Thomas Jefferson traced the right to pursue happiness to Aristotle and the need for the right to bear arms to the classical world: 'the necessity of obliging every citizen to be a soldier; this was the case with the Greeks and Romans, and must be that of every free State. Where there is no oppression there will be no pauper hirelings.'[5]

There are sixteen towns in the United States called Athens, six Corinths and twenty-five Troys. With classical influences so firmly at the heart of American political and legal discourse, it is not surprising that Greek myth, including myths preserved in tragedy, were adopted by African Americans when arguing for equality. The myth of Prometheus, familiar from the Aeschylean tragedy, became a touchstone text; in *Darkwater* (1920), for example, W. E. B. DuBois (also from Baltimore) addresses the demigod directly:

> Why will this Soul of White Folk, – this modern Prometheus, – hang bound by his own binding, tethered by a fable of the past? I hear his mighty cry reverberating through the world, 'I am white!' Well and good, O Prometheus, divine thief! Is not the world wide enough for two colors, for many little shinings of the sun? Why, then, devour your own vitals if I answer even as proudly, 'I am black!'[6]

More than half a century later, Bobby Kennedy used Aeschylus' *Oresteia* the night that Martin Luther King Jr was assassinated in Memphis. As many cities across the United States burned, Kennedy was brave enough to address a predominantly black crowd in a poor section of Indianapolis as follows: 'For those of you who are black and are tempted to ... be filled with hatred and mistrust of the injustice of such an act, against all white people, I would only say that I can also feel in my own heart the same kind of feeling,' he said. 'I had a member of my family killed, but he was killed by a white man.' Then he continued, 'My favourite poet was Aeschylus, and he once wrote:

> "Even in our sleep, pain which cannot forget
> falls drop by drop upon the heart,
> until, in our own despair,
> against our will,
> comes wisdom
> through the awful grace of God.'
>
> What we need in the United States is not division; what we need in the United States is not hatred; what we need in the United States is not violence and lawlessness, but is love, and wisdom, and compassion toward one another, and a feeling of justice toward those who still suffer within our country, whether they be white or whether they be black.'[7]

Robert Kennedy was assassinated himself just two months later. Greek tragic texts are inscribed in the history of race relations in the US; there is a long history of American novels bound up with racial struggle which have engaged with Greek tragedies at many levels.[8]

But how much does *The Wire* owe to the formal conventions of ancient Greek theatre? Since the series has been the subject of increasing critical comment, written about not only by TV studies scholars but academics from fields as diverse as comparative literature, philosophy and geography,[9] several articles have looked at this proclaimed relationship between *The Wire* and Greek tragedy in more detail. Mark Chou has focused on the figure of the tragic hero in *The Wire*, developing a model previously proposed by classicist Page duBois,[10] while Chris Love examines staging, use of epigraphs and in particular how *The Wire* uses Greek tragic *peripeteia* (reversal), echoic doubling and dramatic irony. He is especially interested in the relationship the show develops with its audience within and beyond the show, to which he sees a parallel in the opening speech of Aeschylus' *Oresteia* (*Agamemnon* 37–39):

> *The Wire* . . . reflect[s] the tragic ironies of postmodern America back to the audience. It is precisely in the spirit of this reconciliation of intentional and unintentional ironies, and of dramatic and tragic ironies, that *The Oresteia* and *The Wire* are confederate.
>
> We remember the Watchman's words at the beginning of *The Oresteia:* '. . . willingly I / speak to those who understand; if they do not understand, I forget everything.'[11]

Another Aeschylean tragedy, *Prometheus Bound*, is referenced explicitly and strategically: Clay Davis, the corrupt African-American senator in *The Wire*, waves a copy of the play on his way to court, as the expression of the burden he has to bear. The translation is that by James Scully and C. John Herington (Oxford University Press 1975). Both Davis' character and his writer reference the longstanding significance of Prometheus in the rhetoric of African-American liberation,[12] and implicitly the place of Greek myth at the centre of American life.

One of the Greek theatrical conventions most clearly adopted in *The Wire* is the chorus. The series takes place in a war zone. Or something worse. As the two cops 'Herc' Hauk and Carver say in the very first episode.

> Carver: You can't even call this shit a war.
> Herc: Why not?
> Carver: Wars end.[13]

The characters here function as a chorus, and this is a feature of both sides linked by *The Wire*. Both cops and Corner boys comment on the action and draw the lessons for the audience and one another, as in the much-admired extended metaphor about chess and checkers where D'Angelo explains to Bodie and Wallace the rules of the game and the various pieces and how it relates to the Barksdale organization they work for (see further below).

The trope of eavesdropping, fundamental to all the wire-tapping in *The Wire*, is something else shared with (or taken from) the form of Greek tragedy. Not only do individual scenes require one character to overhear secretly what others are saying (for example, Phaedra listening to the terrible encounter between her nurse and Hippolytus), but the audience, of which the characters on stage are entirely unaware (there is no breaking of the 'fourth wall' in Greek tragedy), are permanently eavesdropping on the tragic action.

Love's article reminds us that overhearing is what an audience of tragic theatre does:

> . . . through the detectives' wiretap, viewers of the show traverse physical, cultural, political, and institutional barriers that the show's protagonists rarely breach. To view the detectives operating the wiretap investigation as they listen in on the targets of their investigation is to participate in a similar form of sanctioned voyeurism. After all, it is a kind of wire through which each premium cable viewer gains ingress into David Simon's fictional Baltimore. As the drug dealers, murderers, money launderers, stickup artists, sex workers, and corrupt politicians of Baltimore remain the targets of the police department's investigation, so too do the various fictional constructions of *The Wire* remain the objects of our own spectatorial scrutiny.[14]

Baltimore is a highly suitable setting for the act of dangerous 'listening-in'. It is a liminal city, a place where all kinds of Americans come together and are connected through the port to the rest of the world. It was founded for the export of one drug, tobacco; it was significant in the import of alcohol during Prohibition and, as the dramas in *The Wire* show, is key in the distribution of another addictive substance. Baltimore was the chief black metropolis of the nineteenth century. And yet communication between black (southern) and white (northern) Americans has always been complicated. Recent research has emphasized the instrumentality of the telephone in reconfiguring America spatially, and revealed how marketing conducted by the telecomms firm AT&T was focused far less on north to south communication than east to west. North–south conversation was always more problematic.[15] Baltimore – 'too south to be north and too north to be south', as Baltimore writer D. Watkins calls it[16] – is the place where these two worlds co-exist. But in *The Wire* there is always something potentially dangerous in this act of listening, which crosses ethnic and colour boundaries and has unexpected consequences. As each wiretap ultimately proves as discomfiting to the authorities as it does to those targeted, this is a world in which knowledge is always a double-edged sword.

Only 'The Greek', the menacing head of 'The Greeks' – a transnational criminal confederation which makes its money from trafficking both drugs and human beings – seems able to cross these barriers as he chooses. Like Zeus himself, The Greek is like an all-powerful *deus ex machina* who can shapeshift and assume different identities; moreover he can make fungible all that he touches.

At the end of Season Two, The Greek looks over Baltimore from his eyrie, secure in the knowledge that he has FBI protection. His sidekick says, 'they know my name, but my name is not my name. And you … to them you're only "The Greek"'. The Baltimore gods demand not only your loyalty but also your identity, and yet they grant neither loyalty nor identity in return. In this hierarchical society, all the characters (except The Greek) are in hock to the institutions in one way or another. Those at the bottom on both sides are at the whim of their superiors, while (as visionary cop Bunny Colvin eloquently puts it), 'middle management means that you got just enough responsibility to listen when people talk, but not so much you can tell anybody to go fuck themselves'.

Even those at the top know that they are always likely to be replaced, like corrupt union boss Frank Sobotka. In the staging of his death, we see another level of the influence of Greek drama on *The Wire*. Chris Love's analysis of the final episode of Season Two shows how Nick Sobotka and the members of the IBS union (International Brotherhood of Stevedores) watch, like a Greek tragic chorus, their leader's bloated corpse being lowered onto the ground. As the camera moves round to behind the corpse, positioned on its stretcher on the equivalent of the *skene*, the television viewer sees that Nick and the dockworkers fan out in a semicircle, as if in the circular *orchestra*.[17] This means that the audience assumes a 'dual role as spectator and fellow bystander … We are forced, therefore, to regard the stevedores as both "players" and victims. They are players both in their roles as actors in a fictional televised drama and as actors – human beings with agency – who live and operate within the universe of the fictionalized Baltimore created for them.'[18]

The wake scenes in *The Wire* act as points where these different circles of characters, performers, and audiences come together in mourning. We see this most clearly in the on-screen wake for Robert Colesbery, co-creator and producer of the series who played cop Ray Cole, and who died in the making of the show. The fictional police mourn a colleague just as the actors and crew are mourning a workmate. The speech includes references to Colesbery's credits on *Mississippi*

Burning and *After Hours*.[19] The audience participates in both of these acts of mourning and is brought to reflect upon the complex relationship between fiction and reality that they raise: 'This self-conscious theatricality – this staging of the stage, so to speak – performs forward to reality and backward to the ancient Greek tragedy behind the curtain of cable television.'[20]

Love's discussion includes an excellent point about the role of social media in maintaining and sustaining the audience of *The Wire* and enabling its debate around it. *The Wire* was one of the first drama series to benefit from these new possibilities of interacting with critics and other viewers. The show was blogged about intensively by critics and newspapers and a remarkable amount of the most interesting critics and articles dealing with *The Wire* exist online, creating a critical community reminiscent of the ancient Athenian society's relationship with its established drama festivals. Slavoj Žižek gave an hour-long talk about the series at Birkbeck College in which he explored the nature of its roots in Greek drama.[21] He made the point that *The Wire* 'provides a kind of collective *self-representation* of a city, like the Greek tragedy in which a *polis* collectively staged its experience . . . This act of self-representation incorporates much of what is not at first glance part of the city'.

No other American TV show has had such an intense sense of place as *The Wire*, which retells tales of Baltimore filmed in Baltimore with people from Baltimore. As Ducker has commented, it is 'as close as you get to an east coast, rust belt, postindustrial city telling its own story'.[22] But the storytelling world of *The Wire* is not parochial. On the contrary, it shows that Baltimore, like any city, is comprised of many kinds of narrative, and these include its own myths and those who create them, as writers or subjects. As Lorrie Moore points out in an acute essay on the show in the *New York Review of Books*. Baltimore was 'home of Edgar Allan Poe, H. L. Mencken, Babe Ruth, and Billie Holiday'. She continues:

> Baltimore is not just a stand-in for Western civilization or globalized urban rot or the American inner city now given the cold federal shoulder in the folly-filled war on terror, though it is certainly all these things. Baltimore is also just plain itself, with a very specific cast of characters, dead and alive. Eminences are pointedly referenced in the course of the series: the camera passes over a sign to Babe Ruth's birthplace, tightens on a Mencken quote sculpted into the office wall of *The Baltimore Sun*; 'Poe' is not just street pronunciation for 'poor' (to the delight of one of *The Wire*'s screenwriters) but implicitly printed onto one horror-story element of the script; a phrase of Lady Day wafts in as ambient recorded music in a narrative that is scoreless except when the credits are rolling or in the occasional end-of-season montage.[23]

Moore then describes the many real locations and references to the city that appear in the show from churches to hot dog joints which now 'reside in *The Wire*'s televized amber' and form 'part of the texture and mythology that *The Wire*'s producers are putting on display both with anger and with love'. As David Simon said in an online Q and A session on the HBO Bulletin Boards when asked about his favourite character: 'My favorite character would be the city of Baltimore, God bless her.'

Yet this mythologized Baltimore is bigger than Baltimore because it also includes not-Baltimore. Other performers who mingle with the 'real' include Steppenwolf-trained Jim True-Frost who plays Prez, black British actor Idris Elba from Hackney, and Aidan Gillen from Ireland. These all bring what might be called 'urbanity' to the narrative. Cities borrow from all the cultures that inhabit them. But this surely is what makes myth (including the civic myths and contexts portrayed in Greek tragedy) transformational: its ability to create a world using both self and other, and thus create something both strange and familiar, both fiction and non-fiction, drawing on a number of modes of representation, from actual participants in the events dramatized, to stylized performances from a range of acting traditions.

The Wire's relationship with Greek mythology is not just structurally and technically indebted to Greek theatre, but also particular and specific, especially in its relationship with Homeric epic. We see this most clearly in the character of Omar Little, probably the most loved character in the series (and singled out as such by President Barack Obama).[24] Omar is a lone gunman with a warrior's code of honour who holds up drug dealers and does not shoot civilians; even when he robs a store, he still pays for his cigarettes. Played by Michael K. Williams, who moves through Baltimore streets with a dancer's grace, in the long dustcoat familiar from Sergio Leone films, and whistling his own theme tune, he is a highly stylized, almost mythical character who was nonetheless inspired by real-life stick-up-man Donnie Andrews (who also appears in the series). After the bloody murder of his lover, Brandon, Omar agrees to testify against the Barksdale drug gang who killed him. As he waits to give evidence, a courtroom sheriff wrestles with a crossword clue: 'God of War, four letters. "Mars" doesn't fit.' But Omar knows the answer: 'Greeks called him "Ares". Same dude, different name is all.' Then Omar adds: 'See, back in middle school and all, I used to love them myths. That stuff was deep. Truly.'

In the previous season, Omar was brought by cop McNulty to the precinct morgue to identify Brandon's body. As Omar weeps for Brandon, there is a direct echo of what Omar called 'them myths', specifically the moment in the *Iliad* where Achilles sees the body of Patroclus after retrieving it from battle:

> But the Achaeans gladly drew Patroclus out from amidst the spears and placed him on a bier, and his close comrades stood around him, weeping. And swift-footed Achilles followed them, shedding hot tears, when he saw his trusty companion lying on the stretcher, lacerated by sharp bronze.[25]
>
> (*Iliad* 18.231–236)

When McNulty enters the police station, he sits his two sons down in the corridor. One of them holds a soccer ball, the other plays a video game, and we hear the beeping of electronic weaponry. The children's point of view of war as a game is counterpointed by the solemn faces of heroic cops – probably killed on the job – on the wall above them.

Meanwhile McNulty ushers Omar into the inner sanctum where the dead Brandon lies. The white sheet covering the body is pulled back to reveal Brandon bearing signs of torture. One eye has been gouged out. Omar bends over the body in long shot, then weeps as McNulty turns tactfully away. We are reminded of Achilles' explanation of his grief to his mother Thetis:

> . . . my most beloved friend is dead, Patroclus, the one I honoured more than any of my comrades, the one I loved as much as I love myself. Him I have lost.[26]
>
> (*Iliad* 18.80–82)

Like the scene in the *Iliad*, the one in *The Wire* is about love and loss. But it is also about the power and violence of the gangs which Omar has challenged. Simone Weil opened her famous essay 1940 on the *Iliad* with the statement that the poem's true hero, the true subject at its centre, 'is force. Force employed by man, force that enslaved man, force before which man's flesh shrinks away'.[27] Omar knows all these manifestations of force, as perpetrator and as victim. His witnessing of the consequences of that force leads him to the courthouse where he will testify to jail the perpetrators, but also identifies himself as a lover of Greek myth who knows the names of the god of war, and who, like him, has a double existence in two worlds. As he said: 'Same dude, different name is all.'

The video game watched by McNulty's sons is just one of many games, from basketball to dice, which are used to stand in for what Omar calls 'The Game'.[28] Later, Prez, the cop-turned-teacher says about an American football game: 'No one wins. One side just loses more slowly.' In this context, the standard Panglossian transformational myths of America in life or drama are not sufficient – what Sarah Palin, mocking Obama, called the 'hopey-changey thing' makes no sense in Baltimore.[29] The absence of hope is another form of violence. As Noam Chomsky put it in an interview at the time of the Occupy Wall Street movement: 'I don't usually admire Sarah Palin, but when she was making fun of this "hopey-changey" stuff, she was right, there was nothing there.'[30] *The Wire* explores this 'nothing', in the space 'wedged between two competing American myths', as David Simon puts it. The first, he elaborates is this: 'if you are smarter … if you are shrewd or frugal or visionary, if you build a better mousetrap, you will succeed beyond your wildest imagination.' And the second is diligence rewarded: 'if you are not smarter … or clever or visionary, if you never do build a better mousetrap … if you are neither slick nor cunning, yet willing to get up every day and work your ass off … you have a place … and you will not be betrayed.' According to Simon, it is 'no longer possible even to remain polite on this subject. It is … a lie'.[31]

Just as the muse of the *Iliad* is inspired to sing of the wrath of Achilles, Simon's anger about these lies and injustice fuels the telling in *The Wire*. In the so-called Bible to the series, a document which seems to be his original pitch for the show to HBO, Simon lays out the principles of the drama: 'Nothing should happen on screen that hasn't *in some fashion* happened on the streets.' (Emphasis mine.) Simon continues:

> Each story gravitates to one common feature, a prolonged wiretap surveillance effort that reveals intricacies and connections in the urban landscape that would ordinarily pass unseen to even the best street cops. And each wiretap ultimately proves as discomfiting to the authorities as it does to those targeted. This is a world in which knowledge is always a double-edged sword … But within a brief span of time, the officers who undertake the pursuit are forced to acknowledge truths about their department, their role, the drug war and the city as a whole. In the end, the cost to all sides begins to suggest not so much the dogged police pursuit of the bad guys, but rather a Greek tragedy. At the end of thirteen episodes … the conclusion is something that Euripides or O'Neill might recognize: an America, at every level at war with itself.[32]

The aim is to make visible 'the intricacies and connections in the urban landscape' and in making them visible turn them into drama. It is significant, I think, that in the earliest internal documents about the series, Simon is referencing Greek tragedy – not a means of selling something as high culture after production, but as an aspiration beforehand.

The desire that everything that happens in the show needs to correspond to something in reality is just one aspect of the process of continual cross-referencing between fictional and real narratives and meta-narratives, which is the stuff of *The Wire*. It is also a way in which the characters reference the world beyond *The Wire* and show the relationship between fiction and reality, and the way in which it becomes harder and harder to tell the difference. I want to explore the nature of these tellings and retellings, and look at how *The Wire* draws on Greek myth and in its repeated retellings of the tale of the attempted surveillance of the drug dealers of Baltimore has created its own mythology, in which the boundaries between fiction and history have been blurred forever. Many of the stories in *The Wire* are being told by David Simon for the third or fourth time. He first wrote about them in some depth in *Easy Money: Anatomy of a Drug Empire*, five articles written for the *Baltimore Sun* published between 11 and 15 January 1985. He then addressed them in two non-fiction books, *Homicide: A Year on the Killing Streets* (1991) and *The Corner: A Year in the Life of an Inner-City Neighborhood* (1997), in a TV series based on those two books, and finally in *The Wire* itself.

Co-writer Ed Burns was likewise involved in these narratives, both as a policeman on the original surveillance project, and later as a teacher in Baltimore. Each role involved not only participating in a narrative, but assembling – or helping others to assemble – one. The process of narrative is at the heart of police work, which in its attempt to establish causation through evidence is a form of history. Sheila Rowbotham made this point on a piece she wrote for a British Library blog: 'These police in *The Wire* are just like historians after all, slowly piecing together all those bits of information.'[33] Teachers are also trying to offer an alternative narrative of the world to the Corner kids – but as District Commander Bunny Colvin points out to an administrator from Baltimore Schools' Central Office in series four episode 10, 'they're not learning for our world; they're learning for theirs'.[34] Simon describes the process of writing as follows:

> You cannibalize everything you have in front of you. There's a lot of oral history in the show. We got to write a lot of stories down on cocktail napkins and put them in the show. I think that's what made the show idiosyncratic and, for lack of a better word, real.[35]

It seems to me that it is this double telling as simultaneously fiction *and* history that makes *The Wire* so distinctive – and so good. It is in the repeated retelling that the events and characters are transformed into myth, speaking simultaneously about what happened (or may have happened) in the past and what might happen in the future. And as the stories are retold, the DVDs are replayed, both past and future are summoned all over again. Aristotle said (*Poetics* 1451a37–1451b7) that history was about the particular, and poetry (he meant epic and tragedy) about universals: *The Wire* is both.

Many of the people in *The Wire* are 'real people'. Felicia Pearson who plays Snoop was in prison at the age of fourteen – and in 2011, after the show had finished, was found guilty of supplying heroin. Country and Western singer and recovering addict, Steve Earle, plays recovering addict Walon; Robert Chew, who plays drug dealer Proposition Joe, is a local actor and acting teacher. And there are a host of extras from every walk of life: cops, dealers, journalists, schoolkids and everything in between. Yet many of the characters from life are playing not themselves but other selves. Policeman Jay Landesman plays a policeman, but not the character called 'Jay Landesman', whilst Melvin Williams, who plays the Deacon, was a Baltimore drug kingpin (arrested by series writer Ed Burns in 1984 in the events that inspired the original show).[36]

Greek tragedy, it has been argued, trained its citizen-spectators in cognitive skills as well as moral and rhetorical ones.[37] Frederic Jameson has argued that, in *The Wire*, 'there it is not an individual criminal responsible for an enigmatic crime, but rather a whole society that must be opened up to representation and tracked down, identified, explored, mapped like a new dimension or a foreign culture.'[38] Trackings and mappings occur constantly in the drama.[39] To take just one example from Season Two: the port workers map their interactions with docker colleagues as they collect photos of the surveillance van sent to spy on them, which they have put in a container and sent around the world. The Polaroids sent back from other ports indicate an international solidarity, which now seems as outmoded as the technology that records them, an inadequate response to the global flow of power and money that is controlling the drugs trade, and their destinies. In Season One, Lester Freamon, the wise old detective who takes the investigation forward, describes the mapping thus: 'You follow drugs, you get drug addicts and drug dealers. But you start to follow the money, and you don't know where the fuck it's gonna take you.' By Season Five he expresses himself differently: 'A case like this, where you show who gets paid, behind all the tragedy and the fraud, where you show how the money routes itself, how we're all, all of us vested, all of us complicit.'

For all the Corner boys, narrative, complicity, identity and geography are close together. Their Corner is all they know and they rarely leave their city-state. There is a scene in which Bodie leaves Baltimore for the first time and is astonished to discover that radio stations are different in other cities. As Bodie and a friend search for music, they happen on the unmistakable tone of Garrison Keillor reading *News from Lake Wobegon*. On one level this is an ironic comment for a knowing and sophisticated audience: what could be farther from Bodie's life on a corner in Baltimore than the fictional village recounted in Keillor's drawl? But on deeper reflection, the clip emphasizes the connection between storytelling, place and audience. Keillor's Lake Wobegon, like Simon's Baltimore, is another fictional world inspired by the real, which has achieved mythological proportions.

We see the relationship between characters, place and destiny explored in a different way when D'Angelo is asked at a prison book club what Fitzgerald meant when he said there are no second acts in American lives,[40] and he responds thus:

> He's saying that the past is always with us. Where we come from, what we go through, how we go through it — all that shit matters ... Like, at the end of the book? Boats and tides and all? It's like, you can change up. You can say you somebody new. You can give yourself a whole new story. But what came first is who you really are, and what happened before is what really happened.

This is more than one text referencing another here. F. Scott Fitzgerald, whose work they are discussing, is another writer who lived in Baltimore (and who also made substantial use of classical literature, including Greek tragedy).[41] The writing teacher encourages D'Angelo to speak in more ways than one: he is played by novelist and screenwriter Richard Price who runs writing workshops in prison and is the author of a number of episodes of *The Wire*.

This is the final speech before D'Angelo is murdered. The character who has commissioned this murder is Stringer Bell, who reads Adam's Smith's *Wealth of Nations* and is described by Lorrie Moore as 'the enigmatic Gatsby figure, yearning for legitimacy'.[42] Bell works as *consigliere* to gang boss Avon Barksdale, D'Angelo's uncle. Barksdale believes in a physical geography of control – whilst Stringer Bell believes in the transformation of capitalism and 'going legit'. Avon, like his nephew, believes that change is neither possible nor desirable: 'I bleed red and you bleed green. I look at you these days, String, you know what I see? I see a man without a country. Not hard enough for this right here and maybe, just maybe, not smart enough for them out there.' Avon wants a physical expression of his empire: 'I ain't no suit-wearin' businessman like you. You know, I'm just a gangster, I suppose. And I want my corners.'

The derivation of the name Stringer Bell apparently comes from two Baltimore gangsters, Stringer Reed and Roland Bell; yet it is the perfect name, combining Stringer, the freelance journalist, with Bell, the inventor of the telephone. Stringer Bell, as his name suggests, is attempting, like *The Wire* itself to connect two worlds each remote from and fascinated by the other. If most of us secretly want to be gangsters, Stringer is the gangster who secretly wants to be us. And as we eavesdrop on him, it's as if the character is eavesdropping on us, on civil society, trying to find out how things work. But he's not going to get what he's looking for.

To be a drug dealer involves being a warrior, where you are ultimately dependent on your ability to survive. The life involves killing and being killed and you are dependent on your skill with weapons, your alertness and your strategy. You inhabit and protect a territory through ruthlessness and betrayal. And if you make a mistake there is unlikely to be a second act.

These narrative deceptions become more intricate as the series develops. In Season Four, Marlo deliberately stages false information for a police surveillance camera, whilst Season Five is dominated by an entire fake serial killer narrative, written and presented by McNulty in order to get necessary funds for police work. The audience piece together these different narratives, which combine ultra-realism with an intense and formal poetics, and which evidence different levels of conscious performance, within and beyond the drama. As *The Wire* was influenced by other stories, it soon started to appear in other narratives. Rap and hip-hop stars like Snoop Dogg immediately incorporated references to *The Wire*. Skillz further interrogated the relationship between history, performance and mythology:

> And these youngins wanna act like Michael on *The Wire*
> 'Til they realize that Michael just an actor on *The Wire*.[43]

This mythologizing of black violence drew an extended critique from Tommy J. Curry. He argues that *The Wire* failed to depict 'the actual lives of the urban Black underclass. The focus on poverty and class, the supposed realism, ultimately distort the lens through which we understand racism, and Black deprivation in the USA.' Moreover, the public 'would not accept such images of police brutalization and violence towards any other race'.[44]

Curry's article shows how fraught potential communication can be, and why many might prefer silence as an alternative. We see the advantage of silence at the beginning of Season Four, when the focus on unexplained deaths adds a metaphysical dimension to the cognitive puzzles presented by the narrative. Snoop and Chris Partlow are committing a series of invisible murders and burying bodies in lime in a boarded-up warehouse; the murder statistics fall. When the killings are brought to light, they become problematic. When murders are known, they have to be accounted for and the cluster of bodies will ruin the statistics, which become another unreliable narrative, to be told the way you want it to, and yet which take on the status of the gods, because though they are constantly gamed (while mythological characters seek to escape their fate), they are in the end relentless and implacable. Bunny Colvin makes this metaphysical connection between statistics and fate explicit. He takes the bold decision to present the crime statistics as they are. When asked about his poor results by his superior Major Rawls, he replies 'Sometimes the gods are uncooperative . . .' That is not good enough for the Police Commissioner, Ervin Burrell, whose response is this: 'The gods are fucking you, you find a way to fuck them back. It's Baltimore, gentleman. The gods will not save you.'

The doctored statistics (and the people living and dead whose stories are omitted from them) are just one example of the many ways in which the events of *The Wire* are redacted from official accounts. In a talk at the University of Southern California in 2008, David Simon made the point that none of the narratives in the show appear in the local newspaper, in fiction or reality: 'Everything that you know about *The Wire* up to this point never appeared in the newspaper.'[45] He then recounted the many plot points taken from Simon's real-life Baltimore experiences: the corrupt mayor asking for cooked crime statistics; the elementary school test scores spawned from students being taught the tests; the deaths of Prop Joe and Omar – all indicators of the city's real problems that never appeared in the *Sun*'s pages, in reality or on HBO. 'Watching a TV drama to get the truth, that's the real joke', Simon added.

Normally the events and characters exist not only in different physical worlds from their audience but in different story worlds, each one of which is unaware of the other's existence. It is only when the stories at either end of *The Wire* are brought together that the tales on either side are recounted as history and synthesized as myth. For me, the most profound version of this synthesis can be seen in the attempted killing of Omar in police custody, and it is, therefore, this with which I want to conclude my essay. Omar sits in his cell – he knows there is a price on his head. Two burly guys enter and one eyes him ominously before letting Omar know that Butchie (his blind mentor) has sent them; he hands Omar a plastic shiv. When they return, Omar is reading *Ghettoheat* (2004), a book of poetry by Hickson. Knowing what is expected, Omar takes his shirt off as the men tape printed matter including, prominently, an atlas, around him for protection. In the breakfast queue, the attack comes. But protected by his invisible shield, Omar survives and buggers the attacker with his shiv. The figure who brings Omar salvation is played by Donnie Andrews, as noted above, a former stick-up guy and inspiration for the Omar character. Donnie protects the fictional character he gave birth to by swaddling him in the written word. Can one imagine a more powerful metaphor for how literature – ancient or modern – can make a man immortal, lend him the heroic *kleos*, the eternal fame and reputation, that the Homeric narrator explicitly claims his poem is bestowing on his heroes?

Bibliography

Alvarez, Rafael (2004), *The Wire: Truth Be Told*. New York: Pocket Books.

Anderson, Paul Allen (2010), '"The Game Is the Game": Tautology and Allegory in The Wire.' *Criticism*, 52: 373–398.

Anderson, Jeffrey (2009), Last Word – Nathan 'Bodie' Barksdale and Kenny Jackson tell their versions of Baltimore's street life in *The Baltimore Chronicles: Legends of the Unwired* http://www2.citypaper.com/news/story.asp?id=17966&p=1

Barton, Chris (2008), '*The Wire*': David Simon schools USC http://latimesblogs.latimes.com/showtracker/2008/03/the-wire-david.html Accessed 26 June 2014.

Bolf-Beliveau, Laura and Ralph Beliveau (2015), 'Educational reform and the epistemology of ignorance: a critique of No Child Left Behind', in Arin Keeble and Ivan Stacy, *The Wire and America's Dark Corners: Critical Essays*, 208–220. Jefferson, NC: McFarland & Co.

Bryant, Adam (2009), 'The Reporter: David Simon Creates Commentary Disguised as a Cop Drama on *The Wire*', 7 December 2009. Available online at http://www.tvguide.com/News/Reporter-David-Simon-1012876.aspx Accessed 26 June 2014.

Chou, Mark (2011), '"We like them bitches on the chessboard": Tragedy, Politics and *The Wire*', www.ctheory.net/articles.aspx?id=677. Accessed 26 June 2014.

Curry, Tommy J. (2013), '*Capital Noir*: White Supremacy, the Political Economies of the War and the Road to Perdition,' in David Bzdak, Joanna Crosby and Seth Vannatta (eds), *The Wire* and *Philosophy*: *This America, Man*, 165–177. Chicago: Open Court Press.

duBois, Page (2004), 'Toppling the Hero: Polyphony in the Tragic City,' *New Literary History* 35.

DuBois W. E. B. (1920), *Darkwater: Voices from Within the Veil*. New York: Harcourt Brace.

Ducker, Eric. (2006), 'The Left Behind Inside *The Wire*'s World Of Alienation And Asshole Gods', available online at http://www.thefader.com/2006/12/08/listening-in-part-iv/#ixzz35qijzTyK Accessed 26 June 2014.

Fitzgerald, F. Scott (1965). *The Stories of F. Scott Fitzgerald*, Volume 2. Harmondsworth: Penguin.

Goodman, Amy (2012), Interview with Noam Chomsky, 14 May 2012, available online http://www.democracynow.org/2012/5/14/chomsky_occupy_wall_street_has_created Accessed 26 June 2014.

Hall, Edith (2009), 'Deianeira deliberates: precipitate decision-making and *Trachiniae*', in Simon Goldhill and Edith Hall (eds), *Sophocles and the Greek Tragic Tradition* (Festschrift for Pat Easterling), 69–96. Cambridge: Cambridge University Press.

Hall, Edith (2011), 'The problem with Prometheus: *Myth, Abolition, and Radicalism*', in E. Hall, R. Alston and J. McConnell (eds), *Ancient Slavery and Abolition*, 209–246. Oxford: Oxford University Press.

Hamilton, Edith (1930), *The Greek Way*. New York: W. W. Norton.

Hornby, Nick (2007), 'David Simon: Creator-Producer-Writer of HBO's *The Wire*', *The Believer*, August, http://www.believermag.com/issues/200708/?read=interview_simon. Accessed 26 June 2014.

Jameson, Frederic (2010), 'Realism and Utopia in *The Wire*', *Criticism*, 52: 359–372.

Jefferson, Thomas (2009), *Thoughts on War and Revolution*, ed. Brett F. Woods. New York: Algora Publishing.

Lavik, Erlund (2011), 'The Poetics and Rhetoric of *The Wire's* Intertextuality', *Critical Studies in* Television, 6.4.

Love, Chris (2010), 'Greek Gods in Baltimore: Greek Tragedy and *The Wire*', *Criticism*, 52: 487–507.

MacDougall, Robert (2006), 'The Wire Devils: Pulp Thrillers, the Telephone, and Action at a Distance in the Wiring of a Nation', *American Quarterly*, 58: 715–741.

Moore, Lorrie (2010), 'In the life of *The Wire*', *New York Review of Books*, 57.15.

Rawlings III, Hunter (2013), 'Classical influences on the Founders: Myth or reality?', *The Chautauquan Daily*, 21 July, available online at http://chqdaily.com/2013/07/21/morning-lecture-guest-column-classical-influences-on-the-founders-myth-or-reality/. Accessed 26 June 2014.

Reinhold, Meyer (1984), *Classica Americana: the Greek and Roman Heritage in the United States*. Detroit: Wayne State University Press.

Richard, Carl J. (1994), *The Founders and the Classics: Greece, Rome, and the American Enlightenment*. Cambridge, MA: Harvard University Press.

Rosen, Gary (1996), 'James Madison and the Problem of Founding', *The Review of Politics*, 58 (3): 561–595

Rowbotham, Sheila (2012). 'From Whitman to *The Wire*' blog, posted 17 April 2012, http://britishlibrary.typepad.co.uk/americas/2012/04/sheila-rowbotham-writer-in-residence-from-whitman-to-the-wire.html Accessed 26 June 2014.

Schlesinger, Arthur M. (1978), *Robert Kennedy and His Times*. Boston. MA: Houghton Mifflin Company.

Sellers, M. N. S. (1994), *American Republicanism: Roman Ideology in the United States Constitution*. New York: New York University Press.

Simmons, Bill (2012), Interview with Barack Obama, 1 March 2012. Available online at http://grantland.com/the-triangle/b-s-report-transcript-barack-obama/

Simon, David (2000), '*The Wire* Bible', version dated 6 September 2000, available online at http://kottke.org/09/04/the-wire-bible Accessed 26 June 2014.

Simon, David (2004), 'Introduction' in Rafael Alvarez, *The Wire: Truth Be Told*. New York: Pocket Books.

Simon, David, Blog http://davidsimon.com/kwame-brown-another-federal-case-another-head-shot/ Accessed 26 June 2014.

Simon, David (2005), HBO Bulletin board conversation 10 June 2005, archived at http://www.hollywoodjesus.com/wire_about.htm Accessed 26 June 2014.

Skillz (2008), 'Don't Act Like You Don't Know' featuring Freeway, Koch Records.

Watkins D. (2014), 'Stoop Stories', *Aeon Magazine* (online at – http://aeon.co/magazine/living-together/these-are-the-two-baltimores-black-and-white/).

Weil, Simone (1956), 'The *Iliad*,: or, The Poem of Force', trans. Mary McCarthy. Pendle Hill pamphlet 91. Wallingford, PA: Pendle Hill.

Zeitlin, Froma (1994), 'The Artful Eye: Vision, Ecphrasis and Spectacle in Euripidean Theatre', in Simon Goldhill and Robin Osborne (eds), *Art and Text in Ancient Greek Culture*, 138–196. Cambridge: Cambridge University Press.

Žižek, Slavoj (2012), 'The *Wire*, or What to do in Non Evental Times', in *The Year of Dreaming Dangerously*. London and New York: Verso.

8

Writing a New Irish Odyssey: Theresa Kishkan's *A Man in a Distant Field*

Fiona Macintosh

In 2004 the Canadian poet/novelist Theresa Kishkan published her second full-length novel, *A Man in a Distant Field*, set both on the west coast of Canada in Oyster Bay, Sechelt Peninsula, British Columbia and in Delphi, Co. Mayo, on the west coast of Ireland. As Kishkan's protagonist explains, the Irish Delphi received its name from the Marquis of Sligo, who had built his hunting lodge in the valley after noting the topographical affinities between the two places following his sojourn in Greece in the company of Lord Byron.[1] Indeed, in many ways, Delphi, Co. Mayo acts as a kind of world-navel or *omphalos* for Kishkan's protagonist – pulling him back from his place of enforced exile in Canada to his motherland.

For the author too, Greece/Ireland exert their magnetic effect: as a student, Kishkan spent time in both Greece and Ireland. *A Man in a Distant Field* was not the first turning she had taken towards Ireland for inspiration – an earlier novella, *Inishbream* (1999) had provided a fictitious account of her stay in the early 1970s on an island off the west coast of Ireland. She also returned in person with her young son to the west coast in the new millennium, to the 'new' Ireland forged by the Good Friday Agreement of 10 April 1998 and the British–Irish Agreement of 2 December 1999. The novel is clearly founded upon those earlier personal experiences, just as it meditates upon the deeper resonances of those immediate, political milestones. It is also Kishkan's first attempt to bring the different strands of her earlier itinerant life – in Greece and in Ireland – into fruitful dialogue with life in her native British Columbia.

Translating the *Odyssey*

Kishkan pronounces in her preface to the novel that she is no Greek scholar and that she has relied on Liddell and Scott's *Greek–English Lexicon* and Cunliffe's

Lexicon of the Homeric Dialect,[2] as well as the Loeb edition as guide to her reading of Homer's *Odyssey*.[3] And there are some wonky transliterations and citations of the Greek that bear this disclaimer out. The title itself, as becomes apparent from one of the novel's epigraphs, is taken from Robert Fitzgerald's 1961 translation of the *Odyssey* (5.487–490). This is the simile in which Odysseus, on landing on the island of Scheria, is said to take the same care of his exhausted self by burrowing under a bed of leaves as the 'man in a distant field' does of the firebrand that he buries in the embers of the fire in order to preserve a spark for the next day. Kishkan's Odysseus is indeed a slow burner: his exile on the other side of the world, attendant on the wanton violence directed at both his family and home, sees him buried under a metaphorical bed of leaves, only to provide him eventually with the necessary strength for return to new life in the Irish Free State.

The novel opens with the protagonist, Declan O'Malley, a former Irish schoolmaster on the run, now in exile in a tiny coastal hamlet in British Columbia appropriately called World's End. Like Odysseus' first appearance on the shore of Calypso's island at the beginning of Book 5 of the *Odyssey*, we first discover O'Malley lying in his boat, rocking inconsolably, unable to articulate in words the full extent of the pain he feels at his loss and his sense of homelessness. It is the spring of 1922 – significantly the year of the publication of Joyce's *Ulysses* as well as the year that ushered in the Irish Free State – and O'Malley, we slowly learn, has been on the run for at least the past nine months. He had been forced to flee his native soil following the savage torching of his family home, and the attendant incineration of his wife and two daughters. O'Malley, we gradually discover, still has the smell of burning flesh in his nostrils; the taste of hell in his mouth (84–85). The barbarous attack on his home and family was carried out by the Black and Tans (the brutal and brutalized British soldiers, veterans of the First World War, who were recruited from 1920–1921 to repress any revolutionary insurgency in Ireland). O'Malley and his family had become victims of a violent reprisal on the tenuous ground that as a schoolteacher, and ardent advocate of Irish independence, O'Malley had been in some way responsible for a recent republican burning of the Big House owned by the local Anglo-Irish landed gentry (83).

Now cast away on the Pacific Ocean – he was unable to remain on the east coast of the United States because the Atlantic bore too many unbearable associations – O'Malley returns to an earlier rough translation of Homer's poem of loss and exile that he had made in the schoolhouse in Delphi long ago. As a scholar of Latin and Greek, ancient languages learned from priests when he himself was a pupil, O'Malley follows in the strong tradition of classical learning in the Gaelic-speaking parts of Ireland. Since at least 1695, when the unofficial hedge schools were set up to elude the ban on Catholic schools, priests had instructed the Irish peasants in Latin and Greek; and O'Malley's background is given credence and substance by the reader's presumed acquaintance with Brian Friel's play *Translations* (1980), itself set in a hedge school in Co. Galway in the 1820s.[4]

O'Malley's translation begins to provide focus and a purpose to his solitary days. As he tells his landlady: 'To save my life, Mrs Neil, I am working on a project of translation' (20). Equally, the translation becomes a means of enabling him to communicate once more with fellow human beings. His landlady has heard of Ulysses through her brother's recital of Tennyson's eponymous poem long ago; and it is through his teaching of the *Odyssey* to her daughter, Rose, that O'Malley is able to communicate most fully; and essentially it is through working on the *Odyssey* with her that he is able commune once again with his own beloved, dead daughters. Translating the *Odyssey* provides him with correspondences to his own life that enable him to salvage some meaning out of its chaos: 'To find equivalences for olives, the magnanimity of kings' (24). To the homeless, impoverished and consequently dependent itinerant, O'Malley's stories 'were all he could think to offer' (47). Since his own stories are still too raw to proffer, Homer's serves as his gift to others. Indeed, as he explains to Rose, 'And isn't that the beauty of a story, that sometimes we feel as though it is our story that's being told?' (48). Eventually, through his work on the *Odyssey*, his own story and that of Odysseus appear to merge. O'Malley realizes that he has a role to play by returning home to the world that he has lost: unlike Odysseus, as he is bitterly aware, he has no Penelope (87, 104); but ultimately he realizes that even though his family won't be waiting, he does have a home and a nexus of relationships that function as equivalences for his Penelope ('a home is something more, is it not, than simply the walls of a house' (163)).

If this makes *A Man from a Distant Field* sound as if the classical freight is destined to drown the fiction rather than keep it afloat, it is important to note that the Homeric content is not simply invoked in counterpoint; it has also shaped in notable ways the form of the novel as well. As O'Malley says:

> The poem was leading him on a merry dance. So many false starts for the homecoming, so many obstacles ... He was not pursuing it from beginning to end but entering parts almost at random and hoping for the poetry to speak to him.
>
> (139)

For this reason, there is a freshness afforded by the recognition of the ancient parallels: we encounter Scylla and Charybdis before the Sirens (137, 105); we voyeuristically watch Nausicaa on the beach together with O'Malley on two occasions, the second time (73ff, 141ff.) shockingly by way of Joyce; and we also revisit Hades on numerous occasions because in many ways it is Odysseus' *katabasis* that characterizes O'Malley's entire time in Oyster Bay (93–96, 109f., 164ff.). Even though O'Malley's journeying is limited to the islands in and around Oyster Bay, his mental and verbal peregrinations are as myriad and convoluted as those of his ancient forebear.

Whilst the first part of the novel in Oyster Bay, Kishkan's Scheria, is often beautifully observed and lyrical, and suitably dreamlike as it takes its bearings from the magical realism of the contemporary novel, Part Two – which is set in Ireland – by contrast rudely reawakens the reader. Here we often find discordance in the Irish speech rhythms, especially in the rendering of the Anglo-Irish-isms of Una, who becomes O'Malley's soulmate in adversity and loss. Most of the syntactical structures are taken from J. M. Synge's language in his plays – a highly wrought, elaborate and intensely lyrical Hiberno-English;[5] but in Part Two the borrowings ring often less than true. We learn that Una, whose family house was burned down just before O'Malley's, is a cousin of the real-life, aristocratic, Anglo-Irish Protestant, Constance Gore-Booth/Markiewicz, who joined the barricades during the Easter Rising of 1916.[6] Whilst parallels with mythical counterparts are often illuminating, those with real-life historical figures are less so here. On account of the insecurity of Kishkan's grasp of her subject-matter – life on an island off the west coast might not have resulted in acquaintance with many of Una's class and background – the reader is forced to draw on their own knowledge of any such proclaimed affiliation to flesh out the detail.

The Irish Literary Revival and Comparatism

The shortcomings to Part Two notwithstanding, this a novel worthy of serious consideration. Kishkan is clearly well aware of the deeper reasons why the trajectory of the plot and its mythical analogue should work. She remarks in the preface:

> I am not a Greek scholar but tried to figure out the kind of translation a passionate but amateur reader of the *Odyssey* in a late-nineteenth-century edition might come up with.
>
> (8)

The translation that O'Malley purchases from Vancouver to assist him in his work is the 1879 prose translation by S. H. Butcher and Andrew Lang. O'Malley finds this and other English translations woefully inadequate, 'as though the good parts had been taken out' (21), and Odysseus were an 'English magistrate' or a 'Minister of God' (70). To render Odysseus as either English or priestly is not only wholly and intrusively anachronistic, it is also total anathema to O'Malley, the atheistic nationalist, whose faith was dashed the night of the fire and who casts the local priest, when he seeks to explain O'Malley's loss in narrowly theological terms, as a Joycean monocular (and bigoted) Cyclopean figure (107).[7]

Despite O'Malley's objections, Butcher and Lang's translation was an excellent crib for the Irish schoolmaster to possess: not least since it provided O'Malley's contemporaries with a familiar window onto Homer's world, one that drew the very correspondences he himself seeks in order that Rose might understand. It was also an especially effective translation for an early twentieth-century Irish speaker of English. For Butcher and Lang's translation, as with the Lang, Leaf and Myers translation of the *Iliad* (1883), bears remarkable similarities to Augusta Gregory's 1902 hugely influential translation of the redaction of tales about Cuchulain, *Cuchulain of Muiremne*.[8] The similarities between the translation of Homer and Lady Gregory's rendering of Celtic saga material are not simply a result of a coalescence of voices at this time; they were underpinned by syncretic studies of both Homeric and Celtic mythologies by both classical and Celtic scholars from at least the middle of the nineteenth century onwards.[9] Whether Kishkan is aware or not of the serious and demonstrable links between Homeric poetry and Irish bardic tales – her conscious nodding in the direction of Friel's *Translations* would imply at least some familiarity with the nineteenth-century discussions (68, 69–70) – these interconnections continued to be explored in the twentieth century by such eminent classical scholars as George Thomson (on comparative oral poetics), George Huxley (on bards), J. V. Luce (on Homer and the Great Blasket Island), and lexically through the comparative philological studies in the 1960s by the classicist Kevin O'Nolan, brother of the Irish novelist, Flann O'Brien.[10]

So for O'Malley's generation, reared on Lady Gregory's version of Irish saga, Butcher and Lang's translation of the *Odyssey* was broadly familiar territory. In this sense, Kishkan's novel is rooted firmly in the late-nineteenth-century, Literary Revival's Celtic/Hellenic syncretic method. Although the bipartite structure of the novel clearly reflects the move in the *Odyssey* from the journeying to Ithaca, the first part equally calls to mind J. M. Synge's ethnographical account of his visits to the Aran Islands over a number of summers from 1898 onwards, which he eventually published in 1907.[11] Synge's observations of the customs of the Irish peasants with whom he lives provide striking parallels with the rituals of ancient Greece;[12] and in the novel O'Malley's observations about the Aboriginal peoples of Canada resemble passages from Synge's diaries (like Synge before him, he watches silently, hoping his gaze appears neither intrusive nor impolite (114)).[13] It is by no means implausible, then, for the Irish-speaking O'Malley to be translating the Homeric epics in 1922 and, like both Odysseus and Synge, to be both explorer and ethnographer.

In marked contrast to Synge, whose knowledge of the Irish language alone provided him with access to knowledge of the inhabitants of the Aran Islands, O'Malley shares with his new friends the common experience of colonial oppression. Alex says to him: 'It is good for us to know you and let you see something of how we used to live. You are a man who has lost something too' (153). Indeed, O'Malley's fascination with the burial rituals of the Aboriginal peoples leads to his own *katabatic* experiences as he not only acquires the coffin-canoe of a dead person, he also spends his most restorative times lying in it, communing with his own dead mother, amidst the Canadian equivalent of Achilles' asphodels, the dead camas. Mirroring Odysseus' erection of an oar over Elpenor's grave at *Odyssey* 12.14–15, which Elpenor's shade has requested in the Underworld (11.75) following his frighteningly arbitrary, accidental fall from the roof of Circe's palace at the end of book 10, O'Malley carries the oar he is given as a present by his Aboriginal friends back home and erects it in the place of his family's collective grave.

An Irish *Odyssey*

Kishkan's decision to write an Irish *Odyssey* can only have been undertaken with a degree of trepidation. As W. B. Stanford wrote in 1954:

> ... no author in ancient or modern times has attempted to rival the comprehensiveness of Homer's account until the present century, when an Irish novelist and a Greek poet have produced two contemporary interpretations of the much enduring hero: James Joyce in his *Ulysses* (1922) and Nikos Kazantzakis in his *Odyssey* (1938).[14]

Like O'Malley, Joyce had used Butcher and Lang's translation as his source; and there is much of Joyce's hero, Leopold Bloom, in Declan O'Malley – in his defence of 'otherness' and natural justice in his support of both the Aboriginal peoples and women's equality; also in his love of music. Kishkan's reworking of the

Nausicaa episode, especially the second time the parallel is invoked when O'Malley awakes from his snooze in his coffin-canoe and espies the pre-pubescent, naked twelve-year old Rose on the beach below (141ff.), gestures, knowingly or not, towards the hugely controversial parallel scene in *Ulysses* when Bloom masturbates on the beach as he pruriently looks up Gerty MacDowell's skirt.[15] O'Malley recognizes his sin, which given his lust for a twelve-year-old, is clearly more culpable than Bloom's lust for the seventeen-year-old Gerty. When Rose's father banishes O'Malley for teaching his daughter to read and write without his permission, O'Malley knows that, like Actaeon, he in fact deserves punishment for voyeurism (160–161).

Like many of her predecessors, notably Derek Walcott in *Omeros*, Kishkan cannot help but include – consciously or otherwise – Joyce's epic novel as intertext. But unlike many Irish predecessors, she has opted to do so in prose rather than in poetry. Indeed all other Irish *Odysseys* after Joyce have been in verse in line with the general trend in Anglophone receptions of Homer in the twentieth century.[16] This 'lyricizing'/'miniaturizing' of epic is evident in, say, the arch and whimsical poem, 'A Siren', by the expatriate and notoriously adulterous Derek Mahon, and in his moving and apologetically masculinist 'Calypso'.[17] It is also demonstrated by the feminist re-readings of Eiléan Ní Chuilleanáin, notably in her collection *The Second Voyage* (1977). But perhaps, the most extensive and consistent lyrical engagement with the *Odyssey* more recently has been in the beautifully crafted poetic renderings by Michael Longley (in, say, his 'Laertes', and his 'Anticlea' poems), which have enabled the poet, as in O'Malley's case, to say things about himself that the raw material of his own life cannot yield publicly.[18]

So why has Kishkan chosen the novel form, when she is herself a poet? One reason is that her *Odyssey* requires space – across time, across place and across the generations of history. As O'Malley realizes, rootedness is always linked to death, to history; his landlady Mrs Neil would never easily leave World's End, where she has buried the child she lost:

> That was a thing to anchor a woman to a place, he supposed. A woman would want to nurture a child, even after its death, remember its birthday, croon a lullaby to the seeding grasses. He'd read of tribes who buried dead children around their cooking fires so they wouldn't get cold. A woman would understand that, he thought, even if she might not do it herself.
>
> (133)

Similarly reflecting upon the devastating effects of the Great Famine in Ireland, O'Malley comments on the importance of what literally lies beneath one's feet:

> There had been families living in folds of the earth, tucked into ravines, who were gone with hardly a trace: a wisp in an aging memory, rituals carved in the bark of a tree, a placement of stones to assist one's footing on a steep ridge.
>
> (54)

Just as his mother had passed the memories of the dead from the Famine onto him, so had O'Malley made his pupils realize that stepping stones can also be hallowed markers of our own mortality.

The first part of the novel runs from the spring to the fall of 1922, the same year as the publication of Joyce's *Ulysses* (written between 1914–1920 and published initially in parts in the *Literary Review* 1918–1920). Of course, the events of *Ulysses* take place on 16 June 1904 but the prominence granted to the year 1922 in the section headings is significant here, not least because of its association with Joyce's monumental *Odyssey*. But there are further historical reasons for the choice of date: Kishkan's novel is not only cut in half by its geographical shift; its second part is made possible purely by a seismic historical shift – the signing of the Anglo-Irish Treaty on 6 December 1921 that had granted dominion status, as with Canada, to Ireland. Without the declaration of the Free State, as an outlaw O'Malley would not have been able to return to his country of birth without arrest; and the novel, in turn, would have been denied the *nostos*. By the middle of the second part of the novel, from June 1922 onwards, the civil war between those who supported the Free State as a first step towards full independence of the Crown and those who rejected it altogether was fully underway. If the burning of Troy that leads to the ten-year *nostos* of the *Odyssey* is replaced here by the burning of Ireland by the Black and Tans, the settling of scores against the suitors on Odysseus' return is now rewritten in the bloody acts of revenge carried out on both sides in the civil war.

Part One focuses mostly on O'Malley's relations with women – with Mrs Neil and Rose, his Arete and his Nausicaa (although it should be noted that Mrs Neil, in particular, is a composite figure – by the end of Part One, at least, she is Calypso as much as Arete). This Odysseus, furthermore, does not have a son, only two dead daughters. O'Malley is increasingly struck by his similarities to Odysseus, but also painfully aware of his differences:

> Declan had journeyed a long way by sea but alone. And the biggest difference between them? Odysseus was struggling homeward to a wife and son. Declan had no one.
>
> (88)

But on his return, it is still his Penelope, or rather her living surrogates, who provides the focus of Part Two.

The only surviving object of the fire that O'Malley can salvage is the harp belonging to his daughter Grainne; and he learns with the help of two women how to bring it back to life. Assistance comes first from Una, whose grandfather had owned the Big House and who now resides in the groundskeeper's cabin, the only remnant of the fire. It is her cabin that provides a warm enough environment for the harp's wood to breathe. Second, Grainne's former teacher, Bernadette Feeny, teaches O'Malley how to string the instrument. The harp, like O'Malley himself, had survived at great personal cost; but such self-sacrifice, it is suggested, is what guaranteed its ultimate survival:

> Perhaps it had been a blessing that the strings had broken and melted as they might otherwise have caused the harp to pull itself apart from the tension.
>
> (237)

Clearly the harp is not simply Grainne's powerful legacy to her father; it represents, as in popular iconography, the symbol of Erin, Romantic nationalism's allegorical figure of Ireland.[19]

Whilst Ireland 'pull[s] itself apart from the tension of civil war', O'Malley the nationalist, but strictly non-violent, proto-republican, joins forces with Una, the daughter of the Protestant Ascendancy now turned feminist activist in the women's republican movement, Cumman na mBan.[20] In a world in which O'Malley is bequeathed a skiff by a relative of one who had died in France in the First World War, fighting on the same side as the Black and Tans who had denied him both his livelihood and his loved ones (61), reconciliation and reunion take on wide political significance. Before the destruction of the Big House, connections – affection almost – had existed between O'Malley and Una's houses:

> . . . despite their class and religious and differences, the two families had been friendly. The woman of the desmesne had consulted Eilis [O'Malley's wife] about her arthritis, sharing the aches and pains of aging over a cup of tea in sunlight by the cabin door, roses wreathed above the entrance, while the woman's horse waited, tethered to a bit of gate. The mister brought cartons of children's books to the school for the young scholars, and their daughters, Grainne and Maeve, loved the same music, played the same instrument. It made no sense.
>
> (90)

As Una and O'Malley now share knowledge – of botany and ancient Greek respectively, and of their respective losses of family homes and of loved ones – they signal the possibility of a new Ireland, for Protestant and Catholic, male and female, the individual and the community. When Una arrives back, carrying a puppy in her arms that reminds O'Malley of his dog Argos in Canada, she tells him of the child that they are expecting together.

Longley's poem 'Ceasefire', published in *The Irish Times* on the eve of the Good Friday Agreement, turned to Homer's *Iliad* to delineate the delicate balance of the peace process. Figuring Ireland as a composite country, with multiple voices, multiple agendas and decidedly without violence, was a no less urgent and necessary undertaking at the start of the new millennium in the wake of the series of Belfast Agreements 1998–1999. Kishkan's *Odyssey*, for this reason alone, still merits attention today. *A Man in a Distant Field* may be a tamed – and occasionally cloyingly sentimental – *Odyssey* compared to Homer's, and very definitely compared to Joyce's; but it too is expansive, warm-hearted, often hard-headed and intelligent, and worthy of scrutiny.

Bibliography

Arbois de Jubainville, Henri d' (1899), *La civilisation des Celtes et de l'épopée homérique*. Paris: Ancienne Librairie Thorin et fils.

Butcher, Samuel Henry and Andrew Lang, trans. (1879), *The Odyssey of Homer*. London: Macmillan.

Foster, R. F. (2014), *Vivid Faces: The Revolutionary Generation in Ireland, 1890–1913*. London: Allen Lane.

Gregory, Augusta (1902), *Cuchulain of Muirthemne, the story of the men of the red branch of Ulster, arranged and put into Engl. by Lady Gregory*. London: Putnam.

Huxley, G. L. (1969), *Greek Epic Poetry from Eumelos to Panyassis*. London: Faber and Faber.

Joyce, James (1971), *Ulysses*. Harmondsworth: Penguin.

Kiberd, Declan (1992), *Synge and the Irish Language*. Dublin and London: Macmillan.

Kishkan, Theresa (2004), *A Man in a Distant Field: A Novel*. Toronto: Simon & Pierre Fiction.

Land, Andrew, Walter Lead and Ernest Myers (1883, trans.), *The Iliad of Homer*. London: Macmillan.

Longley, Michael (1991), *Gorse Fires*. London: Secker and Warburg.

Luce, J. V. (1969), 'Homeric Qualities in the Life and Literature of the Great Blasket Island', *Greece & Rome* 16: 151–68.

Macintosh, Fiona (1994), *Dying Acts: Death in Ancient Greek and Modern Irish Tragic Drama*. Cork: Cork University Press.

Macintosh, Fiona (2015), 'Shakespearean Sophocles: (Re-)discovering Greek Tragedy in the Nineteenth Century', in N. Vance and J. Wallace (eds), *Oxford History of Classical Reception in English Literature: Vol. 4*, 299–323. Oxford: Oxford University Press.

Mahon, Derek (2005), *Harbour Lights*. Loughcrew: The Gallery Press.

Ní Chuilleanáin, Eiléan (1977), *The Second Voyage: Poems*. Dublin: Gallery Press.

O'Nolan, K. (1969), 'Homer and Irish Heroic Narrative', *Classical Quarterly* 19: 1–19.

Platt, Mary-Hartley (2015), 'Epic Reductions: Receptions of Homer and Virgil in Modern American Poetry', unpublished D.Phil. thesis, University of Oxford.

Stanford, W. B. (1976), *Ireland and the Classical Tradition*. Dublin: Figgis.

Synge, J. M. (1982) in Alan Price (ed.), *Collected Works II*, Prose. Gerrards Cross: Colin Smythe.

Thomson, George (1929), *Greek Lyric Metre*. Cambridge: Cambridge University Press.

9

The Minotaur on the Russian Internet: Victor Pelevin's *Helmet of Horror*

Anna Ljunggren

Victor Pelevin's *The Helmet of Horror* (*Shlem uzhasa*) was first published in Russian in 2005, with the English translation appearing in 2006 as part of the Canongate Myth series, an international publishing project with a self-consciously global scope, initiated by the independent Scottish publishing house Canongate Books. It was one of seventeen short novels based on myths from all over the world chosen by the authors, an international team from countries including Israel, Japan, China and Brazil as well as Europe, Canada and Australia. All the writers were well established already, but had made their names in different genres of the novel, ranging from detective to historical fiction. The novels included, for example, Margaret Atwood's retelling of the *Odyssey* as *The Penelopiad* (2005) and A. S. Byatt's adaptation of episodes from the Norse *Edda* in *Ragnarök* (2011). Pelevin's *Helmet of Horror*, which is a response to the ancient Greek myth of the Minotaur, first appeared as an audiobook in Russian, then as a conventional book in printed form, and shortly afterwards as an interactive play entitled *Shlem.com*, with '*shlem*' meaning 'helmet' in Russian. The work is experimental; it was written in the form of an internet chat, so that communication through advanced technology and an ancient myth are combined; however innovative, this approach is not so surprising when we consider that we still record and store narratives just as the ancient Greeks did, although we use electronic disks to preserve them rather than inscribing them on wax tablets with styluses.

In this chapter I argue that Pelevin is using ancient Greek myth to think about the nature of the new community created by the internet. This process involves briefly considering some of the cultural, aesthetic and philosophical influences on Pelevin's novel, including some earlier 'receptions' of the Minotaur myth in fiction and cinema, while analyzing some of the new story's key features: its *topos* (the virtual space in which the 'action' takes place); its dematerialized characters;

the key symbol of the mask of the Minotaur (which is the titular 'Helmet of Horror'); and the erasure of personal names, subjectivities and true identities in the creation of a carnivalesque virtual online community.

In his earlier novel *Babylon* (2000, of which the original title, published in 1999, was *Generation 'P'*), Pelevin drew on Mesopotamian myth to present the world of media and advertisements as it created, and even became a substitute for, political 'reality' in Russia of the 1990s. *The Helmet of Horror* treats another contemporary medium – the internet – and relates it to the philosophical question of subjectivity as the 'prison of the mind'. This metaphor extends back at least as far as Plato's myth of the prisoners in the allegorical cave of his *Republic* book VII, as well as to Buddhist doctrine, and was most influentially explored in the subjective idealism of the early modern thinker George Berkeley. We can see Pelevin engaging with this philosophical question, for example, when interviewed by Kristina Rotkirch in 2007:[1]

> ROTKIRCH You are probably a pioneer among Russian writers in using the internet, and if I am not mistaken, the internet for you is a kind of space of freedom. In *The Helmet of Horror*, however, the internet becomes a labyrinth, even a prison.
>
> PELEVIN The internet is not a space of freedom. Only the mind can be a space of freedom. Everything into which the mind is put becomes its prison.

For Pelevin, everything – including the internet – is a prison of the human mind. *The Helmet of Horror* reveals the illusionary nature of virtuality and exposes its limits.

As many contemporary works of scholarship (including the essays in this present volume) illustrate, the use of mythological elements in today's global mass culture is increasingly common.[2] In Pelevin's case, we see classical mythology being assimilated to a philosophical exploration of the potential of the virtual world expressed 'undercover', in the guise of rough, contemporary computer slang. Yet *The Helmet of Horror* has antecedents in writing from long before the invention of the internet. It is stylistically indebted to the Russian absurdist theatre of OBERIU (The Association for Real Art), a group of futurist writers, circus artists and musicians that existed in Leningrad in the 1920s–30s,[3] as well as to Joseph Brodsky's drama *Marbles* (1982) with its ironic and macaronic use of antiquity. *Marbles* links modern technocratic civilization with the classical world in a manner not dissimilar to Pelevin's novel: it is a humorous and absurdist Platonic dialogue, which observes the classical 'unities' of time and place, conducted by two individuals with the classical Roman names Publius and Tullius, but set in a prison cell two centuries after our own era.[4]

Although *The Helmet of Horror* was commissioned by Canongate, the choice of the Minotaur myth is not accidental. The half-bull and half-human beast is an image in line with Victor Pelevin's earlier work, such as the humanoid insects in *The Life of Insects* (1996) or the werewolf in *A Werewolf Problem in Central Russia* (1998). Nor is it the first time that Pelevin has placed a mythical image at the centre of the story: recall the virtual Tower of Babel in Moscow during the Perestroika 1990s in *Babylon*. Pelevin is one of the most established and popular writers – as well as one of most controversial – of the first post-Soviet generation. He has been criticized for distorting the Russian literary language by using borrowed words and slang; he is considered by his critics to be a threshold or marginal figure, rooted in the unofficial late Soviet Moscow culture.[5] He is much indebted to the artistic strategies of the iconoclastic movement known as 'Moscow Conceptualism', which parodied Soviet state symbols and official art.[6] It divested them of their meaning in order to reach the 'void', a key concept in the Buddhist theory of consciousness (on which see further below), but also of the conceptualist movement.[7] The aesthetic method of parody and stylization – previously used by Pelevin with great success – began to be experienced as a dead-end during the first years of the millennium. *The Helmet of Horror* was written at about this time, when a certain distance from the Soviet experience had been gained, and the Soviet state and its propaganda no longer seemed to be a valid target.

The Helmet of Horror has a subtitle in the English translation: *The Myth of Theseus and the Minotaur*. The subtitle shortens the Russian original *Kreatif o Tezee i Minotavre* in order to avoid the problem presented by the word '*kreatif*', from Russian-language computer slang, meaning 'an entry', often a visual 'piece.' The 'piece' is written in the distorted non-normative language of computer slang, interspersed with obscenities that are replaced simply by 'xxx', but the meaning concealed by these letters is quite transparent for a native speaker.

Neither plot nor characters, in the traditional sense, exist in *The Helmet of Horror*. The setting is cyberspace, where the eight characters are each imprisoned in a room, which apparently contains little more than a computer screen and a keypad to write on. One of the characters, who uses the virtual moniker 'Ariadne', launches a discussion (or 'thread'). The thread is going to take the form of series of dream interpretations. Ariadne dreams about the Minotaur, and other characters offer philosophical interpretation of her dreams by trying to discover the meaning of the myth. When the interpretation reaches a final stage, Theseus appears in the chat room. When the culmination is reached, the characters create a group, who exclaim in unison, 'MOO!'

Here the very process of interpretation replaces action and the plot. The text grasps at the myth to fill the void, the absence of meaning, and it rejects it at the same time. All of the elements are marked with questions: *Who is the Minotaur? What is the labyrinth? And Theseus?* It should perhaps be added here that Victor Pelevin positively enjoys mysteries and mystifications. The author avoids being interviewed, is usually pictured wearing sunglasses, and likes to bewilder or joke with the reader. The text of *Helmet of Horror* actually ends with a disclaimer:[8]

> Not a single fictitious Ancient Greek youth or maiden was killed during the creation of this text.
>
> (274)

Here the ontological status of the actions not only in ancient myth, but also in cyberspace discourse and the modern novel, becomes the source of ironic humour.

Interpretation and inquiry play a central role in *The Helmet of Horror*. In a world where there is no single answer, inquiry itself is parodied. One should also bear in mind the omnipresence of irony as an idiom in youth culture at the time when the novel was written. Indeed, according to the code of the youth subcultures of the 1990s and early 2000s (including rave and internet culture), there was almost an obligation that serious questions should be asked ironically.[9] The opening lines of *The Helmet of Horror* contain a riddle: at the very beginning, Ariadne, the initiator of the chat, types on the screen, thus starting her 'thread', by proposing a labyrinthine game: 'I shall construct a labyrinth in which I can lose myself together with anyone who tries to find me – who said this and about what?' This puzzle refers to a recurring image of a labyrinth in the work of Jorge Luis Borges, both in prose (*The Garden of Forking Paths* [*El jardín de senderos que se bifurcan*], 1941 and 'The House of Asterion' ['La casa de Asterión'], 1947) and in poetry (a diptych 'A Labyrinth' / '*Labyrinth*' ('El laberinto' / '*Laberinto*') from the '*Eulogy to the Shadow*' ('*Elogio de la sombra*', 1969), where the Minotaur is treated as 'the other' who will be discovered in the darkness. Pelevin reveals his debt to Borges when his epigraph to *Helmet of Horror* explicitly salutes the older writer, before the reader ('anyone') is invited to play the game of the riddle, the riddle of the labyrinth and Minotaur. The characters are trying to interpret the dreams of Ariadne in order to find the way out from wherever they are. So, where does Pelevin place them within his virtual labyrinth?

Topos

Each of the characters is sitting in a cell, dressed in a Greek tunic (*chiton*); inter-cell communication takes place via computer screens. Every cell resembles a hotel room: it is somewhat individualized, but not a home, being a so-called *heterotopia* (to use the term Michel Foucault defined and explored in his influential 1967 essay),[10] a virtual counter-site existing in ontologically unstable relationship to material reality. The toilet paper in each room is decorated by the imprint of a star pattern, a sort of asterisk, which reminds the reader of Greek myth, since Asterion was both the name of a Cretan king who was ancestor of the Minotaur, and an alternative name for the Minotaur himself.[11] But it is also a reminder of the story which is the seminal *literary* ancestor of *The Helmet of Horror*, since in Borges' 'La casa de Asterión' (1947), after evading the reader, the narrator, Asterion, is ultimately revealed to be indistinguishable from the Minotaur himself. It is little surprise that Pelevin's characters wonder at first whether they are dead or just dreaming, with *heterotopia* being a way to represent both death or a dream as a different place. These anonymous 'other places' stand for 'virtual reality' in the game that they play.

Each participant first explores his or her different yet similar cells, then the adjacent parts of the labyrinth, which is modeled on the *Labyrinthe de Versailles* with its statues, as described by the super-intellectual 'IsoldA':

> Yes, I forgot to say. The plan that was hanging everywhere looked more like an old engraving than something modern ... And written on it in this strange oblique typeface was: *plan du labyrinthe de Versailles*. What could that mean? Is it from the word 'verse'? Because there are characters from fables in the fountains? (63)

There each one encounters their individual visions, projected 'mirrored' images. While Borges' 'The Garden of Forking Paths' offers an image representing the relativity of time and its multiple possibilities, Pelevin's labyrinth is about the 'self' and about projecting fears and desires: the dialogue between IsoldA and Romeo-y-Cohiba, for example, suggests that they swiftly become intimate with and desire one another, raising readers' hopes of secret assignations. UGLI 666, on the other hand, is a Christian fanatic, who yearns for a canon to explain the meaning of labyrinthine ecclesiastical mosaics, while an alcoholic called Sartrik comes across two refrigerators of alcohol and almost disappears from the text.

Dematerialized Characters

This exploration of the labyrinth continues in tandem with the deciphering of Ariadne's dreams. However, even before we read Ariadne's monologue, the direction of thought is set by the very first lines spoken by the characters.

> *Organizm (-::* What's going on? Is there anyone here?
> *Romeo-y-Cohiba*: I'm here.
>
> (1)

> *Nutscracker*: But where is here exactly?
> *Organizm (-::* How do you mean?
>
> (4)

The words 'anyone', 'here' and 'I' are instances of the rhetorical concept of deixis: their content is determined by their relationship to the speaker, otherwise they are void in meaning or referent. The underlying theme of subjectivity, and its textual representation, is thus immediately introduced from the beginning.

When the characters start presenting themselves, all elements that are related to the outside 'real' world are erased from their self-descriptions, and replaced with series of 'x's, the same procedure which was used in the text with obscenities. A character who calls himself Monstradamus (the self-appointed moderator and chairman of the Socratic dialogue) answers the question 'Who are you?' as follows:

> *Monstradamus*: xxx. I live in xxx and I am an xxx.
>
> (10)

But compare the response of Romeo-y-Cohiba:

> Hey, you, whoever you are! I demand that you allow me to contact my family immediately! And the xxx embassy!
>
> (9)

Or, once again:

> *UGLI 666*: I'm female since it interests you so very much. My name's xxx, I am a xxx by profession, and a xxx by education, but by vocation I've always been a xxx.
>
> (31)

Each of the characters inhabiting the virtual world of the 'cell' is thus partly stripped of their personal attributes, and is thereby dematerialized. This aesthetic experiment of erasing personal attributes challenges all our self-representations and targets our identities, the ways we define ourselves through belonging to a group, a profession or a place.

The Helmet of the Minotaur

The title, *The Helmet of Horror,* refers metonymically to the Minotaur. Ariadne has three dreams about the Minotaur: in the first one, the Minotaur appears as an animate figure but wearing a masked helmet; the second one contains the design of the helmet; and the third is about 'the archives', a mysterious resource where the solution to the theme of the Minotaur in her dreams is found. This is the glimpse which Ariadne catches of the Minotaur in her first dream:

> He wasn't like a man. He was absolutely massive, and I thought for a moment he was like an overgrown mushroom with a big cap of blackish-green metal [...] And on his head he had a bronze helmet, like a gladiator's mask – a head-piece with a wide brim and a plate with holes in it where the face should be. There were two horns on the helmet....
>
> (25)

This description is sufficient to establish the link between the Minotaur's head in Pelevin, which can be removed as a mask, and a famous episode in Federico Fellini's movie *Satyricon* (1969). In the latter, the gladiator impersonating the Minotaur removes his horrifying helmet when Encolpio begs for his life in the arena, revealing the grinning face of the man behind the monstrous mask.[12] The relationship between the sensational cinematic treatment of the Minotaur's helmet and the comedic-novelistic one is perhaps further complicated since, in the movie, the gladiatorial games are staged at the festival of the god of laughter (Momus).[13] Pelevin was certainly familiar with *Satyricon*, although one could also suggest two more visual prototypes from famous works of cinema: the first is Darth Vader from George Lucas' *Star Wars* movies (the first of which was released in 1977), wearing a skull-like black iron mask which actually functioned as part of his life-support system, and the second is an earlier source widely known in Russia – Teutonic knights wearing helmets with horns from Sergei Eisenstein's *Alexander Nevsky* (1938).[14]

As the exploration of the labyrinth by all of the characters progresses, a moment arrives when Ariadne experiences another dream in which the helmet reappears as a blueprint. It is a representation of the human mind or rather the mechanical parody of a human brain, somewhat akin to a computer. This is her description:

> I remember that the helmet of horror consisted of several major parts and a lot of secondary ones. The parts had strange names: the frontal net, the now grid, the separator labyrinth, the horns of plenty, Tarkovsky's mirror and so forth.
>
> (77)

These are not technical names for parts of the brain: some of them evoke themes in the story (net, labyrinth, horns). But 'Tarkovsky's mirror' would be instantly recognized by Russian readers, and experts in arthouse cinema further afield, as a programmatic reference to Andrei Tarkovsky's film *The Mirror* (1975), an experimental, plot-less, semi-autobiographical work evoking dreams and memories rather than reality. After this description, Pelevin's Ariadne then describes how the helmet, i.e. the machine of the mind, actually works:

> The grid sublimates the past contained in the upper section of the helmet, transforming it into vapour, which is driven up into the horns of plenty by the force of circumstances.
>
> (78)

The central metaphor of the whole text, 'the helmet of horror', which has been described already as a mechanical *imitation* of the mind, is now extended further to represent the mind itself. One gradually learns that the Minotaur is none other than Theseus, wearing the helmet of horror while seeing his own reflection in the mirror. Seeing a 'reflection in the mirror' implies 'projection'. Mirroring – reflection – shifts the focus from the projected object to the sphere of the subject once again, following the patterns of Buddhist learning (in which Pelevin has long been interested[15]) that are applied here to what is seen as 'behind' the mirror:

> Theseus is the one who looks into the mirror, and the Minotaur is the one he sees, because he's wearing a helmet of horror.
>
> (220)

The very familiarity of the ancient myth, and the concreteness of the imagined mirror, help the reader here to grapple with the complexities of the philosophy of mind, of the subject, and of cognition.[16]

Helmet, Mask and Internet-Carnival

The mechanical 'material body' relates the helmet to the computer, yet the fact that it can be put on (and removed) makes this helmet similar to the mask:

> ... we can hardly call it a 'real' person. More like an empty mask: Or maybe a 'helmet'.
>
> (224)

So, the empty mask hides no one, no 'I'. As I have already shown, this statement is well in keeping with the device of erasing the personal properties of the contributors to the 'thread', replacing them with x's, and thereby 'emptying' them. The same phenomenon of erasure is also quite ostensible in the sphere of personal names. As a group of substantives, personal names or *nomina propria* have the property of designating one sole object – its bearer. We identify strongly with our names, and the loss of a name is mostly experienced negatively as a depersonalization; this happens when we are given a number or even just a category label in place of a name in the army, in a hospital or, most radically, enslavement. In one situation, however, the loss of a name has a positive value: it is seen as a liberation from the pressure of social hierarchy in the world of the 'carnival', as defined by Mikhail Bakhtin in *Rabelais and his World*, the first (Russian) edition of which was published in 1965. That is, a subversive and emancipatory literary idiom named after raucous festivals which challenge the 'normal' world and its hierarchies by deliberate implementation of chaos and humour.

There are only three 'stable' names in *The Helmet of Horror*, and they are the mythical ones: Ariadne, Minotaur and Theseus. Strictly speaking, other characters have no names, only computer pseudonyms functioning as masks. They are, in the strict sense of the word, anonymous. Wearing the mask of a computer nickname grants considerable freedom to its users and relates to the virtual space of the carnival. Today the online world in Russia is the heir to the unofficial dimension of the polarized culture of the late Soviet period. Irony, obscenity and distorted language are features that mark the difference, the intentional deviation from the 'normative' world.[17] Its general tone is 'liberated' from the seriousness of the 'normative' discourses, although the contents can be philosophical, as in Pelevin's case. Moreover, the relationship between the 'I' and an online forum is a new phenomenon in modern communication. It can be defined as being 'alone together'. So are the ancient archives described in the third dream of Ariadne:

> An entire shelf full of cross-examinations of Minotaurs by themselves – they were called 'Alone Together'?
>
> (244)

Solving the Puzzle: The Carnival Group Instead of the Character

When Ariadne starts a 'thread' in the beginning, the characters appear on the computer screen in the following order:

> Organizm(-:
> Romeo-y-Cohiba
> Nutscracker
> Monstradamus
> IsoldA
> UGLI 666
> Sliff_zoSSchitan (Sartrik)

Just one character's nickname is changed in the English translation: 'Sliff_zoSSchitan' ('Post OK') becomes 'Sartrik', i.e. 'little Sartre' in the English version. The main reason for this permutation was probably to make it more recognizable to the Western reader, while at the same preserving the initial letter 'S'.

At the end of the novel, Ariadne arrives at the final conclusion of the interpretation:

> You are free, and your freedom lies in the fact that the mind has no body [. . .] Even the body has no body, and therefore there is nothing on which to set the helmet of horror.
>
> (255–256)

Here, appearing at the same time as a terrifying noise, the name of Theseus appears on the screen and the names of characters form a constellation together making an anagram, the name of the Minotaur:

> *Theseus*: MINOTAURUS!
> *Monstradamus*: Ah?
> *IsoldA*: Ah?
> *Nutscracker*: Ah?
> *Organizm(-:*: Ah?
> *Theseus*: Ah?
> *Ariadne*: Ah?
> *UGLI 666*: Ah?
> *Romeo-y-Cohiba*: Ah?
>
> (258)

The collective body of Minotaur says in unison 'MOO!' and the *jeu de lettres* continues as the group takes on different configurations.[18] It 'performs' together the birth of the Minotaur from Minos:

> *Monstradamus*: My son!
> *IsoldA*: My son!
> *Nutscracker*: My son!

> *Organizm(-:*:My son!
> *Sartrik*: My son (-:
>
> (261)

Then the collective newborn transforms itself into a serpent named 'Minosaur' (probably morphologically analogous with the noun 'dinosaur'). The character called 'Organizm(-:' explains:

> So what, now we will be the Minosaur. The ancient serpent.
>
> (271)

The text ultimately ends, dissolving itself, stating that the action – as well as all of the beginnings and the endings – took place in the helmet of horror; that is, in the *mind* of the audience/the reader.

The Helmet of Horror translates the philosophical question of human subjectivity (and fear) into terms of contemporary internet culture. It is the internet communication which provides it with its vocabulary and the means aesthetically to shape 'the other', virtual space. The Buddhist notion of void turns out to be compatible not only with the aesthetics of unofficial late Soviet art, but also with contemporary virtuality. One can see three modes of unreality in the text: first, the *heterotopia* of the chat room inhabited by dematerialized characters; second, Ariadne's dreams that lead the narrative and give it its coherence; and finally the myth of the Minotaur, the nucleus of the dream. The myth here does not stand for the solid foundation of shared reality. It is shared by a new collective carnivalesque body of 'together loners' ('Alone Together' (249)). The myth is used, and at the same time it is discarded and parodied in the coded mode of internet culture. One could say that the Minotaur in *The Helmet of Horror* is slaughtered not by Theseus but rather by interpretations and endless parodic mirroring. Interpretation, as an instrument of liberation, functions as an instrument of semantic destruction; it dismantles rather than enriches the meaning. Interpretation undermines not only the validity of the myth but the validity of the subject as well, 'the self'. The anonymous participants are dissolved in a group that 'performs' as an archaic figure – Minotaur or Minosaur, 'the ancient serpent.'

Pelevin suggests in an interview that the exit from the labyrinth is 'to stop thinking you are in a labyrinth'.[19] There is, however, no exit from this cerebral labyrinth of infinite relativization, and it is explicitly compared to a dead end in the text. In *The Helmet of Horror*, dilemmas of contemporary culture are strongly sensed and aesthetically explored with the assistance of one of the most familiar of ancient mythical narratives. If it is read seriously, it leaves us with a vision of a new collectivity with a weakened subject and a philosophical void. We are not, however, invited to read it seriously.

Bibliography

Ågren, Mattias (2010), 'In Pursuit of Neo: The Matrix in Contemporary Russian Novels', *Canadian Slavonic Papers,* 52: 3–4, 249–271.

Armstrong, Richard (2011), 'Eating Eumolpus: *Fellini Satyricon* and Dreaming Tradition', in Jan Parker and Timothy Mathews (eds), *Tradition, Translation, Trauma: The Classic and the Modern.* Oxford: Oxford University Press..

Bobrinskaya, Ekaterina (2013), *Chuzhie? neoficial'noe iskusstvo. Mify. Strategii. Koncepcii.* Moscow: Breus.

Brodsky, Joseph (1989), *Marbles,* translated as *Marbles: a Play in Three Acts* by Alan Myers with Joseph Brodsky. New York: Farrar, Straus & Giroux.

Genis, Alexander (1999), 'Borders and Metamorphoses: Victor Pelevin in the Context of Post-Soviet Literature', in Mikhail Epstein, Alexander Genis and Slobodanka M. Vladiv-Glover (eds), *Russian Postmodernism. New Perspectives on Post-Soviet Culture.* New York: Berghahn Books.

Groys, Boris (2010), *History as Form: Moscow Conceptualism.* Cambridge, MA: Harvard University Press.

Hall, Edith (2007), 'Subjects, selves and survivors', *Helios,* 34 (2): 125–159.

Kerényi, Karl (1951), *The Gods of the Greeks.* London: Thames & Hudson.

Kharms, Daniil (1994), *Rasskazy i sceny.* Vol. 2. Moscow: Viktori.

Ljunggren, Anna and Kristina Rotkirch, eds (2008), *Contemporary Russian Fiction: A Shortlist. Russian Authors interviewed by Kristina Rotkirch.* Moscow: Glas.

Lövgren, Håkan (1996), *Eisenstein's Labyrinth. Aspects of a Cinematic Synthesis of the Arts.* Stockholm: Almqvist & Wiksell International.

Moog-Grünewald, Maria, ed. (2010), *The Reception of Myth and Mythology.* Leiden and Boston: Brill.

Pelevin, V. (2006), *The Helmet of Horror: The Myth of Theseus and the Minotaur.* Edinburgh and NewYork: Canongate.

10

Diagnosis: Overdose. Status: Critical. Odysseys in Bernhard Schlink's *Die Heimkehr*

Sebastian Matzner

When Bernhard Schlink's *Die Heimkehr* (*Homecoming*) was published in 2006, expectations for the follow-up to his international bestseller *Der Vorleser* (*The Reader*) of 1995 were so high that the novel was practically set up to fail. The opinions voiced in initial reviews accordingly ranged from disappointment to condemnation. In his review, entitled 'All and nothing', Leopold describes the novel as the unconvincing work of a now overambitious author:

> *Homecoming* is the attempt to land a big coup, though it is hard to say what exactly this big literary coup is supposed to consist in. The novel is thematically full to the brim, and yet its narrative centre does not really emerge even after more than half of its almost four hundred pages.[1]

Marginally more balanced, Cavelty acknowledges under the caption 'Odyssey as Obsession' that the novel may well be a 'remarkable intellectual adventure', but hastens to add that its 'literary quality seems questionable'.[2] The central lines of criticism which recur in virtually all reviews are that the novel contains too many interwoven narrative strands,[3] covers too many phases of German history,[4] comes with too much erudition, and is too conspicuously constructed to be emotionally engaging.[5] Or, as Weidermann sums up his verdict under the charming headline 'Dross is dangerous for little souls':

> Bernhard Schlink ... storms through world history, through literary history and through the beds of ladies with peachy cheeks, he fights against templates and is himself caught in a locked groove of kitsch. A pitiful sight.[6]

If we want to engage with the book on its own terms, we should take the reading experience articulated in these reviews seriously and focus precisely on the convoluted Odyssean construction that is given such prominence in Schlink's novel. Instead of assessing the book's aesthetic value, this chapter will therefore concentrate on how its peculiar use of myth relates to the German struggle of *Vergangenheitsbewältigung* ('coming to terms with the past').

Needless to say, the year 1989, the watershed chosen for this volume, is of tremendous significance for Germany and her literature. The fall of the Berlin Wall and the subsequent reunification gave new urgency to lingering questions of German national identity.[7] The literature of the 1990s, though widely concerned with processing the diverging experiences of life in the two German states and the present intracultural rapprochement,[8] was dominated by a renewed engagement with the National Socialist (NS) past.[9] This joint return to the most recent shared past no longer focused exclusively on the Shoah, but extended to further victim groups, increasingly also including reflections on German experiences during the war and post-war era.[10] This new interest in German wartime suffering – Müller even speaks of a 'new German delight in the victim discourse'[11] – was and remains fraught with problems. It is often seen as a consequence of the one-sided empathy taboo that resulted from the 1968ers' indignant confrontation with and condemnation of the generation of perpetrators and followers,[12] which found literary expression in the so-called *Väterliteratur* ('fathers' literature') that explored the lives and actions of the parent-generation during the Third Reich.[13] More recent attempts to revisit the past thus not only risk being branded revisionist, but their access to the past is also inevitably inflected both by preceding and competing contemporary modes of remembering. What and who is to be remembered, and how, remains a challenging issue to be negotiated in the self-reflexive medium of literature, which is a central site of what Fuchs calls 'German memory contests'.[14] Schlink's *Vorleser* is a prominent example for the re-evaluation of the memory politics of the generation of 1968,[15] and *Heimkehr* continues to address these issues by combining two further trends in post-unification German literature: the privatization of history in family and generational narratives, and the 'mythical turn'.

Friedrich has argued that the privatization of history resulted from the way the trauma of the Second World War was initially dealt with. He distinguishes between two conformations of victimhood: *victima*, the passive experience of having one's life taken away; and *sacrificium*, the offering of one's life for a greater good. The Germans' collective disavowal of Nazi Germany after the war, according to Friedrich, rendered it impossible for them to give their own wartime suffering a meaning of *sacrificium*, which blocked its incorporation into a collective narrative of national identity.[16] Instead of heroization and mythologization on a national level, wartime experiences were thus commemorated and processed on the small scale of family narratives.[17] The veritable 'remembrance boom'[18] after the reunification in the context of the search for a new national identity, however, makes this ostensibly private form of memorial literature less innocent than it might seem: while individually upholding, by and large, the discursive taboo of interpreting German suffering as *sacrificium*, the appearance of individual, private accounts of *victima* suffering en masse collectively introduces into the public sphere an emotionally highly charged body of texts which shifts the balance and boundaries in the (self-) perception of Germans as perpetrators and victims.[19] Although these family narratives tend to adopt a metacritical perspective, actively reflecting on the concepts of memory and victimhood that underlie this genre,[20] as a group they nonetheless give rise to the 'perception of the nation as a family and of history as family history'.[21] Thus, the 'family narrative represents the shattered or damaged post-war German family as a symptom of the impairment of the nation as a whole'.[22]

The mythical turn, on the other hand, illustrates once more how *die Wende*, the turning point of the reunification in 1989, connects to the turning point of 1945: as Stephan has pointed out, literary reworkings of myth tend to increase in times of crisis and change when individual and national identities become unstable, and the surge in neomythical writings over the course of the last two decades appears to point back to a similar surge in such texts after the collapse of fascism.[23] While these two trends might seem somewhat disparate – the family narratives deliberately zooming in on the individual and the particular, narratives with a mythical theme zooming out from the historical to a universal level – they share a concern of probing family relations and gender roles as focal points for the interrogation of past and future constructions of national identity.[24] In combining a mythological hypotext with a post-war family narrative, Schlink's *Heimkehr* situates itself at the very centre of these literary discourses and offers critical comments on their possibilities and limitations.

Leaving aside for the moment the ubiquitous references to Homer's *Odyssey*, the novel can be summarized as follows: the narrator, Peter Debauer, searches for the lost ending of a pulp fiction story he had begun to read as a child at his grandparents' home and which never ceased to grip his imagination. On his search for the author, he meets and falls in love with Barbara Bindinger. She is already married but, given her husband's extended absence, a relationship develops nonetheless and ends only when her husband returns. Peter leaves, seeks a new start and moves to Berlin to experience the contemporaneous events of the German reunification at first hand. Some time later, he unexpectedly meets Barbara again. She has separated from her husband and they resume their relationship. Peter's continued search for the pulp fiction author reveals that the latter is actually his father, whom he had been brought up to believe had died in the war. Instead, he is alive and now working under the name John de Baur at the Political Science Department of Columbia University. Although anxious not to put his relationship with Barbara at risk again, he decides to go to New York to meet and confront his father. Under a false identity, he joins one of his courses, gains an insight into his life and work, and takes part in a group experiment de Baur has staged for his students as a dramatic, formative illustration of his political theory. Peter ultimately fails to openly confront his father, but feeling that he has accomplished as much as he could, he returns home to find happiness in the comforting routine of love he shares with Barbara. This is the myth-free version of the story; a fairly straightforward addition to the aforementioned 'fathers' literature'.[25]

So where does the *Odyssey* come in, how does it add to the story, and how does it relate to the memory contests about German history? The *Odyssey* is present on various and interconnected levels.

The Inset Narrative

The pulp fiction novel that haunts Peter tells the story of a band of German soldiers who escape from internment in Siberia after the Second World War and struggle to return home; and it does so by closely following the model of the *Odyssey*. Thus, the wind god Aeolus becomes Mr. Aolski who, rather than providing a bag of winds, gives the group leader Karl – who represents Odysseus – access to an aeroplane;[26] Karl does not meet his mother in Hades but they do meet in a dream;[27] he does not stay for seven years with Calypso but for nine months with Kalinka,[28] to give just a few examples. When Peter recognizes the Homeric hypotext, all allusions, thinly veiled though they are, are explained *expressis verbis*.[29] The only significant departures from Homer are the absence of a Telemachus and the fact that Penelope (Karl's wife) has remarried and has two children with her new husband. The novel's final pages, which narrate the moment of Karl's homecoming and confrontation with the new situation at home, are lost and the search for them is a key drive of the main narrative.

The Inset Political Theory of de Baur

The intrafictional author of this post-war *Odyssey* adaptation not only turns out to be Peter's father, once known as Johann Debauer, he also emerges as a twentieth-century Odysseus himself. Peter traces his father's movements from his native Switzerland, where he studied Law, to Germany, where he emigrated out of excitement for the totalitarian political developments there. Having changed his name to Vonlanden, he wrote for an NS propaganda paper before the war, then changed his name to Scholler and wrote for a communist propaganda paper in the German Democratic Republic (GDR) after the war. He subsequently emigrated to the US under the name John de Baur, and became an academic writing on liberal democracy, 9/11 and the war on terror. What remains constant behind this man's many *personae* is his political theory, which can be recognized in all his writings; eventually dubbed 'Deconstructionist Legal Theory', it is formulated in a book entitled *The Odyssey of Law*.[30] This not only makes the allusion to Paul de Man, who likewise wrote for a collaborationist newspaper during the Second World War,[31] abundantly clear; it also heightens the reader's awareness of the role of the *Odyssey* within the novel as a nexus of decidedly theoretical reflections on narrative, morality and history.

The Narrative: Plot Progression Through Role Reversals

Just like the inset narrative, the novel's main narrative also follows patterns borrowed from the *Odyssey*. Peter recognizably assumes the roles of a series of male characters from Homer's epic as, through his search for the author of the pulp fiction novel, his own life interlocks with the inset narrative: when he falls in love with Barbara, he recognizes the house she lives in as the one described in the pulp fiction story as the returning soldier's final destination. From the angle of the inset narrative, Peter thus corresponds to Odysseus. The re-appearance of Barbara's husband, however, soon recasts him as a suitor, who flees upon the return of the rightful husband. With his search for his father, that man of many wiles (and, hence, an Odysseus of sorts), Peter becomes a modern-day Telemachus – thereby neatly filling the one position the inset narrative itself had left conspicuously open. On the last part of his journey, however, the role reversals come full circle: having resumed his relationship with Barbara, he again takes up the position of Odysseus, experiencing on his adventures abroad a strong yearning for Barbara, who is cast once more as a Penelope *rediviva*.[32]

The Narrator: Self-stylization

A further way in which the *Odyssey* is emplotted in the main narrative consists in the protagonist's temporary, conscious self-stylization as a new Odysseus. After losing Barbara to her returning husband, Peter changes his job, has an emotionally chilling one-night stand with a journalist, for which he is falsely accused of rape, and then embarks on a truly epic midlife crisis: re-reading books 9 and 10 of the *Odyssey*, Peter interprets the journalist as his very own Ciconian, and his assistant Bettina, who indulges him without asking for anything in return, as a comforting lotus-eater.[33] Enamoured with this reading of his own life, he becomes obsessed and deliberately searches for women who fit the narrative: a voluptuous sales assistant becomes his Laestrygonian princess; in a mixed choir he finds the equivalent to Aeolus' family and seduces one of the 'daughters'; a beautician is chosen as his Circe.[34] Peter abandons his 'project'[35] only when a former girlfriend's son, Max, with whom he has a quasi-paternal relationship, shows up on his doorstep and temporarily moves in with him.

Framing Intrafictional Interpretation: Personal Relationships and National History

While the active emulation of Odysseus is confined to this episode, his story never ceases to serve Peter as a foil for interpreting his experiences. Be it in his reading of Barbara's reaction upon the return of her husband,[36] be it in explaining why he enjoys his 'adventure' in New York despite genuinely missing her,[37] Peter continuously and explicitly reflects on his relationship with Barbara in terms of Odysseus and Penelope's bond. Simultaneously, the *Odyssey* is used as an interpretative framework for German history: witnessing the reunification in Berlin, Peter discusses the historic developments with an American journalist and draws on the *Odyssey* to explain why there will be no violent settling of scores after the fall of the Wall:

> Odysseus hat nur deshalb bei seiner Heimkehr die Freier erschlagen und die Mägde, die's mit den Freiern getrieben hatten, aufhängen können, weil er nicht geblieben ist. Er ist weitergezogen. Wenn man bleiben will, muß man sich miteinander arrangieren, nicht miteinander abrechnen. Es stimmt doch, daß in Amerika nach dem Bürgerkrieg nicht abgerechnet wurde? Weil Amerika nach der Spaltung wieder zu sich heimgekehrt ist, um bei sich zu bleiben. Auch wenn Deutschland wieder zu sich heimkehrt, will es bei sich bleiben.

> [The only reason Odysseus could kill the suitors and string up the women who had reveled with them was that he did not go on to stay. He kept moving. When you stay on, you have to get along with people, not get back at them. There were no reprisals in America after the Civil War, were there? Because the country had to heal the split if it's going to stick together. Well, Germany too will have to heal the split if it's going to stick together.][38]

Given this all-pervasive presence, it is easy to see why reviewers took issue with Schlink's *Odyssey* overdose. Yet a critical voice is already embedded within the novel. The series 'Romane zur Freude und zur guten Unterhaltung' ('Novels for Your Enjoyment and Reading Pleasure'), in which the inset story appeared, was edited by Peter's grandparents. While his grandfather had a penchant for tales of historical battles, his grandmother detested war,[39] and while her husband had a professional attitude towards the stories they edited, Peter notes that his grandmother

> liebte ... Literatur, Romane wie Gedichte, hatte ein sicheres Gespür für literarische Qualität und muß unter der Beschäftigung mit den banalen Texten gelitten haben.
>
> [... loved literature, fiction as well as verse, and had a sure feeling for it; she must have suffered from having to spend so much time on such banal texts.][40]

With this comment, the inset story is soundly rejected, its tale of the returning WWII soldiers in the guise of Homer's *Odyssey* intrafictionally dismissed as bad literature. Indeed, the grandmother forbids Peter to read pulp fiction novels: the post-war shortage of paper means that young Peter must use the novels' proofs as scrap paper, but until his adolescence he adheres to his grandmother's prohibition and does not read the stories on the back. This whole scenario poignantly encapsulates the memory constellation after the Second World War, in which the post-war generation receives its own education against the backdrop of a fundamental taboo, resulting in a problematic palimpsest that powerfully explodes when the generation of 1968 eventually 'turns the page'. However, the grandmother's literary verdict is of importance in its own right. It questions whether a neomythic approach to individual and collective histories within a light and entertaining framework is in fact appropriate. Whenever Peter expresses interest in the topic of a pulp fiction novel, his grandmother discourages him from reading them and instead directs him to 'the better book'.[41] Inevitably, this puts the question mark of irony over the main narrative itself: if an intrafictional character openly characterizes a thinly veiled adaptation of Homer's *Odyssey* as painful to read, can the extrafictional reader be expected to think very differently of the strikingly similar narrative technique that underlies much of the main narrative? For, what is the difference between the inset narrative evoking Homer's Calypso in Karl's stay with Kalinka, and Peter Debauer admitting in the main narrative an indiscretion during his New York adventure by saying 'On New Year's Eve [...] I ended up in bed with a woman who told me her name was Callista. I liked the name'?[42] An ironic reading of this overt reproduction of the same mode of classical reception gains plausibility not least from the fact that the novel is perfectly capable of more discreet allusions: the delayed mention of the protagonist's name, for instance, which does not appear until page 102(/71), is reminiscent of the same technique in Homer, where Odysseus is named only at the very end of the proem in verse 20. Similarly, the secret of the immovable bed in the *Odyssey* finds a reflection in *Die Heimkehr*, where Peter and Barbara get to know each other while hunting for furniture in antique shops, semiconsciously buy matching furniture, and eventually consolidate their commitment to a relationship by bringing their matching furniture together in a shared flat.[43] Given such subtle allusions, the predominant mode of less understated Homer reception raises even more questions.

Following the grandmother's advice to turn to 'the better book', a comparison with Schlink's own *Vorleser* suggests itself. Here, too, the *Odyssey* plays a prominent role. It is the first text the protagonist Martin Berg reads to Hannah Schmitz, the analphabetic woman with whom the schoolboy has an affair and whom he meets again years later as one of the defendants in an NS war-crimes trial. Homer, Cicero, Lessing, and Schiller – the canon that formed the cultural core of traditional German *Bildungsbürgertum* (the ideology and identity of the upper bourgeoisie) – are all there at the start of their relationship.[44] The *Odyssey* then reappears at the end of the novel when Hannah is imprisoned and Michael resumes his position as Hannah's reader by recording tapes of literary texts, beginning again with the *Odyssey*.[45] Aided by Michael's recorded readings, Hannah teaches herself to read and write. She uses these skills to write to Michael but also to read historical accounts of the Holocaust, as Michael learns when he comes to pick her up on the day of her release, only to discover that she committed suicide at dawn.[46] In *Der Vorleser*, Hannah's (re-)introduction to the *Odyssey* thus initiates a process of education and, as it were, empowering enlightenment which ultimately leads to historical understanding, but also to death. In a sense, the crisis of the entire enlightenment project at large, a central feature of post-war German intellectual debates, finds a dramatic echo in Hannah's suicide.[47]

In *Die Heimkehr*, the presence of the *Odyssey* elicits different, but also damaging effects. As in Hannah's case, Peter's encounter with (Karl's version of) the *Odyssey* triggers historical enquiries: as he researches the pulp fiction author's fate, Peter reads Josef Martin Bauer's 1955 work *So weit die Füße tragen* (*As Far as Feet Will Carry*).[48] Yet it is not just the subject of wartime suffering and specifically his parents' past that captures Peter's interest; it is the pulp fiction novel's mythopoeia, its way of retelling lived experience by merging it with myth, that fascinates him;[49] a fascination borne out by his mythological readings of his own life and actions.[50] This obsession with the *Odyssey*'s suggestive narrative structure, however, time and again gets in his way. During Peter's midlife crisis, it is the emotionally shallow imitation of myth in his own life that distracts him from the people and questions he really cares about. Likewise, during his stay in Berlin, his experience of the reunification is flawed by the intrusion of myth. Peter regrets not having engaged with the 1968 student revolution because he was too busy earning money and wants to prevent this from happening again.[51] Yet in Berlin he realizes that there is no big history show on display, that real life continues, and ponders:

> Was hatte ich von der Begegnung mit der Geschichte erwartet? Daß die Menschen demonstrieren? ... Die Polizei angreifen und entwaffnen? Die Mauer einreißen? Offensichtlich hatte es die Geschichte nicht eilig. Sie respektiert, daß im Leben gearbeitet, eingekauft, gekocht und gegessen werden muß .... Was soll man den ganzen Tag in der gestürmten Bastille? Was an der offenen Mauer?
>
> [What had I expected from my encounter with history? Demonstrations? ... Police interventions? The destruction of the Wall? History is clearly not in a hurry. It respects daily activities like work, shopping, cooking, and eating .... What is there to do at a Bastille already stormed? Or a Wall already scaled?][52]

Still, when it comes to the meeting with the American journalist mentioned above, Peter is quick to draw on the *Odyssey*, foregoing his own genuine but limited and ordinary experiences in favour of the lofty heights of epic grandeur. The value of his historical-mythological comparison, however, is at once thrown into doubt by the journalist's response: 'Lachte er mich an, oder lachte er mich aus? Ich war mir nicht sicher.' ['Was his smile a smile of goodwill or of derision? I was not sure.'][53] Similarly, when Peter finally meets his father amidst his new American family, he cannot bring himself to confront him openly and instead forces a conversation about Penelope, Telemachus and Odysseus in order to gauge his father's feelings about abandoning his first family.[54] Even the long-awaited reconciliation with the man his father turns out to be occurs only in an imagined conversation about homecomings: that of Odysseus, Karl, his father's and his own.[55] All this taken together creates the strong impression that the pervasive layer of myth invariably gets in the way of truly meaningful personal interaction and engagement. This is especially true of the protagonist's continuous struggle with father–son issues, which gives the novel the air of a *Bildungsroman*. Without unfolding this complex at length, it is important to note that the turning point in Peter's development (i.e. in finding his role as a partner, son, 'father') lies in his recognition of similarities between himself and his trickster father: both consistently avoid making genuine, concrete commitments, and cover up their evasiveness by self-deluding reasoning.[56] The *Odyssey* here offers a blueprint for the exploration of fraught post-war father–son relations,[57] gives narrative shape to Peter's own emotional escapism, and features prominently in de Baur's pseudo-deconstructionist theory that legitimizes his immoral behaviour.[58]

Precisely through this excessive and high-profile emplotment of the *Odyssey*, Schlink's *Heimkehr* builds up a critical momentum which draws attention to the mechanisms of narrativization in general and of mythical narratives in particular,[59] a concern it shares with Adorno and Horkheimer's chapter 'Odysseus or Myth and Enlightenment' in their *Dialektik der Aufklärung* (*Dialectics of Enlightenment*) of 1947.[60] *Die Heimkehr* experiments with the myth of Odysseus' homecoming as an ordering paradigm for the erratic events in the lives of individuals and of the nation – and repeatedly stages its failure. An important case in point is the character of de Baur and his theory, which provide the foil against which Peter's development is cast into relief. De Baur resembles Homer's and Adorno's Odysseus in his readiness to (repeatedly) sacrifice his own identity and name to ensure his survival.[61] Porter, commenting on Adorno and Horkheimer, notes that '[i]n reducing himself to a nameless cipher … he [Odysseus] breaks the chain of mimesis between names and essences, and thereby cunningly reinvests language with a purely rational and intentional content'.[62] De Baur represents this move on two levels: his life exemplifies the calculating rationality of Odysseus as the prototype of the bourgeois individual in all its moral dubiousness while his self-justifying theory develops its philosophical underpinnings. Combining (literary) deconstructionism with (legal) decisionism, De Baur argues:

> Was wir für Wirklichkeit halten, sind nur Texte, und was wir für Texte halten, nur Interpretationen. Von der Wirklichkeit und den Texten bleibt nur, was wir daraus machen. In der Geschichte gibt es kein Ziel … Wir können sie interpretieren als ob sie ein Ziel hätte … als ob Wirklichkeit mehr wäre als Text … als ob es das Gute und das Böse, Recht und Unrecht, Wahrheit und Lüge gäbe … Unsere Wahrheit, die uns unsere Entscheidung treffen läßt, erfahren wir

nur in der existentiellen, der extremen Ausnahmesituation. Die Richtigkeit unserer Entscheidung erweist sich in dem Einsatz, mit dem wir sie verwirklichen, und der Verantwortung, die wir für ihre Verwirklichung übernehmen.

[What we take for reality is merely a text, what we take for texts are merely interpretations. Reality and texts are therefore what we make of them. History has no goal ... We can interpret it as if it had a goal ... as if good and evil, right and wrong, truth and lies actually existed ... We come to our truth, which enables us to make decisions, in extreme, existential, exceptional situations. The validity of our decisions itself is felt in the commitment we make to carrying them out and the responsibility we take for carrying them out.][63]

The literary implications of this view are illustrated in his assessment of the *Odyssey*:

Alles sei im Fluß: Ziel und Sinn der *Odyssee*, Wahrheit und Lüge ... Das einzig Bleibende sei, daß die *Odyssee* den uralten Mythos von Aufbruch, Abenteuer und Heimkehr zu einem Epos gewandelt habe, zu einer Geschichte, die zu einer Zeit und an einem Ort spielt. Sie habe die abstrakten Größen Raum und Zeit geschaffen, ohne die wir keine Geschichte und keine Geschichten haben.

[[E]verything was in flux: the work's entire intent and meaning, its portrayal of truth and lie ... All that remained was that *The Odyssey* transformed the primordial myth of departure, adventure and return into an epic, a story set in a specific moment and place, thereby creating the abstract quantities of space and time without which we would have no history and no stories.][64]

Note the proximity to Adorno and Horkheimer:

The translation of the myths into the novel, which is accomplished in the narration of Odysseus' adventure, does not so much falsify them as pull myth into time, revealing the abyss that separates myth from homeland and reconciliation.[65]

De Baur's notion of Homer's poetry as the turning point where free, authentic myth becomes calculatedly controlled epic picks up central ideas of Adorno and Horkheimer, for whom 'Homer represents the "precipitate" of archaic mythology, the mere unity of his plots standing for a wilful imposition of intentionality on their chaotic, massive sprawl'.[66] Although reframed in deconstructionist–decisionist terms, these are the very problematics addressed by de Baur. Moreover, the ideological adaptability of the theoretical kernel of de Baur's *Odyssey of Law* is not only disavowed as an intellectual cover-up for spineless opportunism, it also contrasts sharply with the problematic rigidity of the *Odyssey* as a structuring device imposed on lived experience for narrative framing. In this sense, *Die*

Heimkehr can be read as a narrative realization of Adorno and Horkheimer's critique of instrumental reason: in and with its narrative form, it problematizes the cunning inherent in the rational ordering of narrated myth.

Theoretical reflections on the value of myth for poetic production traditionally emphasize its combination of a durable narrative core and a flexible shape.[67] Modern critics have added to this the notion that myths have the power to turn the contingency and absolutism of reality into aesthetic plausibility.[68] In Schlink's novel, these notions are both expressed (in de Baur's theory and Peter's reflections) and resisted (in the narrative). The resulting frustrations and absences point to the irreducibly human that gets lost when confronted with (pre-)fabricated narratives. In de Baur's theory as in Peter's life, myth becomes all shape and no core. Schlink's novel neither rewrites myth nor corrects it, but rejects mythologization by narratively demonstrating its inadequacy.[69] From this perspective, it is especially significant that the reader is left feeling uneasy about the novel's tortuously interwoven compound of myth-family-nationhood. The recurring parallelization of the myth of Odysseus and Penelope, of Peter and Barbara's relationship, and of Germany's reunification here comes into view as a fundamentally troublesome and flawed perspective:[70] the notion of Germany's 'homecoming' to its former unity after its historical errant wanderings is both suggested and critiqued. Narrative 'failures' thus gain significance as a marked reaction against the traditional German longing for myth,[71] and as warnings against the risk of implicitly redemptive narratives.[72] If, as Adorno and Horkheimer write, '[a]ll demythologization has the form of the inevitable experience of the uselessness and superfluousness of sacrifices',[73] then one effect of this reading of Schlink's novel is that it restores *ex negativo* – through manifest narrative obstruction – the rawness of individual experiences (including *victima*-suffering) as something not containable in collectively shared, pre-scripted narrative frames. It thereby resists the movement of Odyssean myth as a cunningly told story, which turns suffering into *sacrificium*, both on the individual and collective level. Schlink's *Heimkehr* critically positions itself within the context of German memory contests as it denounces the tempting grand-scale narrative perspective of myth by letting it collide, repeatedly and variously, with the irreducible reality of individual historical experience. Against Frye's assertion that '[o]f all fictions, the marvelous journey is the one formula that is never exhausted'[74] and Adorno and Horkheimer's verdict that '[o]nly by first becoming a novel does the epic become a fairy tale',[75] this novel turns the *Odyssey* against itself and into a stumbling block for mythologization: by exhausting it, it undercuts the epic's signature move of turning life into a fairy tale.

Bibliography

Adler, Jeremy (2002), 'Bernhard Schlink and "The Reader"', *TLS* (London), 03.03.2002.

Adorno, Theodor W. and Max Horkheimer (1947), *Dialektik der Aufklärung* (Amsterdam: Querido); here cited from 'Odysseus or Myth and Enlightenment', trans. R. Hullot-Kentor, *New German Critique* (1992) 56: 109–114.

Assmann, Aleida (2006a) *Der lange Schatten der Vergangenheit. Erinnerungskultur und Geschichtspolitik.* Munich: Beck.

Assmann, Aleida (2006b) *Generationsidentitäten und Vorurteilsstrukturen in der neuen deutschen Erinnerungsliteratur.* Vienna: Picus.

Bartov, Omer (2000) 'Germany as Victim', *New German Critique* 80: 29–40.

Beßlich, Barbara, Katharina Grätz and Olaf Hildebrand, eds (2006), *Wende des Erinnerns? Geschichtskonstruktionen in der deutschen Literatur nach 1989.* Berlin: Schmidt.

Blumenberg, Hans (1979), *Arbeit am Mythos.* Frankfurt: Suhrkamp; here cited from *Work on Myth* (1985), trans. R. M. Wallace. Cambridge, MA: MIT Press.

Börnchen, Stefan (2008), 'Derselbe Krieg mit anderen Mitteln? De Man, Derrida und die Dekonstruktion in Bernhard Schlinks Roman Die Heimkehr', in M. W. Rectanus (ed.), *Über Gegenwartsliteratur, Interpretationen und Interventionen. Festschrift für Paul Michael Lützeler zum 65. Geburtstag,* 87–104. Bielefeld: Aisthesis.

Bohrer, Karl Heinz (1983), 'Vorwort', *idem* (ed.) *Mythos und Moderne,* 7–14. Frankfurt: Suhrkamp.

Calvino, Italo (1981), 'Odysseys within the Odyssey', *Why Read Classics?*, trans. M. L. McLaughlin, 11–19. London: Cape; first published in *La Repubblica* (Rome), 21.10.1981.

Cavelty, Gieri (2006), 'Die Odysee als Obsession', *Neue Züricher Zeitung* (Zurich), 22.04.2006.

Eigler, Friederike (2005), *Gedächtnis und Geschichte in Generationenromanen seit der Wende.* Berlin: Schmidt.

Emmerich, Wolfgang (2005), 'Entzauberung – Wiederverzauberung. Die Maschine Mythos im 20. Jahrhundert', in M. Vöhler. B. Seidensticker and W. Emmerich (eds), *Mythenkorrekturen. Zu einer paradoxalen Form der Mythenrezeption,* 411–435. Berlin: de Gruyter.

Emmerich, Wolfgang (2008), 'Generationen – Archive – Diskurse. Wege zum Verständnis der deutschen Gegenwartsliteratur', in F. Cambi (ed.), *Gedächtnis und Identität. Die deutsche Literatur nach der* Vereinigung, 15–29. Würzburg: Königshausen & Neumann.

Evans, Richard J. (1997), *In Defence Of History.* London: Granta.

Fischer, Gerhard and David Roberts, eds (2007), *Schreiben nach der Wende: Ein Jahrzehnt deutscher Literatur, 1989–1999.* 2nd edn. Tübingen: Stauffenburg.

Friedrich, Gerhard (2008), 'Opfererinnerung nach der deutschen Vereinigung als "Familienroman"', in F. Cambi (ed.), *Gedächtnis und Identität. Die deutsche Literatur nach der Vereinigung,* 205–222. Würzburg: Königshausen & Neumann.

Frye, Northrop (1957), *Anatomy of Criticism: Four Essays*. Princeton, NJ: Princeton University Press.

Fuchs, Anne, Mary Cosgrove and Georg Grote, eds (2006), *German Memory Contests: The Quest for Identity in Literature, Film and Discourse since 1990*. Rochester, NY: Camden House.

Fuchs, Anne (2008), *Phantoms of War in Contemporary German Literature, Films and Discourse: The Politics of Memory*. Basingstoke: Palgrave Macmillan.

Fulda, Daniel (2006), 'Irreduzible Perspektivität. "Der Brand" von Jörg Friedrich und das Dispositiv des nicht nur literarischen Geschichtsdiskurses seit den 1990er Jahren', in B. Beßlich. K. Grätz and O. Hildebrand (eds), *Wende des Erinnerns? Geschichtskonstruktionen in der deutschen Literatur nach 1989*, 133–156. Berlin: Schmidt.

Hall, Edith (2008), *The Return of Ulysses: A Cultural History of Homer's Odyssey*. London: I. B. Tauris.

Hamacher, Werner, Neil Hertz and Thomas Keenan, eds (1988), *Wartime Journalism 1939–1943 by Paul de Man*. Lincoln, NE: University of Nebraska Press.

Hamacher, Werner, Neil Hertz and Thomas Keenan, eds (1989), *Responses: On Paul de Man's Wartime Journalism*. Lincoln, NE: University of Nebraska Press.

Knobloch, Hans-Jörg (2007), 'Eine ungewöhnliche Variante in der Täter-Opfer-Literatur: Bernhard Schlinks Roman *Der Vorleser*', in G. Fischer and D. Roberts (eds), *Schreiben nach der Wende. Ein Jahrzehnt deutscher Literatur, 1989–1999*, 89–98. Tübingen: Stauffenberg.

Krauss, Hannes (2008), 'Das Vergangene erzählen – Erinnerungsdiskurse nach 1989', in F. Cambi (ed.), *Gedächtnis und Identität. Die deutsche Literatur nach der Vereinigung*, 45–56. Würzburg: Königshausen & Neumann.

Leopold, A. (2006), 'Alles und nichts', *taz.die tageszeitung* (Berlin), 04.03.2006.

Mauelshagen, Claudia (1995), *Der Schatten des Vaters: deutschsprachige Väterliteratur der siebziger und achtziger Jahre*. Frankfurt: Lang.

Moritz, Karl Philipp (1791), *Götterlehre oder mythologische Dichtungen der Alten. Zusammengestellt von Karl Philipp Moritz: Mit fünf und sechzig in Kupfer gestochenen Abbildungen nach antiken geschnittnen Steinen und andern Denkmälern des Alterthums*. Berlin: Unger.

Müller, Achatz von (2003), 'Volk der Täter, Volk der Opfer. Deutschland auf dem Weg der Selbstversöhnung', *Die Zeit* (Hamburg), 23.10.2003.

Niven, Bill (2003), 'Berhard Schlink's "Der Vorleser" and the Problem of Shame', *The Modern Language Review*, 98 (2): 381–396.

Paver, Chloe E. M. (1999), *Narrative and Fantasy in the Post-War German Novel: A Study of Novels by Johnson, Frisch, Wolf, Becker, and Grass*. Oxford: Clarendon Press.

Porter, James I. (2010), 'Odysseys and the Wandering Jew. The Dialectic of Jewish Enlightenment in Adorno and Horkheimer', *Cultural Critique*, 71: 200–213.

Schlant, Ernestine (1999), *The Language of Silence: West German Literature and the Holocaust*. London: Routledge.

Schlink, Bernhard (1995), *Der Vorleser*. Zurich: Diogenes; *The Reader*; trans. C. B. Janeway (1997). London: Phoenix.

Schlink, Bernhard (2006), *Die Heimkehr*. Zurich: Diogenes; *Homecoming*, trans. M. H. Heim (2008). London: Weidenfeld & Nicolson.

Schmitz, Helmut, ed. (2007), *A Nation of Victims? Representations of German Wartime Suffering from 1945 to the Present*. Amsterdam: Rodopi.

Schmitz, Michaela von (2012), 'Heimkehr als Utopie. Buch der Woche: "Die Heimkehr" von Bernhard Schlink', *Deutschlandfunk* (Cologne), 09.04.2012.

Schrödter, Hermann, ed. (1991), *Die neomythische Kehre. Aktuelle Zugänge zum Mythischen in Wissenschaft und Kunst*. Würzburg: Königshausen & Neumann.

Stephan, Inge (2007), 'Die bösen Mütter. Medea-Mythen und nationale Diskurse in Texten von Elisabeth Langgässer und Christa Wolf', in G. Fischer and D. Roberts (eds), *Schreiben nach der Wende. Ein Jahrzehnt deutscher Literatur, 1989–1999*, 172–180. Tübingen: Stauffenberg.

Taberner, Stuart (2002), 'Introduction', *idem* (ed.), *Berhard Schlink: Der Vorleser*, 7–38. Bristol: Bristol Classical Press.

Vöhler, Martin, Bernd Seidensticker and Wolfgang Emmerich (eds) (2005), 'Zum Begriff der Mythenkorrektur', *Mythenkorrekturen. Zu einer paradoxalen Form der Mythenrezeption*, 1–18. Berlin: de Gruyter.

Vogt, Jochen (1998), 'Er fehlt, er fehlte, er hat gefehlt . . . Ein Rückblick auf die sogenannten Väterbücher', in S. Braese *et al.* (eds), *Deutsche Nachkriegsliteratur und der Holocaust*, 385–399. Frankfurt: Campus.

Weidermann, Volker (2006), 'Schund ist gefährlich für kleine Seelen. Odyssee des Bösen: Bernhard Schlink auf Irrfahrt durch den Dschungel der Geschichte', *Frankfurter Allgemeine Zeitung* (Frankfurt), 15.03.2006.

Wöhrle, Georg (1999), *Telemachs Reise. Väter und Söhne in Ilias und Odyssee oder ein Beitrag zur Männlichkeitsideologie in der homerischen Welt*. Göttingen: Vandenhoeck & Ruprecht.

11

Narcissus and the Furies: Myth and Docufiction in Jonathan Littell's *The Kindly Ones*

Edith Hall

At a climactic moment in Jonathan Littell's *The Kindly Ones*, the narrator Maximilien Aue is describing his illness – both physical and mental – during the battle for Stalingrad in the winter of 1942–1943. He was serving there as a German SS officer, an *Obersturmbannführer*. As the Soviet army gained ground, his mental disintegration accelerated. His squadron was temporarily housed in a wrecked university building. He buried himself in a translation of Sophocles on which he had fortuitously stumbled. Reading to escape from the dire reality around him, he recalled the day he starred at the age of fourteen in the role of Electra, in a school performance of Sophocles' play (410–411):[1] 'I wore a long white dress, sandals, and a wig whose black curls danced on my shoulders: when I looked at myself in the mirror, I thought I saw Una, and I almost fainted.' Una is Max's twin sister. Since he first mentioned her (139), the reader has gradually come to suspect that he has, since early childhood, felt an uncontrollable sexual passion for Una which he could feel for no other human being, either male or female. He tells us, for example, although the reader is by no means clear as yet that he means Una, that the one person he had ever truly loved was the Isolde to his Tristan (200); when he visits Chekhov's house in the Crimea he meets the caretaker Masha, Chekhov's sister herself, who makes him think of the incestuous relationships between pharaohs and their sisters (204).

In the Stalingrad sequence, Aue's memory violently fuses the myth dramatized in Sophocles' *Electra* and the myth of Narcissus, who loved his reflected image. At the climax of the novel, when Max is in desperate flight to Berlin while the Russian tanks advance through Pomerania, he finally becomes a fully fledged Narcissus beside the River Persante (925): 'my reflection drew my gaze; it was blurred, deformed by the movements of the surface; I leaned over to see it more clearly, my foot slipped and I fell.' Although a few previous critics have carefully discussed some aspects of the Atridae myth in *The Kindly Ones* – first published in French as *Les Bienveillantes*[2] – they have overlooked the increasing importance of Narcissus, as the novel unfolds, to understanding Aue's status as a narrator. This essay therefore traces the interplay of the two mythical narratives within the novel, and argues that they are central to Littell's ambitious concept of a documentary fiction, incorporating both real and surreal elements, with scope and intellectual richness adequate to even the gravest and most incendiary historical material.[3]

Aue hurls classical mythology at the reader, along with data from many other spheres of knowledge, in an excess that is unpalatable. After his Proustian recollection of teenage Sophoclean theatricals, and autoerotic recognition of his feminine avatar in the mirror, Aue quotes bloodthirsty lines from the ancient tragedy. The jarring, overblown classical rhetoric culminates in Aue's torrid confession of the parallels his teenage self could see between his psychological predicament and the violence of the play: 'I was sobbing, and the butchery in the House of Atreus was the blood in my own house' (411). This theatrical image of the cross-dressed SS officer sobbing at mythological butchery is one of many invitations to realize the novel's action in terms of high-cultural performance media.[4] In the third sentence we are told that the story is 'a real morality play' (3). Soldiers shouting 'Heil Hitler' are likened to a theatrical chorus (29). At Lemberg, the massacre of the Jews is 'performed' by squads in bizarre costumes they have stolen from the local theatre: 'some were even wearing masks, amusing, hideous, ridiculous' (47).[5] In Paris, Aue reads an essay on Sartre's *Les Mouches* – an Existentialist treatment of the Electra/Orestes myth – reminding readers that the French play premiered in occupied Paris in 1943 (499–500). Aue is an aficionado of classical music as well as theatre, and the titles of his memoir's chapters are 'Toccata', 'Air', 'Gigue' and so on, which forces the reader to imagine him replaying mentally the horrors of the war, as if on a gramophone, to the tinkling accompaniment of Bach's *Partitas* for harpsichord.

Yet it is precisely the sense of violent assault and inundation by coolly presented information, elite cultural references and extreme fantasy, which lends *The Kindly Ones* its compulsive readability and intellectual power. These were the reasons why its publication was regarded as a major publishing event. Ecstatic reviews acclaimed the novel as heralding the return of serious historical fiction, as inaugurating a new age of fictional photo-realism, or as comparable with Tolstoy's *War and Peace*. It won two literary prizes – the prestigious Le Prix Goncourt and Le Prix de l'Académie Français – and sold nearly a million copies within months of publication.

The subject matter could be neither more sensitive nor more grisly. Aue is attached to the *Einsatzgruppen*, mobile execution squads. They followed the main German advance, wiping out Jews, Russian partisans and 'undesirables'. Aue's account reveals how 'ordinary men' became killers. We follow in every muddy footstep of his squad's squalid work ('Aue' means 'marsh'). His men, although viciously anti-Semitic and excited by inflicting pain, are given 'normal' personalities and habits: Littell is indebted to Hannah Arendt in his commitment to exposing the 'banality' that atrocity can acquire.[6] As massacre follows massacre, the Germans are progressively brutalized. They eat sausages and drink beer in pauses during the Kiev *Aktion*, which saw more than 30,000 Jews killed in two days. By the time Aue arrives at Auschwitz, the collective desensitization has reached a new extreme. Industrialized death on a vast scale, a method partly conceived and technologically developed in order to spare troops direct involvement in mass killing, is presented as a rational, indeed inevitable, solution to 'the Jewish Problem'.

Littell is half-Jewish, although completely secularized. His mother is French and his father is the American author Robert Littell, famous for spy novels set during the Cold War. They are highly researched and respected; he is regarded as the US John le Carré. His son knows that the medium of fiction does not excuse historical inaccuracy. But there are people alive who were involved in the Holocaust; *The Kindly Ones* has outraged many, including Jews, Poles and Germans. Michael Mönniger, Paris correspondent of *Die Zeit*, accuses it of being 'scandalous kitsch in places. It's the poetics of horror that turn a very talented contemporary author into a pornographer of violence'.[7] Dominick LaCapra condemns its 'seemingly fatalistic mingling of erotic and genocidal motifs and its disavowal or underestimation of the difficulty and necessity of understanding victims of the Nazi genocide'.[8] The influential journalist Iris Radisch thunders, 'Why on earth should we read a book by an educated idiot who writes badly, who is stricken with sexual perversion and who has abandoned himself to an elitist racist ideology and an archaic belief in destiny?'[9]

A compelling answer is that the book offers a reliable account of the historical period 1941 to 1945, especially the events occurring on the Eastern Front, in a medium more digestible than any factual narrative offering equivalent detail. Littell's research took five years. He walked the route across Ukraine taken by the Germans, and wrote every word, while immersing himself in Russian archives, during a winter spent in Moscow. His meticulousness has been demonstrated comprehensively. Take Claude Lanzmann, the creator of *Shoah* (1985), the canonical documentary on the Holocaust which includes the oral testimony of both victims and such convicted war criminals as Franz Suchomel, *Unterscharführer* at Treblinka. Lanzmann originally condemned *The Kindly Ones* as 'a poisonous flower of evil',[10] alleging that such fiction threatened to displace 'authentic' witnessing. But once Lanzmann had met Littell, he changed his view. He was so impressed by the younger man's knowledge and serious attitude that he publicly praised the accuracy of the work, claiming that only he and Raul Hilberg, author of *The Destruction of the European Jews* (1961), were sufficiently expert to judge.[11] Robert Manne, an Australian historian descended from Jewish refugees, concurred. He put Littell's research 'on trial' by investigating evidence for Aue's discussion of the Caucasian *Bergjuden*. Manne was astonished. There was only one academic article on the topic, which had appeared too late to be consulted by Littell. 'Littell's account was both consistent with and more illuminating than its academic counterpart. *The Kindly Ones* is perhaps the first novel I have read where I yearned for footnotes.'[12]

I am no expert on the Holocaust and must take Lanzmann and Manne at their word. But the accuracy of Littell's portrait of Nazi culture is suggested through his evocation of their saturation in classical images and myths. Aue is not the only classicist amongst the Fascists we encounter. When young, he engaged in discussions about the Roman origins of the symbolism of the fasces (511), and whether there was a 'Fascist' literary canon: the authors proposed had included Plutarch as well as Corneille and Stendhal (505). Aue's engagements with the philosophical justifications for anti-Semitism are larded with esoteric references to Plato, Josephus, Augustine, Tertullian and other Church Fathers (e.g. 187, 252, 326–327, 546–547, 671) as well as to Kant and Hegel. The behaviour and rhetoric of the German officers is often evoked in Homeric terms (e.g. 814, 893). As the German army moves across Ukraine, Herodotus' account of these regions is prominent. Arrival at the river Dnieper, where the bridges have been almost entirely destroyed, prompts a conversation about the pontoon bridge Xerxes built over the Hellespont (137). Aue offers us references to Herodotus' accounts of the Scythians, Amazons, Aryans, and the 'scorched earth' strategy the Scythians deployed against Darius (196, 302, 341, 388).

We are given an admiring description of the qualifications of the new chief of Aue's execution squad, Dr Thomas: a psychiatrist, he had been awarded 'the Iron Cross and spoke French, English, Greek and Latin' (134). Dr Mandelbrod's assistant had studied for a Frankfurt doctorate in Latin and German Philology (675); Aue labels her 'a German Artemis' (706). But our narrator wants to prove that he is the most cultured classicist of all. He often produces a classical reference when imparting shocking details about the victims of the Holocaust; this is no softening mechanism, but a horribly inappropriate aestheticization and accentuation of disgusting information. He quotes Sophocles' *Oedipus at Colonus* (1224), 'not to have been born is best',[13] after several pages of harrowing comparison of the rate at which Germans, Jews and Russians had died per minute (13–17). He refers to the Slavs to be deployed in the fields as 'helots' (133). When narrating the Kharkov massacre, he *first* describes the carved muscular Atlas figures, 'impressive caryatids', with white arms supporting the balcony of an elegant town house, between which the corpses of the enemy dangle (167). He discusses the classical roots and comparands of words in daily use – 'besiege' (386), for example, or 'death', '*mors*' and '*thanatos*' (630). These priggish academic excurses both emphasize and occlude the real suffering which prompted them. When discussing the minimum calories required by workers in labour camps just to stay alive, he draws a parallel with the diet of Roman and Egyptian slaves (640).

In an appalling episode, a soldier kills a woman who is in labour by slicing open her stomach and extracting the baby: *Untersturmführer* Ott then dispatches the newborn by smashing its skull against the stove (155). The slaughter recalls two gruesome passages of classical Greek detailing the brutality of Agamemnon. In the *Iliad*, he urges his brother that they need to destroy every Trojan, even the unborn baby boys in their mothers' wombs (6.57–59); in the *Iphigenia in Aulis* of Euripides, Clytemnestra reminds Agamemnon that he tore her first baby from her breast to dash him to the ground (1151–1152).[14]

Greek tragedy provides Aue with his most pyrotechnic displays of literary allusion when essaying philosophical questions. Eichmann, we are told, was guilty of hubris (786). 'Necessity, as the Greeks knew already, is not only a blind goddess, but a cruel one too' (589), Aue remarks when considering a fellow officer's bad luck for having being born German and therefore being accused of inhumanity. The same officer prompts Aue to reflect on the causes of the heroes' suffering – chance, error, or delusion – in Sophocles' *Oedipus* and Euripides' *Heracles Mainomenos* (592–593). The knowledge of much more obscure tragedies, including the *Rhesus* (893), shows that not only Aue, but his creator Littell, have done their homework on Greek tragedy. Greek myths surface in prodigal overabundance. Max desires to impress us with his erudition. The result is, however, to horrify us with his insensitivity.

There is a long and moving (although inexplicit) 'Prometheus' sequence in the Caucasus – one of the places in which Littell shows his powerful understanding of the real geographies underlying both ancient literature and the route taken by the Germans into Ukraine. Aue's Prometheus is Nahum ben Ibrahim, an elderly peasant, originally from Daghestan. He addresses Aue in 'strangely accented but understandable classical Greek' (278). He is very ancient – over a century old, Aue calculates – and educated. Max takes him up the mountains, fascinated, and allows him to choose the place – with a spectacular vista – where he is to die. The old man defiantly refuses to dig his own grave, and continues a conversation in Greek with Aue, who eventually has to help his sullen orderly dig the grave himself. When the articulate old rebel is finally shot (by the orderly), Max is surprised by his own sense of desolation (284).

Yet, as implied by the novel's French title, *Les Bienveillantes* (the noun traditionally used in that language to translate the title of Aeschylus' *Eumenides*[15]), the most significant Greek tragic text underlying the novel is Aeschylus' *Oresteia*. This choice in a novel exploring the mentality of the Third Reich is hardly coincidental. The *Oresteia* had been directed by Lothar Müthel at a massive gala staged in association with the notorious Olympics of 1936. The National Socialists had adopted the trilogy as a supreme manifestation of the Greek-Teutonic primeval culture from which they claimed the German *Volk* was descended. One of the reviews praises Aeschylus for being a 'Greek prophet and cultic author, who had a "typically Nordic" conception of life';[16] the stages of evolution of the state in the *Oresteia* were deemed to offer a parallel to the evolution of Germany from monarchical *Kaiserreich*, through the perceived decadence of the Weimar Republic to the heroic renewal of the Third Reich.

This genealogy was articulated by Alfred Rosenberg in *The Myth of the 20th Century* (*Der Mythos des 20. Jahrhunderts. Eine Wertung der seelisch-geistigen Gestaltenkämpfe unserer Zeit* (1930)). This manifesto had described the *Oresteia* as a racial 'parable for all time' and a legacy left by 'Nordic Hellas' to 'Aryan Europe'. Rosenberg's book was the most influential Nazi propagandist text after *Mein Kampf*. For him, the *Oresteia* dramatized the epochal struggle in ancient Greece between the unmanly Eastern darkness, represented by the Erinyes, and the victorious, masculine 'new Nordic spirituality' embodied in Athena and Apollo. Rosenberg was pleased that the patriarchal 'Nordic' Olympians triumphed over the matriarchal 'Semitic' chthonic gods, but criticized Aeschylus for allowing the two parties to become reconciled at the end. It had been, Rosenberg argued, the incorporation of the Semitic Erinyes (Furies) which had threatened the Greek race from within.[17] In integrating this favourite myth of the Third Reich into his narrative, Littell reveals his familiarity with the cultural imaginary of the people he is examining.

The tastes of the regime's leaders partly resulted from the prestigious place occupied by Weimar classicism. Weimar itself was 'the spiritual home of German

Kulturpatriotismus', producing a strong association 'between high culture and National Socialism'.[18] There was a personal link in the form of Reiner Schlösser, the *Reichsdramaturg*, chief administrator and censor of the Third Reich's stage. His childhood home was Weimar; his father had been Director of the prestigious Goethe and Schiller Archive. The *Reichsdramaturg* therefore collected a large group of literary and dramatic Nazis around him associated with Weimar, and many actually from it.[19] Along with his ministry chief, Joseph Goebbels, Schlösser did not favour direct propaganda, but 'a carefully chosen repertoire . . . to provide ideological mood music',[20] and rousing stories from the past over pessimistic social critique. Greek tragedy and German adaptations of it, especially Goethe's play about Orestes and his friend Pylades meeting Orestes' other sister in Artemis' realm in the Crimea, *Iphigenie*, fitted the bill to perfection.

The intensity with which Greek tragedies about the House of Atreus spoke to the Nazis was manifested in Gerhart Hauptmann's four plays on the theme of Agamemnon's children, *Iphigenie in Delphi* (1940), *Iphigenie in Aulis* (1943), and *The Death of Agamemnon* and *Electra* (both 1944). Nazi cultural policy prioritized the theatre; theatres were amongst the first Nazi targets, and very highly supervized, partly because theatre was known to have exerted such a strong political influence during the Weimar Republic.[21] More than a quarter of the Propaganda Ministry's total budget was spent on the theatre – far more than on film.[22] Along with another ancient Greek tale of sisterly devotion, Sophocles' *Antigone*, the German Iphigenie plays of Hauptmann and Goethe were prominent at the Berliner Staatstheater at the height of the war. *Antigone* of Sophocles was performed thirty-seven times during the 1940–1941 season,[23] but the season afterwards, in 1941–1942, Hauptmann's *Iphigenie at Delphi* was performed thirty-nine times, and Sophocles' *Antigone* four times.[24] In the 1942–1943 season, Goethe's *Iphigenie* was performed twenty-two times and Hauptmann's *Iphigenie at Delphi* was performed twice; despite heavy bombing and disruptions to the schedule, Goethe's *Iphigenie* was one of the eleven plays known to have been performed in the 1943–1944 season.[25] It is hardly a surprise, therefore, that when the legendary Marxist director Erwin Piscator, by then nearly seventy years old, returned to Germany from the United States in 1962 to direct the Berlin Freie Volksbühne, he opened with a compressed production of Hauptmann's entire tetralogy. He was in no doubts about the symbiosis between the Atridae myths and Germany under National Socialism:

> At a time when Hitler occupied the world with war and death, could there have been a more convincing or persuasive parable than this ancient myth to express

> the chaos emanating from Germany? Did this archetypal picture of a family driven to destroy itself not stand for raving insanity of a nation – the German nation?[26]

I cannot prove that Littell knew Piscator's eloquent explanation of the obsession with Atridae plays during the Third Reich. It would not surprise me, since the disintegration of Littell's narrator's psyche is indeed representative of the disintegration of the German state.[27] But I can be sure that Littell has used the myth, first presented theatrically in Aeschylus' *Oresteia,* to lure his reader on through appalling atrocities. His title has raised in the reader's head the question of what the Erinyes/Eumenides – supernatural females who punished crimes within the *family* – are doing in Aue's story. By dangling the possibility of an analogy between Orestes and Aue from the outset, Littell invites us to piece together what happened between Aue and his mother, stepfather, sister and best friend. This absorbing detective trail is a device by which Littell forces us to concentrate on the horrific historicity of his novel.

We are quickly told of Aue's 'family problems' (5). Soon afterwards, the *Oresteia* begins to be audible (7; compare *Agamemnon* 179–181): 'At night, your dreams fall apart, unfurl, and proliferate, and when you wake they leave a fine, bitter film at the back of your mind, which takes a long time to dissolve.' One of Aue's colleagues, a historical figure named von Radetsky, born in Moscow before being brought up in Berlin, dreams 'of entering Moscow as a conqueror and *of striding across the Kremlin carpets*' (Littell's italics, 32), like Agamemnon returning home to walk up Clytemnestra's carpet, victorious, from Troy.[28] We are subsequently introduced to Aue's closest friend and fellow SS officer, Thomas, an Austrian: a mutual acquaintance asks *in Greek* if Thomas is Max's 'Pylades', and Thomas answers him, in Greek, 'Exactly … And he is my Orestes. Beware the power of armed friendship' (57). It was for excellent service in *Greece* that Thomas had achieved his promotion to *Hauptsturmführer* (59). Thomas himself quotes *Agamemnon* when he opines that Ukrainian peasants are angry with the Jews because the Bolsheviks, he claims, had exploited the Ukrainians through the Jewish merchant class: 'Hence the legitimate anger of the people' (64; compare *Agamemnon* 456–457). When he is staying in the Wehrmacht sanatorium near Yalta, Aue's revelations about his childhood (189–192) render the parallels between his family and Agamemnon's painfully obvious.

For Aue's father had left for World War I when he and his sister were infants. They spent their infancy in the Alsace countryside. The family settled in Kiel, but his father disappeared mysteriously, when Max was eight, in 1921. This was after his father's much livelier younger brother had moved in: Max's sister 'didn't like him so much.' Our suspicion that his mother and uncle had begun an intimate relationship, like Clytemnestra and Aegisthus, is here aroused, but the stepfather who is inflicted upon the children is a Frenchman called Aristide Moreau.

In 1943, Aue returns to convalesce in France, where he reads an essay by Maurice Blanchot on the myth of Orestes, as dramatized by Sartre, in his 1943 *Les Mouches* (499). The *Eumenides* parallel becomes obvious just before he murders his mother and stepfather on the same French excursion. He recalls a discussion with Una of their father; they couldn't be sure whether he was dead or alive, and their mother had effectively killed him by declaring him dead for legal purposes. Aue was disturbed by his mother and stepfather's 'shameful desires' (528). Other characters from the *Oresteia* make appearances: Aue describes Albert Speer (Minister of Armaments and War Production), urging, at an emergency meeting in Berlin, that the Germans weren't producing enough military hardware. 'These weren't Cassandra warnings' because they were scientific and persuasive (659). Aue's Furies are Clemens and Weser, the KRIPO (*Kriminalpolizei*) detectives investigating the deaths of Max's mother and stepfather (733). They catch up with him in Berlin during the last air raids of the war. We learn that the murder had been crazed and sadistic (734).

The parallels with the *Oresteia* become increasingly grandiose and frantic as Aue's mental state further deteriorates. His shoe size becomes crucial to the investigation (755), thus reminding anyone familiar with *The Libation Bearers* of its recognition scene. Aue endures nightmares replaying the Clytemnestra 'ghost' scene in *Eumenides*: Clemens and Weser, 'painted marionettes, poorly made and badly painted, creaked through my dreams, buzzed around me like dirty mocking little creatures. My mother herself sometimes joined this chorus' (827). When they interrogate Aue in Berlin, Clemens describes the murder (967): 'You went upstairs, covered in blood. Your mother was standing there waiting for you … She must have reminded you how she had carried you in her womb, then fed you at her breast, how she had wiped your ass and washed you while your father was chasing whores God know where. Maybe she showed you her breast' (968).[29]

Weser is killed by Russian gunfire near the Tiergarten, Clemens is shot by Thomas. Aue smashes his friend's neck with an iron bar, takes his identity and the policeman's money, and that is the end of the novel. It actually concludes with Aue's overblown statement of his own 'tragic' predicament:

> I was sad but didn't really know why. I felt all at once the entire weight of the past, of the pain of life and of inalterable memory, I remained alone with the dying

> hippopotamus, a few ostriches, and the corpses, alone with time and grief and the sorrow of remembering, the cruelty of my existence and of my death still to come. The Kindly Ones were on to me (*Les bienveillantes m'ont rattrapées*).
>
> (975)

In Aeschylus' *Eumenides*, Orestes is acquitted of guilt by the court of the Areopagus, and returns to Argos as its king. The chthonic beings who have driven him mad – his mother's Erinyes – are transformed into Eumenides, and confined to a cave beneath the Athenian acropolis, where they are now permitted to terrorize their victims solely through the state-run judicial machinery.[30] At the end of Littell's novel, Aue is suspended in a position equivalent to that of Orestes at the end of *The Libation Bearers*. Like so many Nazis, he has never been tried for his crimes. But nor has he eluded his Erinyes, who have never been transformed into Eumenides. Long after the war is over, they remain ever-present in his consciousness, just as they pursue the demented Orestes, with the blood of murder dripping from his hands. It seems to me impossible that Littell did not know of Cicero's explanation of the Furies as the effect of guilt on the human conscience, a passage often reproduced in translations and editions of Greek tragedies:[31]

> . . . the blood of a mother . . . has a great power; it is a mighty bond, of awful sanction. If any stain be conceived from it, not only can it not be washed out, but it penetrates through to the mind to such an extent that raving madness and insanity results . . . These are the constant, secret, Furies which . . . exact punishment on behalf of their parents both by day and by night.
>
> (*Pro Sexto Roscio Amerino* 24.66)

Through his use of the mythic framework, Littell therefore dangles the possibility – never to be fulfilled – of Aue ending up in a court to be tried for either war crimes or domestic murder.

Littell plays similarly with the possibility that Aue will encounter a sister in the Crimea. The most significant Atridae plays in the German repertoire, and a favourite of Weimar Nazism, was Goethe's *Iphigenie auf Tauris*, an adaptation of Euripides' *Iphigenia in Tauris*. It is set in the ancient city of Taurike Chersonesos, on the site of modern Sebastopol. Orestes, in the company of Pylades, is promised a cure for his madness after being reunited with his long-lost sister Iphigenia. Not only did every German schoolchild memorize swathes of Goethe's play, but several famous German and Russian paintings of the nineteenth century portray Iphigenia, alone on the beach at Sebastopol, awaiting reunion with her brother.[32] Littell cleverly poses the question of whether Max will go to Sebastopol from the minute when the Crimea is first mentioned (178); that city was the scene of some of the worst violence of the war. We are tantalized further as the discussion turns more frequently to the Crimea – to the planned liquidation of the Jews of Simferopol (181), just an hour's drive from 'Tauris', and then to the Wehrmacht sanatorium near Yalta to which Aue is sent to convalesce (185). The 'operations' are still continuing at Sebastopol when he arrives (187). It is during his account of this convalescence that Aue begins to confide about his family. He visits the old palace of the Crimean Khans at Bakhisaray,[33] from which he can listen to 'the monotonous rumble of the artillery pounding Sebastopol, resounding gently along the mountain' (218). Our expectations are raised when he mentions the fall of Sebastopol in July 1942 (225–226). He eventually does visit Tauris, commenting on the smoking ruins, the mountain-tops, and how he 'continued to take advantage of the beaches as much as possible' (226). The individual sitting on the beaches of Tauris/Sebastopol is not Aue's older sister 'Iphigenia', but Aue, or Orestes, himself.

The sister who *is* all-important is Una, 'the One', his twin. Una is Electra to Aue's Orestes, but she is also twin sister to his Narcissus, and the extravagant amalgamation of the two ancient narratives is symptomatic of the novel's idiom of bewildering excess. The two ancient myths are in ancient sources unrelated, yet our Orestes/Electra, gazing autoerotically into a mirror, is also a Narcissus. This fusion reaches a (literal) climax when, at the end of the war, Aue's 'obscene, perverse thoughts' flood into him, emerging 'from the corners of the room like mad dogs and rushed at me to tear into me and inflame my body', and he fantasizes uncontrollably, while masturbating, about exchanging clothes and even genitals with Una 'until all distinctions were erased' (888). His agonizing sexual urges, like the crazed dogs to which Aeschylus' Erinyes are repeatedly likened, can only find relief in a drink-fuelled, depraved orgy of masochism, masturbation and truly obscene fantasy.

No sister appears in the familiar version of the Narcissus myth. Narcissus fell in love with his own reflection in the water of a reed bed, and died of love on the spot. But Littell again proves his control of recondite classical sources by giving Narcissus the sister discussed in just one ancient author, Pausanias:

> There is another story about Narcissus, less popular indeed than the other, but not without some support. It is said that Narcissus had a twin sister; they were exactly alike in appearance, their hair was the same, they wore similar clothes, and went hunting together. The story goes on that Narcissus fell in love with his sister, and when the girl died, would go to the spring, knowing that it was his reflection that he saw, but in spite of this knowledge finding some relief for his love in imagining that he saw, not his own reflection, but the likeness of his sister.
>
> (9.31.8)

As a child, Aue had indeed developed an incestuous relationship with his twin. He remembers blissfully swimming and running through the forests, 'twisted together in the dust, our naked bodies indissociable, neither one nor the other specifically girl or boy, but a couple of snakes intertwined'; their 'little bodies became a mirror for each other' (405). In adulthood, before Una put a stop to it, they had once revived their sexual relationship. It suddenly becomes apparent to the reader (although not to Aue) that she had conceived twins as a result (890). Aue is, instead, angry that she had betrayed him by having sex, as he imagines, with another man, and fantasizes about watching her undress as he wanted to watch *himself*, 'not with a narcissistic gaze, or with a critical gaze that searches for defects, but with a gaze that is desperately trying to grasp the elusive reality of what it sees' (896).

This explicit *disavowal* of Narcissism of course makes the reader infer quite the opposite. Here the importance of Greek myth lies in the role Littell knows it played in German psychoanalysis from the time when Paul Näcke defined the term in 1899, and his ideas were taken up by Sigmund Freud.[34] In the novel, the Orestes myth drives the reader through the reality of the Holocaust, but the Narcissus myth illuminates Aue's insanity; the invitation to the reader to think in these terms – which were in common currency by the early 1940s – was earlier extended with the information that Una studied psychology in Zurich 'with a certain Dr. Carl Jung, who has become quite well-known since then' (371). Jung was probably the first to analyze Adolf Hitler's own megalomaniacal personality in psychoanalytical terms; he had met Hitler in Berlin.[35] But academic discussions of the psychopathologies of Hitler and several other senior members of the Third Reich leadership have subsequently focussed on strands including not only misogyny and homosexuality, but specifically clinical Narcissism. This often involves sadomasochism and addictive masturbation.[36]

As Martin Buber already argued in *Ich und Du* (1923), Narcissists often relate to other people as objects, rather than as equals, subjects and agents with capacities to feel emotions equal to the Narcissist's own. This aspect of Narcissism has played a role in psychoanalytical and socio-historical attempts to explain the atrocities which so many SS officers became capable of ordering, especially in Klaus Theweleit's study of the fascist male consciousness and bodily experience in *Männerphantasien* (1977), translated as *Male Fantasies* (1987). Yet, in a final twist, the reader is given strong indications that Aue's objectification of others, self-love and closely allied self-loathing, have a good deal to do with his denial of his own Jewishness. From his descriptions of his sister we know he is slender, with jet-black hair; he is also circumcized (199), which he explains as the unfortunate result of some medical incident in childhood. Una's twins are also circumcized and their stepfather may have been helping Jewish children to escape in France. Aue's mother interrogates him about the Ukrainian Jews, concluding when he disparages Jews to her that he is 'completely mad'. (525). And Aue himself is tortured by dreams in which he shows off his personal library to *Reichsführer* Heinrich Himmler, who promises to protect Aue even though he is a 'little Jew', '*Judelein*' (794). The Narcissus myth and the disorder named after it are thus manipulated by Littell in order to examine the Third Reich's unconscious antipathy to Jewish intellectual culture, as its eroticized internal 'other', which must be eliminated.

Although fixated on himself and his feminine twin/avatar, Aue is a practising closet homosexual. His erotic partners (if that is the right word for the brutal encounters he describes) include other officers, rent-boys, and (significantly) a young Jewish lad destined for extermination. The mentions of homoeroticism are usually presented in glamorizing classical terms, often by allusion to Plato's *Phaedrus* or *Symposium* (194–195, 197, 198). When Aue first fully 'comes out' to the reader as homosexual, he says that he liked the Berlin of the 1930s, because his private needs could be serviced there; he cites in illustration Plutarch's *Life of Alcibiades* (67). He is erotically obsessed with a statue of 'Apollo with Cithara' he saw in a Paris exhibition (500–501) At the Paris École Normale Supérieure he remembers meeting another 'invert', with whom he discussed the Greek inscriptions painted on the walls (503) and who wanted to stare at him as his '*eromenos*' (passive male sexual partner) while masturbating (510).

Aue's autoerotic frenzy takes place as Soviet tanks roll into eastern Germany, where he has taken refuge in his sister's abandoned house near Stettin (now Szczecin in Poland). In his mania he reflects on the reliability of the recollections which he has been describing:

> It's not that my memories are confused, on the contrary, I have many of them and very precise ones, but many of them overlap and even contradict one another, and their status is uncertain.
>
> (870)

This disturbing admission must undermine our trust in everything we have heard from our frustrating narrator. Psychotic delusions are symptomatic of the schizophrenia often associated with Narcissistic Personality Disorder. Yet so much of the material in the novel describing the Holocaust is, as we have seen, regarded even by experts as meticulously accurate. The reader is forced to confront the paradox that the palpably insane narrator, although often unreliable when telling us about his private life, is for much of the narrative, especially the account of his 'professional' activities as an SS officer, relentlessly truthful. His cold, philosophical eye and pen, partly on account of his inability to empathize with other human beings, sees and records the facts with a dispassionate, sometimes even disinterested accuracy.

Aue never speculates on the subjective experiences of his victims (something of which he is pathologically incapable). Littell's skill as a writer is such that the reader can sometimes hear something of the agony of the victims even through his psychotic narrator's speciously clinical prose, for example in the sequence when he is cursed, as if in ancient Greek tragedy, by a professor from Leningrad he is about to murder during the *Aktion* at Minvody:

> 'I know what you are doing here,' the man said coolly. 'It is an abomination. I simply want to wish that you'll survive this war and wake up for twenty years, every night, screaming. I hope you will be incapable of looking at your children without seeing ours, the ones you murdered.'
>
> (242)

As a self-admiring Narcissist, however, Aue is gratified by his capacity to describe what their experiences looked like to *him*. In the most jarring pair of sentences in the entire work, he makes this claim:

> When it comes to suffering, though, I ought to know a thing or two. Every European of my generation could say the same, but I can claim without any false modesty that I have seen more than most.
>
> (12)

Aue thinks he deserves personal credit for having witnessed a record *volume* of suffering.

He is more interested in the emotional experiences undergone by Germans. His descriptions, although apparently contradictory, reflect the moral *conflict* and chaos which made the atrocities possible. Sometimes he implies that the Germans enjoyed the killings, elsewhere that the brutality had been necessary for the perpetrators to repress their 'natural' sense of fellow feeling with other humans (147). He once compares the German soldiers who feasted their eyes on the spectacle of Jewish and Bolshevik corpses with Leontius in Plato's *Republic* (4.439e–440a), obsessed with the 'beautiful spectacle' of the corpses of executed criminals outside the north wall of Athens (98); this passage is one of the rare occasions which forcibly remind the reader that s/he is reading, for motives including the pursuit of recreational pleasure, descriptions of mass executions. The novel is not, by contemporary standards, particularly self-reflexive (I am aware that other critics disagree).[37] Littell has said that his primary aim was to try to understand the consciousness of the perpetrators of the Holocaust.[38] That was the impact the novel had on me even before I researched its genesis. Despite rich references to the classical novels which Aue admires – Stendhal and Flaubert, in particular – there is little theoretical discussion of the nature of fiction or its relationship with reality.

There is one important programmatic passage, however, when Aue asks why Thomas, although intelligent and articulate, would not have made a novelist:

> At the same time he had no imagination, and I had always thought, despite his ability to paint a complex scene in a few strokes, that he would have made a poor novelist: in his reasoning and intuitions, his polestar always remained personal interest; and although, sticking to that, he was rarely wrong, he was incapable of imagining any different motivation for people's actions and words. His passion ... was not a passion for pure knowledge, for knowledge for its own sake, but solely for practical knowledge, providing tools for action.
>
> (690–691)

The accusation that Thomas was motivated solely by 'personal interest' must bring a wry smile to readers' lips, since Aue is so irritatingly self-obsessed himself. But his talk of 'passion' and of 'pure knowledge', 'knowledge for its own sake', is suggestive. Although the book's subject matter is 'genocide over four years, with a few deviations here and there' (Littell's own description),[39] this framework is designed to support extended historical-realist excurses on topics including the Kiev massacres, the linguistic diversity of the Caucasus and infighting within the upper echelons of the Nazi regime.

Littell's narrator is mad but knowledgeable. He adores accumulating data and garish detail. His consciousness is coloured by an elite classical education, and analyzed in terms of psychoanalytical models, current in the protagonist's own day, but named after figures in Greek mythology. Littell has thus created a new type of documentary window, without precedent in fiction, onto some of the darkest recesses of history.

Bibliography

Arendt, Hannah (1963), *Eichmann in Jerusalem: a Report on the Banality of Evil.* New York: Penguin.

Blumenthal, Samuel (2006), 'Jonathan Littell: interview', *Le Monde des Livres*, 17 November, http://www.harpercollins.com/author/microsite/readingguide.aspx?authorID=32781&displayType=essay&articleId=4661

Bourguignon, Hélène (2007), 'Les Bienveillantes', *Vingtième Siècle. Revue d'histoire*, 96 (Oct.–Dec.): 238–239.

Delvaux, Peter (1992), *Antiker Mythos und Zeitgeschehen. Sinnstruktur und Zeitbezüge in Gerhart Hauptmanns Atriden-Tetralogie*. Amsterdam: Rodopi.

Engels, David (2013), 'Narcissism against Narcissus? A Classical Myth and its Influence on the Elaboration of Early Psychoanalysis from Binet to Jung', in Vanda Zajko and Ellen O'Gorman (eds), *Classical Myth and Psychoanalysis: Ancient and Modern Stories of the Self*. Oxford: Oxford University Press.

Fischer-Lichte, Erika (2008), 'Resurrecting Greece in Nazi Germany', in Martin Revermann and Peter Wilson (eds), *Performance, Iconography, Reception: Studies in Honour of Oliver Taplin*, 481–498. Oxford: Oxford University Press.

Friedländer, Saul, ed. (1992), *Representing the Holocaust*. Cambridge, MA & London: Harvard University Press.

Gadberry, Glen W. (2004), 'The Theater in and of the Third Reich: the German stage In Extremis', in Hellmut Hal Rennert (ed.), *Essays on Twentieth-Century German Drama and Theater*, 133–146. New York and Bern: Peter Lang Publishing.

Grethlein, Jonas (2009), *Littells Orestie: Mythos, Macht und Moral in* les Bienveillantes. Freiburg: Rombach Verlag.

Grethlein, Jonas (2012), 'Myth, Morals, and Metafiction in Jonathan Littell's "Les Bienveillantes"', *PMLA*, 127: 77–93.

Hagemann, W. (1936), '"Die Orestie": Aischylos im Staatstheater', *Germania* (Berlin), 6th August, Erste Beilage, 5.

Hall, Edith (1998), 'Introduction' to *Euripides: Medea, Hippolytus, Electra, Helen*, trans. James Morwood. Oxford: Oxford University Press.

Hall, Edith (2004), 'Aeschylus, race, class and war', in E. Hall, F. Macintosh, and A. Wrigley (eds), *Dionysus since 69: Greek Tragedy at the Dawn of the Third Millennium*, 79–97. Oxford: Oxford University Press.

Hall, Edith. (2005), 'Iphigenia and her mother at Aulis: a study in the revival of a Euripidean Classic', in S. Wilmer and J. Dillon (eds), *Rebel Women: Staging Ancient Greek Drama Today*, 3–41. London: Bloomsbury.

Hall, Edith (2007), 'Subjects, selves and survivors', Helios, 34 (2): 125–159.

Hall, Edith (2008), *The Return of Ulysses: A Cultural History of the Odyssey*. London and Baltimore, MD: I. B. Tauris.

Hall, Edith. (2009), 'Greek tragedy and the politics of subjectivity in recent fiction', *Classical Receptions Journal*, 1: 23–42.

Hall, Edith (2010), *Greek Tragedy: Suffering under the Sun*. Oxford: Oxford University Press.

Hall, Edith (2013), *Adventures with Iphigenia in Tauris: A Cultural History of Euripides' Black Sea Tragedy*. New York: Oxford University Press.

Hall, Edith (2015), 'Peaceful conflict resolution and its discontents in Aeschylus' *Eumenides*', *Common Knowledge*, 21: 253–269.

Hofstetter, Elisabeth Schulz (2004), *The Berlin State Theater under the Nazi Regime*. Lewiston, Queenston & Lampeter: Edwin Meller.

Hyland, Philip, Daniel Boduszek and Krysztof Kielkiewicz (2011), 'A psycho-historical analysis of Adolf Hitler: the role of personality, psychopathology, and development', *Psychology & Society*, 4: 58–63. Online at http://www.psychologyandsociety.org/__assets/__original/2012/01/Hyland_et_al.pdf

LaCapra, Dominick (2011), 'Historical and literary approaches to the "Final Solution": Saul Friedländer and Jonathan Littell', *History and Theory*, 50: 71–97.

Lanzmann, Claude (2006), '*Les Bienveillantes*: vénéneuse fleur du mal', *Le Journal du dimanche*, 17 September, 14.

Lanzmann, Claude (2007), 'Littell hat die Sprache der Henker erfunden', interview with Claude Lanzmann, *Frankfurter Allgemeine Zeitung* 277, 28 November, 35.

Littell, Jonathan (2010), *The Kindly Ones*. London: Chatto & Windus. English translation of original French *Les Bienveillantes* (2006; Éditions Gallimard).

McGuire, W. and R. C. F. Hull (1977), *C. G. Speaking: Interviews and Encounters*. Princeton, NJ: Princeton University Press.

Manne, Robert (2009), 'An audacious look into the Nazi state of mind', *The Australian*, 4 March, available online at http://www.theaustralian.com.au/arts/an-audacious-look-into-the-nazi-state-of-mind/story-e6frg8px-1111118953995

Mendelsohn, Daniel (2009), 'Transgression' (review of Jonathan Littell, *The Kindly Ones*, *New York Review of Books* 56, 5 (26 March).

Mercier-Leca, Florence (2007), '*Les Bienveillantes* et la tragédie grecque. Une suite macabre à L'*Orestie* d'Eschyle', *Le Débat* 144 (Mars–Avril): 45–55.

Michaud, Louis Gabriel, ed. (1832), *Biographie universelle, ancienne et modern*, vol. 54. Paris.

Michelakis, P. (2004), 'Greek tragedy in cinema: theatre, politics, history', in E. Hall, F. Macintosh and A. Wrigley (eds), *Dionysus since 69: Greek Tragedy at the Dawn of the Third Millennium*, 199–217. Oxford: Oxford University Press.

Mönniger, Michael (2006), 'The banalisation of evil', *Die Zeit*, 21 September, reproduced in full at http://www.signandsight.com/features/976.html.

Näcke, Paul (1899), 'Kritisches zum Kapitel der normalen und pathologischen Sexualität', *Archiv fuer Psychiatrie* (Berlin), 32: 356–386.

Radisch, Iris (2008), 'Am Anfang steht ein Missverständnis', discussion of Littell's *Les Bienveillantes*, *Die Zeit*, 18 February.

Rosenberg, Alfred (1930), *Der Mythos des 20. Jahrhunderts. Eine Wertung der seelisch-geistigen Gestaltenkämpfe unserer Zeit*. Munich: Hoheneichen Verlag.

Schwarz, Daniel R. (1999), *Imagining the Holocaust*. New York: Palgrave Macmillan.

Stobl, Gerwin (2007), *The Swastika and the Stage, 1933–1945*. Cambridge: Cambridge University Press.

12

Philhellenic Imperialism and the Invention of the Classical Past: Twenty-first Century Re-imaginings of Odysseus in the Greek War for Independence

Efrossini Spentzou

In 2008 Isidoros Zourgos published *Aidonopita* (*A Nightingale's Pie*),[1] a modern Greek historical novel set in the Greek mainland during the War of Independence (1821–1832).[2] The novel recounts, in diary form, the wanderings in 1820s Greece of Gabriel Linton, a fictional American classical scholar and philhellene. At the Olympic Games of August 2004, only four years before the publication of Zourgos' novel, Greece performed for the world, projecting idealized narratives of national identity, pride, inclusion, continuity, ancient achievements and present-day dynamism. There was a great deal of self-belief in these public narratives, but it was also the performance of a small nation, consciously engaged in reasserting familiar and reassuring images that reflected ancient glory to the millions who watched. Performing for others, contemporary Greece utilized a national myth whose origins can be found around the time Gabriel, Zourgos' protagonist, was setting foot in revolutionary Greece, and whose trajectory over the last two centuries has been a product of conscious collusion between Greeks and other Europeans. The world gave its benevolent approval, just as it had previously both solicited and sponsored Greece's classicising self-representation in the nation building of the nineteenth and early twentieth centuries.[3] Present-day Greece, the Greece of Zourgos, never features in this period narration. Yet, as I hope to show, the novel resonates in our present post-heroic, crisis-ridden times, raising questions about how one can be(come) a Greek, and how one can read the Greek *mentalité*: questions that are thoroughly modern and which resist easy resolution.

In *Aidonopita*, Zourgos is a contemporary Greek ventriloquizing the American hero of an early-nineteenth-century epic novel, explicitly both the

Iliad and the *Odyssey*. Zourgos takes an anti-heroic approach to ancient foundational texts of Greek identity, exposing the colonizing myths surrounding modern Greece while at the same time allowing a positive articulation of national self-awareness, albeit one that undermines any unitary narratives of political identity. There are three contexts within which to situate *Aidonopita*. First, and in the foreground, there is the narrative-historical context: the Mediterranean in the earlier part of the nineteenth century, with Greece caught in a revolutionary fever, and with a Philhellenic movement situated in the United States,[4] and to a lesser extent in Europe. Second, *in absentia* but indispensable for our reading, there is the context of contemporary, twenty-first-century Greece. And finally, intricately connected with both these periods, there is a third spectral presence: the classical imaginary sustained throughout the novel by Gabriel's devotion to classical letters.

By means of its spectral presence, the classical layer in the plot fuses the separate historical referents of the story. Gabriel may be a nineteenth-century American, but in his romantic and erudite devotion to the classics, his itinerary also acquires symbolic significance, mirroring, as he does himself, every visitor who has ever made the Greek land their destination in the hope of experiencing the transcendental entity that was Greek antiquity.[5] As Artemis Leontis puts it, speaking in particular about the most coveted of those destinations, the Acropolis: 'Travel annotations, letters, journals, newspaper articles, and scholarly texts representing nearly two centuries of travel to Greece and acquisitions from Greece claim the Acropolis as a home away from home. These texts make the Acropolis European, the traveller Hellenic.'[6] I would like to mark here, and will return to it, the reciprocity of the encounter, where both parties' identities are implicated in the process.[7]

As we will see, Gabriel's encounters with 'real' Greeks[8] were ambivalent, to say the least. Intriguingly, as the novel draws to a close, he abandons Greece for good. Is this a willing departure, or does Greece chase him away? How disturbed is he to discover that the nineteenth-century descendants of Aristotle and Longinus (the two classical figures he holds closest to his heart) led a haphazard, unkempt, illiterate life in a dangerous, precarious land?[9] I will return to Gabriel's departure from Greece in the last part of the chapter. In a novel set during the Greek War of Independence, a key moment in the new nation's effort to acquire and project a national conscience, Zourgos fights shy of the certainties of collective myth-making, reading the Philhellenes of the early nineteenth century with an eye to their self-delusions and misunderstandings. There is, I suggest, an attempt to discuss how misleading, and often plain inadequate, such symbolic histories can be, a message that questions the foundational mythologies of twenty-first-century

Greece as much as those of nineteenth- and twentieth-century (European) Hellenism. Significantly, this Mediterranean *Odyssey* is completed neither by the American diarist nor by the omniscient, occasional narrator, but by Gabriel's Greek widow, Lazarina, part Penelope, part Helen, part Molly Bloom. In themselves, the multiple voices produce a shifting narrative with no single goal or perspective, and yet, as I will suggest, they succeed in articulating core political questions –vivid for our times – about the relationship between history and the individual; Europe and Greece; Orientalism and the Classics; the classical heritage and imperialism.[10]

* * *

Our hero, Gabriel Thackeray Linton, is an orphan from the docks of Boston, adopted by a rich family and drawn to the Greek War by the same romantic urge associated with other celebrated Philhellenes such as his hero, Lord Byron. Gabriel's politics are complicated. Admiration for Greek valour aside, his decision to embark on a voyage to Greece is prompted by his thwarted love for Elizabeth, the daughter of his benefactor, and by a gnawing dissatisfaction with the social and political status quo in America. Gabriel's best friend on old Linton's estate is Raphael, a black servant, loved by, and yet not equal to, the family. Raphael's angelic acceptance of his position reminds Gabriel of his own uncertain, subordinate status. In Gabriel's words to Elizabeth:

> 'I often wonder what kind of democracy this is that we live in. Imagine a five-storey building that we all want to climb. You start from the fourth floor and proceed gently and slowly with a parasol in one hand and a fan in the other; I, on the other hand, run frantically from the basement until I am out of breath.'[11]
>
> (32)

In spite of social prejudice, Gabriel's fortunes are far better than those of Raphael. He is allowed into the local evening school for farmers, and at the time of his departure for Greece he is a promising third-year student in the newly founded School of Classics at Harvard University. This is his other window onto Greece; his beloved ancient authors are, we are repeatedly told, his most valuable belongings. Fuelled by his learned imagination, Gabriel sets off for Europe, hoping to negotiate a passage to Greece from the port of Marseille. He is fired up by the revolution, but also by a desire for a vicarious meeting with his favourite authors, Aristotle and Longinus. The opportunities come, but with mixed results. The first encounter with flesh-and-blood Greeks comes soon after he arrives in Marseille, in the front room of a Greek trader. The account of the meeting comes from Gabriel's diary:

> We started talking amidst big puffs of smoke. I tried to speak to them in Greek, but it proved hard. If it had been Archilochus or Longinus in front of me, believe me, all would have been better and I would have been able to understand what they were saying . . . All these smugglers with huge moustaches are the first Greeks of my dreams. Likeable and unapproachable, heroic and quiet, tessera of a Christian East mosaic. Will I ever put this mosaic together?
>
> (43)

Empathy and incomprehension are blended in Gabriel's writing, and on board the (Christian) ship *Theotokos* (*The Begetter of God*) his heart swells with pride at being able to cross 'the ancient water, mingled with Poseidon's piss for centuries now' (68). And yet, every time he attempts an overture that might establish a link across the ages, he is rebuffed. We read in his diary: 'They feed us every day with bread, olives, salty feta and wine. "Homeric food," I told Thomas [his British companion]. "Gloop," he replied' (69). The Greeks themselves appear no more alive to the link he is trying to forge. From Gabriel's diary, still on board *Theotokos*:

> I asked him [the captain] why he named his ship *Theotokos*. He looked at me, seemingly taken aback. 'What else?' he asked. I could see I was not helping. 'Ariadne, for example', I said without much thought. 'Is this your mother's name?' he asked. I understood I was caught in a whirlwind.
>
> (70)

Enthused and rebuked, Gabriel perseveres against the natural and human adversity that tosses him out in Malta, where a Greek benefactor takes him on and gives him a specific mission: to deliver a letter to an old friend in Thessaloniki. In the first of many strikingly Odyssean moments, and after several starts and stops, our hero disembarks just south of Thessaloniki in a small dinghy. The connection is acknowledged in Gabriel's diary: 'I had arrived just outside Ithaca, but without luggage, naked and frozen' (171). He is particularly shaken because, just as he was setting foot on the dinghy, the box containing the books written by his beloved ancient authors capsized and sank into the waters of the Aegean Sea; his first encounter with the 'real' Greece had seen the destruction of his classical guides. After a night's unsettled sleep, he (and we) are faced with a rather different, and yet instantly recognizable, Nausicaa. Woken by noise, Gabriel makes an appearance through the bush, forgetting his nakedness, to be met by a hunched old man, who seems less perturbed by him than Nausicaa's girlfriends are by Odysseus.[12] But the real shock comes as soon the old man speaks, and a flow of incomprehensible words comes tumbling out. The man about to give our Odysseus shelter, the man Gabriel will call a page or so later in his diary 'my Alcinous, the king of the mud-brick house, my host' (174), is a Turk. If such a humble, poverty-stricken Alcinous does not catch our fancy, we might try to place him in the shoes of Eumaeus; yet even this parallel cannot dispense with the irony that our Odysseus is rescued by one of those against whom he had come to fight.

This is only the first of many such instances where Gabriel's Odysseus loses his footing. I cite just one further example. Days after his encounter with his first Turk, Gabriel arrives at Thessaloniki. Turks control the gates, and Gabriel, disguised as an old woman, is smuggled inside in the back of a cart full of lettuce (187). One cannot miss the transvestite allusion to Odysseus' arrival at the palace in Ithaca.[13] Gabriel diligently acknowledges the parallel, and with a distinctly Cavafian overtone: 'Now that I have delivered Papafis's letter I feel without purpose. What will I do from tomorrow morning? . . . After my Ithaca what? I do not know' (197).

Thus begins Part Two of Zourgos' novel, with Gabriel's new journey, this time an *Odyssey* mixed with Iliadic passages of war. I dip in again. Part Two finds Gabriel galloping across northern Greece heading south, with a group of very strange companions: Nikitas (a klepht), Yiannakos (his retainer), Lazarina from Thessaloniki (Nikitas' newly acquired and pregnant wife), and Panagiotis (the secretary of Lazarina's father). Gabriel feels distinctly isolated from these Greeks, and yet bound to them, and once again without a goal in his Iliadic odyssey around warring Thessaly. The journey is perilous, with all the events, dangers and suspense appropriate for an odyssey, and in its course an irresistible bond is created between Gabriel and Lazarina, another man's wife. Boundaries, and the narrative trajectories of the characters, start to meld and then separate again, as we follow the erratic fates and characters of the protagonists. We have already been told that Nikitas' and Lazarina's marriage was an arrangement between Nikitas and Lazarina's father. Nikitas married the previously raped (and thus dishonoured and unwanted) Lazarina in return for the money he needed to assemble an army to fight the Turks.

The mismatched group that crosses the dangerous fields of Thessaly is, as Gabriel tells us, his Danaoi charging for Ilion. He has at last found his Greeks; he is Odysseus to Nikitas' Ajax, Ares' son, who 'rattles the bronze shield and spreads fear to besieged Trojans and whose superior art sends numerous souls to Hades' (225). But unfortunately, as Gabriel notes, Nikitas is Lazarina's husband, and – we are told – that saddens Gabriel more than he can either admit to himself or commit to paper (226). Unrequited love, love denied, and love bought is the real freight on this perilous journey. When the promised money is proven to be a ruse, Nikitas abandons everyone and runs to the mountains to meet his real love, war. Gabriel then finds himself Lazarina's guardian. New symbolism eases itself into the story. Lazarina gives birth and Gabriel makes her a home in a stable. They later separate and find each other again, setting off on a further journey towards the unknown. I quote from the omniscient narrator: 'They had set off more than three days now. A bearded man, a woman with her baby son and a donkey loaded with bedding and a bit of flour' (336). Searching for his *Odyssey* in the Christian East, Gabriel has found Mary. But this foundational image is also undermined. Despite their apparent togetherness, Gabriel and Lazarina row continuously as they cross the serene landscape exchanging hurtful words and insults. Then Lazarina's son falls ill and dies.

The next episode, and the climax of the book, is resolutely Iliadic. Gabriel and Lazarina are trapped inside Messolonghi, together and now very much in love, but separated by the imperatives of war. Gabriel is at his most content when he writes in his diary: 'my country is Messolonghi, my home the bastion of Franklin ... There is fatigue, thirst, heat, but – what a wonderful thing – someone has censored grief.' And an important postscript: 'Some nights I see her furtively' (375). When his Andromache, as he calls her, comes out on the walls to see him, he is Hector, except that he does not send her back to church to pray, as his famous predecessor did. But it is a common secret to all around that he has another man's wife. At his happiest, at his most resolute, Gabriel is now a Hector and a Paris, two figures of such different natures in the epic, and with Paris a figure of minor significance and unimpressive character in his beloved Homer. He admits this syncretism when he speaks of besieged Messolonghi in his diary: 'Every day my eyes are lost in a marshy field beneath us. It is Ilion, only we are the Trojans' (375).

As the Homeric re-rewriting rushes to its denouement, boundaries and allegiances fall. Like Ilion, Messolonghi falls, and women and children are led into slavery by the hundred. But, in a nice theatrical contrivance, Lazarina and Gabriel (together with a lost child they take into their keeping) survive. As they wander across the wasted fields and villages of the flats of Akarnania in Western Greece, Greek and Turkish villages become one; Greeks and Turks walk and often run together, fleeing the same fate. On their way, Gabriel and Lazarina save two Turkish children from a fire. They then decide to embark on yet another journey, a homecoming for Gabriel, a return to Boston. To raise money, Gabriel will offer to the interested 'Phaeacians' of the Ionian coast an account of their life in Messolonghi. He is ready to be Odysseus again, but his account to the Phaeacians will now incorporate Hector's bravery as well as, and perhaps more crucially, Paris' devoted love for Helen, another man's wife.

* * *

There are many stories that can be, and have been, told about the Philhellenes and Greece in the Greek War of Independence. They may differ, but they are all stories of an observed nation, stories bred by a culture keenly aware of itself as spectacle. There is pride in this (literal) reflection, where an underdog attracts admiration, attention and help from the great and powerful of the time: it is always an enduring, and easily retrievable, trope. I quote from the American Philhellenes Society website:

> The Greek War of Independence against the Ottoman Empire was not only of and for the people of Hellas. This struggle revived the spirit of Philhellenism throughout the world. James Monroe, the President of the United States along with his Administration, offered the Greeks material and psychological support, under the Monroe Doctrine. Emissaries travelled to Greece, individually and in groups, to support the Greeks in their mission.[14]

In the space of just a few lines, a number of complications are smoothed away, not least the famous 'Monroe Doctrine' announced on 2 December 1823, by which European governments of the time were recognized as de facto legitimate, and, subsequently, any official interference in European affairs was halted. Foregrounding the Romantic cult of the individual at the expense of political commentary, the site then fills its space with portraits of selected American individuals, notable among them Dr Samuel Howe, George Jarvis and Jonathan Miller, who did indeed leave an indelible mark through their participation in the Greek War of Independence.

Juxtaposed to these emotional, at times positively gushing, accounts of American, and more broadly Western, involvement in the War of Independence are rather more probing investigations of Philhellenism which read the encounter as one chapter in the complex history of the relationship between East and West. Within this political and theoretical framework, the philhellenic response to the war in the Eastern Mediterranean becomes a stage in the ongoing process of a curious and self-serving scopophilia, a chapter in the reading of Greece from without. Self-possessed travellers with narcissistic memories of a Grand Tour, together with Humboldtian philologists in love with a notionally enlightened ancient Greece, established Philhellenism in a desire to see – or more radically to *become* – what the (Western) self was not; it was a desire to establish identity through difference, and specifically oriental-exotic difference.[15]

The diminutive, yet at the same time distinctive, profile of the Greeks within European consciousness and conscience becomes abundantly clear in Lord Byron's own notes to *Childe Harold's Pilgrimage*, written and published from 1812 to 1818.[16] In the notes we often see Byron drawn to the suffering of a people who 'have been amply punished by three centuries and a half of captivity',[17] rising to their defence against what seems to him a consensus of derogatory evaluations by fellow Europeans, especially the French. Yet these same notes include repeated references to a colonialist ambivalence going hand-in-hand with a somewhat condescending philanthropy.

> The Greeks will never be independent; they will never be sovereigns as heretofore, and God forbid they ever should! But they may be subjects without being slaves ... To talk, as the Greeks themselves would do, of their rising again to their pristine superiority would be ridiculous ... but there seems to be no great obstacle, except in the apathy of Franks, to their becoming a useful dependency, or even a free state with a proper guarantee.[18]

Sketched against this dubious background of self-centred, interlaced motives, Gabriel cuts a solitary figure. His classicism could place him alongside the philologists, except that, as we saw, he loses his classical books, his lifeline to the ancients, just seconds before he sets foot on the Greek mainland. On the other hand, his Romantic enthusiasm for adventure, his love for the fight and for freedom, might suggest that he belongs with the Grand Tourists. But he is a jarring figure in the world of privilege that surrounds those wealthy enough to embark on the *Bildung* experience of the Grand Tour. It is telling, I think, that for all his adoration for Byron, their encounter somewhere outside Messolonghi in the early 1820s, much anticipated by Gabriel, leaves a bitter aftertaste, dominated by the memory of a rather withdrawn Byron, at some remove from his environment, a traveller disconnected from his travels, disappointed by the reality of Greece and closed up within himself. I quote from Gabriel's letter to Elizabeth regarding this meeting:

> I introduced myself and started talking about my studies ... he interrupted and told me that had fate arranged things otherwise, he would not be in Greece now but in America. He had plans, while he was travelling, to leave everything behind. America, he said intently, promises a new start, it is a true destination for poets. (313)

Later on in their discussion, Gabriel speaks about the bodies that ground one in reality: 'the only solution amidst war and rain is the memory of the bodies'. But

Byron 'emptied his glass all at once and replied: "I lived with so many bodies, and now, as I think of it, I can only remember two, Augusta's[19] and that other, the little one, buried in Harrow church, my daughter Allegra's"' (315). The distance between the poet of Greek freedom and the Greeks is heartbreaking for Gabriel, who watches his idol lost in a reverie of pleasure and pain, unable to link these with the real and immediate bodies who ate, laughed, danced and died so close to him and under his orders in Messolonghi. The Greek corporeality is as lost to the poet as is reality within his Romantic imaginary.

A philologist or a well-to-do traveller Gabriel may not be, but he is no fool. During a brief stop at Malta, he has the chance to converse with Ioannis Papafis, an educated expatriate Greek who offers him a sobering lesson in international diplomacy. Still in Malta, he writes back to Edward Everett, the holder of the recently inaugurated Chair of Classics in Harvard and Gabriel's personal mentor, a letter oozing with bitterness:

> I judge, Sir, that the very John Quincy Adams, our current Foreign Secretary, is ready for a tighter embrace with the Turkish Tyranny. The Greeks who have given me hospitality in the past few days, all prominent in their fields and with a broad awareness of the world, are convinced that trade and industry interests will keep our politics favourable, if not enslaved, to Turkish affairs. No-one seems to want to change the balance of trade in the Eastern Mediterranean; indeed many European as well as American merchants rush to declare that they have no desire for a Greek state, and the officialdom associated with it, to start interfering with their affairs.
>
> [116]

Disheartened by the dirty games played by the various capitalists, who are listed later in the letter (slave traders, opium handlers, antiquities dealers), Gabriel exhorts his old mentor to use his influence, and his friendship with Congressman Daniel Webster, to secure a political intervention in the crisis. But with twenty-first-century hindsight, and through our familiarity with imperial realpolitik, we know that this intervention was never likely to take place: Greece was too insignificant to risk disrupting the forces of capital and empire. Gabriel thus enters the action as a fringe figure, representing no one, a vagabond full of enthusiasm but with no agenda, let down by institutions, nations and class, but also unfettered by the obligations and expectations that these structures impose.

There is an air of impermanence and uncertainty in the novel that, one could argue, is its most long-lasting effect. A famous story of return to the familiar, the reassuring, the enduring world of imagined pasts is remade as a story of successive and hurried departures with only temporary respites. Gabriel's odyssey works against the readings of Greece that have kept, and still keep, its people beholden. There is a suspicion of home running through the novel that is both salutary and thoroughly postmodern. Gabriel learns early on that if by reaching 'home' one expects to walk the paths of an ancient Greek landscape and converse with Homer, Alcibiades or Longinus, then one can never hope for arrival. Also, unlike Odysseus, who needs to cling to his identity, to stay the same despite all the disguises in order to return to Ithaca one day, Gabriel's arrival depends on his willingness to shed current identities and embrace new ones, often antithetical to those they replace. Gabriel is an Odysseus, yes, but he is also a Hector, a Paris, briefly an Achilles, even a Joseph for one fleeting moment, and he needs all of these masks to make it through a story in which he finds that it is increasingly hard to separate good and bad, Greek and Turk, victor and defeated.

'Egocentric travellers and dispassionate philologists', Stathis Gourgouris tells us in his expert account of Philhellenic expediency, 'engage in kindred obsessions ... together, they constitute the discursive practices of the Orientalist industry. Inherent in both is contempt for bodies as they exist and function in themselves'.[20] Gabriel, though, immerses himself in the body of Greece, over and above anything else. The bodies of those to whom he has grown close end up dead in his arms, time and time again, not least the small frame of Lazarina's little boy, who dies of fever during their perambulations. Above all, he comes into contact with Greece through the body of Lazarina, a body raped and fallen from social grace, a body sold, but by ruse, and then desired and loved but not possessed, while she was another man's wife. His and hers is a coming-together subjugated to no symbolic meaning, a taste of Greece as fresh and tangible and free as the tastes of the sea, as Gabriel puts it when writing to Elizabeth from inside besieged Messolonghi:

> I am happy. I am now happy. In this town that wails, pressed by the monster onto the sea, I have her hands, her eyes, her breasts, that smell of fresh sea urchin.
>
> (371)

The most important moments in Zourgos' novel are departures. Gabriel's and Lazarina's short stay up in the mountains, literally in a no-man's (free) land, after the fall of Messolonghi, is their most uncomplicated and contented time: an interlude away from the world and its diktats, it is bound to last only a short while. And this part of the book ends with the greatest of flights in the midst of a mighty storm outside Kefalonia in the Ionian Sea, as the new counter-historical familial unit (a Greek woman, an American man, a Greek girl and two Turkish children) push their way west, back towards Boston. It is now 1826 and Gabriel encounters a final fight for his life and those of his makeshift family on board a boat too small for them all, forced by necessity to share the vessel with an Elgin-like English sailor whose loot of classical sculptures threatens to capsize the frail craft. We last see Gabriel alive in the book throwing overboard busts, friezes and metopes, in a desperate attempt to keep the small boat from sinking.

The coda of the book is placed forty-three years later in 1869. Our Odysseus has been dead for a few months by this time. We meet again Lazarina and her three children, a close-knit family with a common home but no common origins. We hear a lot about Gabriel. His Odyssey in Greece, we realize, was only a departure; a start and not an arrival. Gabriel never settled in Greece. He prospered in Boston, but remained adamant in his desire never to return to Greece. Moreover, and this is the last and greatest gesture of self-effacing open-endedness, he never finished his odyssey. In this third and last part of the book, the widowed Lazarina, an erstwhile Helen and a loyal Penelope, becomes the poet, entrusted by Gabriel the week before his death with the task of finishing the last empty pages of his diary. Unwilling to dictate, or to take responsibility for, the Greek home, Gabriel sends his lifelong companion, a Greek woman, a figure that started life in the novel as a raped young girl and thus a dishonoured cast-away, to seek a final arrival. Once again the novel skirts the potency and tyranny of symbols, international dealings and treaties, as Lazarina passes through Athens, the new capital, to her final destination which is a place that no international treaty has yet declared Greek: her birthplace, Thessaloniki.

With its multiple endings, its journeys traced and re-traced, this is not the foundational story of arrival either for the West or the East. The desire to imagine Greece as the classical world continued fails, for Zourgos' rewriting of the *Odyssey* and the *Iliad* denies any complacent myths of belonging. His Gabriel is a plea for freedom, not simply from Turkish oppression, but from the binding assumptions and stereotypes that have kept a nation captive for the last two centuries. Gabriel loved and lived in Greece, but he also let it go. Deprived of resolution or a foundational moment, Gabriel's epic is an episode in a history that is continuous and unfinished. Entrusted with its ending, Lazarina writes into Gabriel's epic her own ancestral, long abandoned hearth in Thessaloniki. Her quest produces a Greek home, in her city of birth. But it is a home *built anew* on the vestiges of her father's old mansion, which, the architect tells her without any hesitation, cannot be restored.

* * *

For all its period setting, Zourgos' *Aidonopita* constitutes a thoroughly contemporary and relevant commentary at a time when European identity is undergoing a systemic, and uncertain, overhaul. Cosmopolitanism, mobility, mass communication and migration have forced European systems of authority to acknowledge distant others as significant neighbours, and to recognize the European imaginary as one based on heterogeneity, multiplicity and intimate interactions between communities at times resentful of each other and between individuals keenly aware of difference.[21] As boundaries shift eastwards, (geographical and cultural) distinctions between core and peripheries also fade rapidly. If in the course of the last two centuries Europe inscribed itself comfortably in a centre legitimated by a common classical and Christian heritage, it now sees itself embracing the 'other' within the homeland.[22] Geopolitical changes also demand a heightened awareness of Islam's chronological primacy of contact with the Hellenic civilization that the West has placed at the core of its identity.[23]

Zourgos' twenty-first-century perspective finds itself uneasy with both a complacent compliance with the prescriptive voices from the West and the false essentialism that has dominated the imaginary of the Greek nation (especially in its self-presentation to the outside world). Disenfranchised from American and European establishments, dispirited as a classicist, a *xenos* (foreigner) in Greece at home with both 'same' and 'other', an Odysseus who never arrives to stay, Gabriel is an apposite conduit through which Zourgos can exorcize both (European) possessiveness and (neo-Hellenic) insularity, offering us a counter-representation of Greekness. Read against the ongoing debate on Romantic Hellenism, Orientalism and the politics of nation-building, Zourgos' affectionate play on a Greek foundational myth inspires us to rethink East–West conflict and to re-imagine the problematics of the past in the invention of the present. In his reworking, Zourgos unsettles the epic tradition's customary velocity towards success, arrival and belonging,[24] as his hero passes through a myth of national redemption to find ultimate peace only in the reality of his love for Lazarina.

Bibliography

Beaton, Roderick (2013), *Byron's War: Romantic Rebellion, Greek Revolution*. Cambridge: Cambridge University Press.

Beaton, Roderick (2014), 'Re-imagining Greek Antiquity in 1821. Shelley's *Hellas* in its Literary and Political Context' in D. Tziovas (ed.), *Re-imagining the Past: Antiquity and Modern Greek Culture*. Oxford: Oxford University Press.

Byron, George Gordon, Lord (1986), *The Major Works including Don Juan and Childe Harold's Pilgrimage*, edited with an introduction and notes by Jerome McGann. Oxford: Oxford University Press.

Gourgouris, Stathis (1996), *Dream Nation: Enlightenment, Colonization and the Institution of Modern Greece.* Stanford, CA: Stanford University Press.

Koliopoulos, John S. and Thanos M. Veremis (2002), *Greece: The Modern Sequel: From 1821 to the Present.* London: Hurst and Company.

Koundoura, Maria (2004), 'Between Orientalism and Philhellenism: Lady Mary Wortley's Montague's "Real" Greeks', *The Eighteenth-Century; Theory and Interpretation,* 45 (3): 249–264.

Lazos, Christos (1983), *America and Its Role in the Greek War of Independence* [in Greek]. Athens: Papazisis.

Leontis, Artemis (1995), *Topographies of Hellenism: Mapping the Homeland.* Ithaca, NJ and London: Cornell University Press.

Marchand, Suzanne (2009a), 'What the Greek model can, and cannot, do for the modern state: the German perspective', in Roderick Beaton and David Ricks (eds), *The Making of Modern Greece: Nationalism, Romanticism, and the Uses of the Past (1797–1896),* 33–42. Aldershot: Ashgate.

Marchand, Suzanne (2009b), *German Orientalism in the Age of Empire: Religion, Race, and Scholarship.* Cambridge: Cambridge University Press.

Miliori, Margarita (2009), 'Europe, the Classical Polis, and the Greek nation: Philhellenism and Hellenism in nineteenth-century Britain', in Roderick Beaton and David Ricks (eds), *The Making of Modern Greece: Nationalism, Romanticism, and the Uses of the Past (1797–1896),* 65–77. Aldershot: Ashgate.

Most, Glenn (2008), 'Philhellenism, Cosmopolitanism, Nationalism', in Katerina Zacharia (ed.), *Hellenisms: Culture, Identity, and Ethnicity from Antiquity to Modernity,* 151–67. Aldershot: Ashgate.

Tzanelli, Rodanthi (2008), *Nation-building and Identity in Europe: The Dialogics of Reciprocity.* Basingstoke and New York: Palgrave Macmillan.

Van Steen, Gonda (2010), *Liberating Hellenism from the Ottoman Empire: Compte de Marcellus and the Last of the Classics.* New York: Palgrave Macmillan.

Vestraete, Ginette (2010), *Tracking Europe. Mobility, Diaspora, and the Politics of Location.* Durham, NC and London: Duke University Press.

Zourgos, Isidoros (1995), *Φάουστ.* Athens: Nea Sinora, A. A. Livani.

Zourgos, Isidoros (2000), *Η Ψίχα εκείνου του καλοκαιριού.* Athens: Patakis.

Zourgos, Isidoros (2011), *Ανεμώλια.* Athens: Patakis.

Zourgos, Isidoros (2014), *Σκηνές από το βίο του Ματίας Αλμοσίνο.* Athens: Patakis.

13

The 'Poem of Force' in Australia: David Malouf, *Ransom* and Chloe Hooper, *The Tall Man*

Margaret Reynolds

Episode from an Early War

This is a poem by David Malouf which was written in 1970.

> *Episode from an Early War*
> Sometimes, looking back, I find myself, a bookish nine
> year old, still gazing down
> through the wartime criss-cross shock
> -proof glass of my suburban primary school. Blueflint gravel
> ripples in my head, the schoolyard throbs. And all the players
> of rip-shirt rough-and-tumble
> wargames stop, look on in stunned surprise:
> Hector, hero of Troy,
> raw-bloody-boned is dragged across the scene
> and pissed on and defiled,
> while myrmidons of black flies crust his wounds and the angelic
> blunt-faced ones, the lords of mutilation,
> haul off and watch.
>
> My way home
> that Friday, like any other afternoon,
> was the same familiar crossing of three streets, past a shop that sold
> Nigger Chews and Bulls' eyes, the fig-tree gloom
> of Musgrave Park where metho-drinkers slept
> in a buzz and flammable haze, the red-eyed flame-in-foxhole nightmare
> the scraping of a match;
>
> I knew then that the war, our war,
> was real: highways of ash

where ghostly millions rise out of their shoes and go barefoot
nowhere, the children herded into vans
for their journey, or white-walled spick-and-span bath houses suddenly
    trapped
by their craving for breath. At night, fog-bound in mid-Atlantic,
my still sleep was choked
with bodies, blind kittens
in the tub where Mrs Allen did our wash
still jerked at arm's distance, kicking their life out in a sack.

Immaculate, still with starch
my shirts after that
creaked, their collars scratched. Our days were green, matter-of-fact
happy. Only at night
far out in the shipping-lanes
I foundered, white fog thickened in my throat.[1]

Beginning by focussing on what is actually in the poem, the first thing to notice here is the play on 'early' in the title. The 'early war' is both the siege of Troy in the *Iliad* from the early history of mankind, and the fact of Malouf's having lived through a war early in life. So there are two 'episodes' here: Achilles conquering Hector in battle; and Malouf relating that story to his own experience as a nine-year-old living in a city at war. The physicality of the vision of Hector's bloodied body is paralleled by the play on the actuality of a northern Australian town as the flies swarm in 'myrmidons'. I suspect here too that there is a reference to that other great novel about children and war, William Golding's *The Lord of the Flies*.[2]

The ordinary streets of an ordinary town are then transformed by the destruction and despair of war. The park where the down-and-outs – the 'metho-drinkers' – sleep, is the refuge of those broken men who have been displaced by war, dreaming their 'red-eyed flame-in-foxhole nightmare'. But even the small apparatus of a child's life, the sweet treats, the 'Nigger Chews' and 'Bulls' eyes' come to us fraught with double meaning – in the black man's suffering and the target hit.

So the war is here, but it is also elsewhere, in newspapers, in gossip, in headlines and photographs, and in the hidden experience of the men who fought it. In the third stanza the speaker thinks of the Nazi death chambers – 'highways of ash / where ghostly millions rise out of their shoes and go barefoot / nowhere'. And then he thinks of the sinking of the SS *City of Benares* – 'At night, fog-bound in mid-Atlantic, /my still sleep was choked / with bodies'. You will notice that in both cases he – the speaker who recalls being a child – speaks about the fate of these particular child victims of the war, who are equivalent, in his imagined vision, to the 'blind kittens' drowned in a sack.[3]

And so, in the last stanza, the 'nightmare' that should be the preserve of the adults – like the veterans who have become desolated meths drinkers sleeping rough – the nightmare of war comes home to the child: 'Our days were green, matter-of-fact happy. Only at night / far out in the shipping-lanes / I foundered, white fog thickened in my throat'. Finally, I think here too of the presence of laundries: '. . . the children herded into vans / for their journey, or white-walled spick-and-span bath houses suddenly trapped / by their craving for breath.' Or the grave of the 'blind kittens' which is also 'the tub where Mrs Allen did our wash'.

What then does this colour imagery suggest? The 'Blueflint gravel', the 'bloody' corpse, the 'black flies', the 'red-flame' nightmare, the 'green' of ordinary childhood days, as opposed to the 'white-walled bath houses' the 'immaculate' and 'starched' collars, and the 'white fog' that 'thickens in the throat'.

All this is there in the poem. But there is more beyond it and around it, and those dates and times are relevant here. The opening incident of which Malouf speaks – his vision of Hector's abused body – happened in 1943 when he was growing up in Brisbane. This is what Malouf said in September 2009 in a speech delivered at the Australian National University (ANU) at the launch of a new degree in Classical Studies:

> In 1943, to be precise, in Brisbane, a wartime city, where as a nine-year-old, I heard the Troy story for the first time on a rainy Friday afternoon when we were unable to go out in the playground as usual for our period of tunnel-ball, and our teacher, Miss Findlay, read to us instead. I immediately identified Troy, under the threat of imminent fall, with our own sand-bagged and blacked-out city that was waiting then, with the outcome of the war still unknown, for the Japs to arrive, and my own childish fears with the horrors of that earlier war. On several occasions afterwards, those old emotions rose up and haunted me in the shape of poems.[4]

As well as the fact of the war in Australia, Malouf would have had family reasons to feel connected to events in Europe and in the Middle East. His father was Christian Lebanese, his mother was descended from Portuguese Sephardic Jews.

In that 2009 speech Malouf goes on to speak about *Ransom* which was published in that year, and of how it took:

> . . . more than 60 years for those anxieties and questions – about force, about war, about the fate of ordinary men and women in war, about what in the midst of such horrors is to be grasped as enduringly human, to find its shape as a piece of fiction.

But he had already written this poem in 1970. And in 1970 Australia was again at war – for this was the time of Vietnam. And here I find that my own experience, as a child growing up in a country at war, very clearly overlaps with his.

Australia was never threatened with invasion during the Vietnam conflict, though Prime Minister Harold Holt's 'All the way with LBJ' propaganda convinced many Australians that it was, and I can well see why this period of the war in Vietnam might have taken Malouf back to those childhood memories of the earlier war.[5]

When I was a child April the 25th, ANZAC Day (Australian and New Zealand Auxiliary Corps), was a very big deal, and the parade of veterans from both the Second and the First World Wars was long and sad. We all heard again the story of the landings at Gallipoli, we all knew about Simpson and his donkey,[6] and we all recited 'At the going down of the sun, and in the morning, we will remember them'. But in the 1960s there were suddenly young men in that parade. Young men who were blind, boys with limbs blown off, names that were read out because their owners were not there. And the reason for this was conscription.

During the First World War Australia twice rejected by plebiscite the introduction of conscription. During the Second World War it was brought in, but only for postings in Australia. In 1964, National Service was introduced in Australia. Each month, the names of those young men who had reached their twentieth birthday were entered in a lottery and those that were selected were required to do two years' military service, including overseas, followed by three years in the reserve.[7] A small group of Australian women formed an organization called 'SOS' – 'Save Our Sons'.[8] One blisteringly hot day as my cousins and I ran under the sprinkler I heard my mother arguing vehemently with my aunt who held her new baby – a boy – on her knee. 'Yes, of course', she said, 'of course I would send Robbie.'

I should add that this same dear aunt was later to feel very differently, and ended up being part of the immensely important protest that took place in November 1983 when a group led by Aboriginal women breached the security at Pine Gap, a secret joint Australian and US military tracking station in the Northern Territory.[9] But at the time my mother and father felt so strongly about the war, and found themselves so isolated, that they packed up their own four children and came to live in England.

The area around Pine Gap is now the only place in Australia designated 'prohibited' land and air space. It has again been the centre of many protests since the beginning of the war in Afghanistan. There was, and is, little appetite for that war in Australia. On 3 July 2012 the then Prime Minister Julia Gillard made another speech: 'Our nation once again has to absorb the news of a loss in Afghanistan. We have lost another brave Australian soldier.' She also then announced that Australia would be bringing forward their date for withdrawal from the end of 2014 to the end of 2013. Under her successor Prime Minister Tony Abbott this promise was carried out, and the last Australian troops finally left Afghanistan on 16 December 2013.

I do not know, but I suspect that this is why David Malouf was reminded of his own self in 1943, his own self in 1970, and why he went back sixty years in time to re-visit war and the *Iliad* in 2009, in a reworking of crucial scenes from the final, twenty-fourth book of Homer's poem.

Ransom

Taking his starting point from that image of Hector's torn and bloodied body in his earlier poem, David Malouf's *Ransom* begins with Achilles, still angry, still grieving the death of Patroclus and clinging to his revenge on Hector. Each day Achilles goes to the spot where he has thrown Hector's body, and each day it is renewed. Hector lies 'as if sleeping', like 'a young bridegroom newly refreshed': 'No need to get down. He can see from where he stands that all is as it was yesterday, and the day before, as it has been each day since the beginning. The gods continue to defy him.'[10] So, yet again, Achilles lashes the corpse to his axle of his chariot and drives furiously across the plain: 'He was waiting for the rage to fill him that would be equal at last to the outrage he was committing.'[11]

The second section focuses on Priam, who decides to break with kingly tradition and go, in plain robes and in an ordinary cart, and ask for his son's body. Hecuba objects, but Priam is firm:

> 'The fact that it has never been done, that it is novel, unthinkable – except that *I* have thought of it – is just what makes me believe it should be attempted. It is possible because it is not possible. And because it is simple. Why do we think always that the simple thing is beneath us? Because we are kings? What I do is what any man might do.'[12]

Priam remembers his own rescue, the 'ransoming' by his sister which gives him his name – 'Priam', 'the price paid'. As a child named 'Podarces' he may have been the prince, but he had hidden among all the other displaced children, ordinary children, as his father's palace was sacked: 'I am just one more slave-thing like the rest, one among many. I look at my blackened hands and feet, the rags I am dressed in, and know that I have no more weight in the world than the droppings of the lowest beggar or street-sweeper.'[13] Because of this, Priam knows, 'What it means for your breath to be in another's mouth, to be one of those who have no story that will ever be told'.[14]

A carrier is summoned with his cart and his mules from the marketplace. He is re-named 'Idaeus', the king's herald. He says 'very well':

> But in fact it is not 'very well' with him, not at all. His name is Somax. It fits him ... It guarantees the breath that passes in and out of his mouth ... Something about the life he has lived all these years, the hardships, the losses he has suffered, and the way he has forced himself to go on and endure, is being set aside and made light of. That is what he feels.[15]

When Priam appears in Achilles' tent, the hero, for one moment, mistakes the old man for his own father: 'The man is clearly not his father, but for half a hundred beats of his heart his father had been truly present to him, and he continues now to feel tenderly vulnerable to all those emotions in him that belong to the sacred bond.' Priam appeals to Achilles: 'We are mortals, not gods. We die. Death is in our nature. Without that fee paid in advance, the world does not come to us. That is the hard bargain life makes with us – with all of us, every one – and the condition we share. And for that reason, if for no other, we should have pity for one another's losses.'[16]

Achilles gives over Hector's body to the laundry where it will receive his 'last commerce with the world in the hands of women', and then returns it to his father, Priam. They both know the gods' 'dark joke', obscured, but there in the future. Achilles will die. Priam will die at the hands of Achilles' son. But meanwhile Priam returns to Troy. Priam has 'done something for which he will be remembered for as long as such stories are told'. And for Somax, the ordinary man: 'Later – when Troy has become just another long, windswept hilltop, its towers reduced to rubble, its citizens scattered or carried off ... into exile and slavery – all he has to tell ... will have become the stuff of legend, half folktale, half an old man's empty bragging.'[17]

The Poem of Force

Not all of this story comes from the *Iliad*. Malouf takes some details and hints from Homer, borrows from other sources – notably Virgil – and adds a great deal of his own. But attention needs to be paid to some of Malouf's key themes and images: the emphasis upon the common man and the shared experience of human beings; the question of naming; the reduction of individual men and women – through slavery, through neglect or through violence – to the status of an object or a thing; and the dreadful contract that Malouf sees here between powerful subject and debased object, where each, in spite of appearances, is as compromised as the other.

In Malouf's novel this last observation is most powerfully expressed in the key death encounter between Achilles and Hector. Hector, crucially, is wearing Achilles' armour, stripped from the body of the dead Patroclus. So Achilles, in effect, does battle with a reflection of himself. And when Hector is dead, Achilles slices the tendons of his ankles – Hector's Achilles heels – in order to use the sinews to tie his degraded body to the axle (see Homer, *Iliad* 22.395–398). The two heroes are each other's mirror image.

Which takes me to Simone Weil's famous 1940 meditation on Homer, 'The *Iliad*: or The Poem of Force'. Her essay begins:

> The true hero, the true subject, the centre of the *Iliad* is force. Force employed by man, force that enslaves man, force before which man's flesh shrinks away . . . For those dreamers who considered that force, thanks to progress, would soon be a thing of the past, the *Iliad* could appear as an historical document; for others, whose powers of recognition are more acute, and who perceive force, today as yesterday, as at the very centre of human history, the *Iliad* is the purest and the loveliest of mirrors.[18]

David Malouf recognizes the influence. In that speech for the ANU in 2009 he quotes this passage from Weil's essay and he notes the time coincidence that links her essay, his poem 'Episode from an Early War' and his novel: '*Ransom* begins, oddly enough, at pretty much the same time that Simone Weil was writing her great essay, in the midst of war. In 1943, to be precise . . .'[19]

A close reading of Weil's essay alongside Malouf's fiction suggests how much he owes to her. At the beginning of the essay Weil defines what she means by 'force' or violence, essentially the prerogative of power used by the strong against the weak:

> To define force – it is that *x* that turns anybody who is subjected to it into a *thing*. Exercised to the limit, it turns man into a thing in the most literal sense: it makes a corpse out of him. Somebody was here, and the next minute there is nobody here at all; this is a spectacle the *Iliad* never wearies of showing us . . . The hero becomes a *thing* dragged behind a chariot in the dust.[20]

This is very much where Malouf's vision begins, just as Weil's vision begins here. But over the page Weil invokes the picture of Andromache calling her maids to prepare a bath for their lord even at the very moment of his murder: 'Nearly all the *Iliad* takes place far from hot baths. Nearly all of human life, then and now, takes place far from hot baths.'[21] Which suggests to me both Malouf's image of the feminine world of the laundry in *Ransom,* and its two ghastly killing doubles – the 'bath-house' gas chambers of the Nazi concentration camps and the washtub grave of the kittens – in his poem 'Episode from an Early War'.

But Weil takes the travesty of becoming a 'thing' beyond the materiality of death even into the living:

> From its first property . . . flows another quite prodigious too in its own way, the ability to turn a human being into a thing while he is still alive . . . Who can say what it costs it, moment by moment, to accommodate itself to this residence; how much writhing and bending, folding and pleating are required of it? It was not made to live inside a thing; if it does so, under pressure of necessity, there is not a single element of its nature to which violence is not done.[22]

This too is there in *Ransom*, in the easy taking over of Somax's cart, his day, his life, his name. And it is the shadow at the edges of Malouf's story, as it is in Homer, in the ending which we all know, where the city lies in ruins, the dead are unburied, and the women are driven into exile and slavery. As Weil says, 'Fidelity to his city and his dead is not the slave's privilege'.[23]

But, according to Weil, it is not just the enslaved and degraded object that suffers. So too does the powerful subject: 'Force is as pitiless to the man who possesses it, or thinks he does, as it is to its victims; the second it crushes, the first it intoxicates. The truth is, nobody really possesses it.'[24] And Weil sees also how violence can become its own end, that breaking the cycle of violence and despair is as equally impossible on either side:

> To be outside a situation so violent as this is to find it inconceivable, to be inside it is to be unable to conceive its end. Consequently, nobody does anything to bring this end about. In the presence of an armed enemy, what hand can relinquish its weapon? The mind ought to find a way out, but the mind has lost all capacity to so much as look outward. The mind is completely absorbed in doing itself violence. Always in human life, whether war or slavery is in question, intolerable sufferings continue, as it were, by the force of their own specific gravity, and so look to the outsider as if they were easy to bear, actually, they continue because they have deprived the sufferer of the resources which might serve to extricate him.[25]

For Weil, one of the essential characteristics of the *Iliad* is its 'incurable bitterness'. She says that it is often only there in 'a mere stroke of the verse, or a run-on line'.

In one phrase used to describe Hector, by his widow Andromache in her last dirge for him (*Iliad* 24.730), 'guardian of chaste wives and little children', is encapsulated its terrible opposite, the mirror reversal where we see rape, mutilation and murder – 'chastity appears, dirtied by force, and childhood, delivered to the sword'. Just as the nine-year-old Malouf was left hanging in 1943, without the end of the story of Troy, and without the end of the war he was living, so he leaves his characters in *Ransom* with that same 'incurable bitterness', the bitterness of no resolution.[26]

Malouf takes issue with Weil in his 2009 speech and finds in the *Iliad* not just 'force' but courtesy, tenderness and 'largeness of spirit' in the 'all encompassing sympathy' with which Homer treats both sides. In his novel, this is the mood that we are left with. That generosity, and the telling of the story by the ordinary man – even if nobody hears: 'His listeners do not believe him, of course. He is a known liar. He is a hundred years old and drinks too much.'[27]

But Malouf slightly skips over one of the key observations of Weil's essay: 'The whole of the *Iliad* lies under the shadow of the greatest calamity the human race can experience – the destruction of a city.'[28] Of course Weil does not just mean a city. For 'city', read race, civilization, culture, religion, community, learning, way of thinking, way of living, way of dying, nationality and identity. She may be speaking about Troy, but she meant so much more. It comes out in an odd coda at the end of the essay where she remarks that:

> Both the Romans and the Hebrews believed themselves to be exempt from the misery that is the common human lot. The Romans saw their country as the nation chosen by destiny to be the mistress of the world; with the Hebrews it was their God who exalted them and they retained their superior position just as long as they obeyed Him.[29]

No one reading her essay in 1940 or in the years thereafter could ignore the implications or the relevance of her remarks to the Shoah and the war she had just witnessed. If, in his novel, Malouf chooses to favour the generosity that connects human beings, rather than the violent oppositions that divide them, then in his poem 'Episode from an Early War' he acknowledges the darker side that Weil also sees:

> highways of ash
> where ghostly millions rise out of their shoes and go barefoot
> nowhere, the children herded into vans
> for their journey, or white-walled spick-and-span bath houses suddenly trapped
> by their craving for breath.

In fact, genocide is also there in Malouf's *Ransom.* It is just not altogether obvious. And, for Australians, genocide is a very difficult topic.

Malouf did something similarly obscure – actually writing about Australia when he appeared to be writing about the classical past – in his 1978 novella *An Imaginary Life.*[30] That book took the form of a 'lost letter' from the Roman poet Ovid, writing to the future from his place of exile among the natives of Tomis. Many Australians then puzzled at an Australian writer taking up an 'irrelevant' classical subject. But, as Malouf said in 2009, *An Imaginary Life:*

> . . . took up the then unknown post-colonial question, as it was later called, of the relationship between the centre and the edge, the metropolitan world and the distant offshoot of that world that is the metropolitan world reconfigured and translated – a very Australian question, of course.[31]

He does not say that this novel also includes a vexed relationship between Ovid, the 'civilized' poet in exile at the edge of the world, and a wild native boy, apparently without language, without culture, who has been brought up by wolves. Also, as it happens, 'a very Australian question'.

I have argued that it seems to me that the pressure of the Vietnam War was one reason for Malouf writing 'Episode from an Early War'. But across the same period, from 1966 to 1975 came the final dismantling of the so-called 'White Australia' policy.[32] This culminated in 1975 with the Racial Discrimination Act, which made racially based selection criteria for immigration to Australia illegal. This legislation relaxed the rules for 'coloured' immigrants, including, of course ironically, those coming from Asia and Vietnam. But this new legislation also raised a spectre which was closer to home and one which was still stalking Australia: the question of the fate of its indigenous people.

From the time of the Federation of the Australian states in 1901, right up until 1967, the Commonwealth Constitution Act, Section 127, dealt with the Census and stated that: 'in reckoning the numbers of the people of the Commonwealth . . . aboriginal natives shall not be counted.' After a referendum in 1967 Australian natives, aboriginals, indigenous peoples, and Torres Strait Islanders were officially included in the census – as people, human beings, ordinary folk, as opposed to racial curiosities.[33]

Across the ensuing years there was a lot of protest, a lot of consciousness raising, and quite a bit of legislation. Finally, on 13 February 2008 the then Prime Minister Kevin Rudd delivered a formal apology to the indigenous peoples and to the so-called 'Stolen Generations'.[34] In 2009 David Malouf published *Ransom.*

At the beginning of 2008 Chloe Hooper published *The Tall Man: Death and Life on Palm Island.*

The Tall Man

The Tall Man: Death and Life on Palm Island makes only one brief mention of the *Iliad* even though it is steeped in ancient myth. The closest it comes in any technical sense to ancient Greek myth is in the fact that one of the string of many small islands off the coast of Queensland of which Palm Island is a part, is called – Orpheus.

Nevertheless, I am offering this text as one of those 'reflections' of the *Iliad* that Simone Weil speaks of: 'For those . . . who perceive force, today as yesterday, at the very centre of human history, the *Iliad* is the very purest and loveliest of mirrors'.

I first came across the story of these events when I was living in Australia towards the end of 2006. I had read Chloe Hooper's first novel, *A Child's Book of True Crime,* when it was shortlisted while I was a judge for the Orange Prize in 2003 – and I was pleased to find an essay by her in a collection of *The Best Australian Essays 2006.*

The essay was not happy reading. At the end, Hooper wrote: 'It's too much. I want to leave. All I want to do is get on a plane and leave. And when I do, I feel myself shaking. I get home and I'm still shaking days later. It's overwhelming: the relief of being able to walk away from this, of this not being my life.'[35]

In the event, of course, it was to go on being her life. As it has become part of mine, part of every Australian's life.

On Friday 19 November 2004 shortly after 10.00 in the morning Cameron Doomadgee was arrested in the street on Palm Island in Queensland and taken to the police station. At 11.22 Senior Sergeant Chris Hurley called an ambulance. The surveillance camera in his cell showed Doomadgee – as Chloe Hooper puts it in her original essay – 'writhing on a concrete floor, trying to find a comfortable position in which to die'.[36]

Doomadgee had been arrested because he was said to have insulted the police. On the morning of 19 November he had been drinking homemade cask wine and 'groom' – methylated spirits mixed with water – and he happened to walk by as Hurley and Lloyd Bengaroo, an Aboriginal Police Liaison Officer, were arresting Patrick Nugent, another drunken man: '. . . you black like me', said Doomadgee to Bengaroo as he passed by this scene, 'Why can't you help the blacks?'[37] Hurley arrested Doomadgee as well, 'for public nuisance' and put both men in the back of the police van.

At the police station, Hurley says that Doomadgee tripped over a step and sustained his fatal injuries in this way. Forensic examination showed that when Doomadgee died he had a black eye, four broken ribs, and his liver was cleaved in two. Patrick Nugent and Roy Bramwell, both present then at the police station, say that Doomadgee struggled with Hurley as he was removed from the van. That Doomadgee hit Hurley and that Hurley punched him back. That the two flailing men both fell over the step and lay side by side. That Hurley then raised himself up, knelt on the Aborigine's chest, and beat Doomadgee: '... he tall, he tall, he tall, you know ... just see the elbow going up and him down like that ...,' said Roy Bramwell.[38]

All the long tortuous investigations that followed – the inquests, the adjournments, the refusal to bring charges, the eventual decision to bring charges, the trial and the acquittal – are minutely documented in Hooper's *The Tall Man*. It is not over yet. Hurley still works as a police officer on Queensland's Gold Coast. In 2011 he was ordered to pay back some of the state compensation awarded to him for the damage done to his house in the riots that followed Cameron Doomadgee's death. Other claims are still outstanding.

In David Malouf's *Ransom*, Achilles considers that, 'War should be practised swiftly, decisively. Thirty days at most ...'. This distinctively Australian war has been going on for more than two hundred years. But the devastating effects are the same. On Palm Island, every one of the four faces of the clock tower is smashed. Naked children play in the dirt amid graffiti and empty beer cans. In 1999 the *Guinness Book of Records* named Palm Island the most violent place on earth outside a war zone. Average life expectancy for the island's 3,500 inhabitants is fifty years.

But there are other parallels too. Just as Somax in Malouf's novel resents his name being taken away, so Doomadgee's sister Elizabeth wants her brother to be referred to as *Moordinyi*. This is a word used in Gulf languages to denote the dead, in order to avoid calling them back by naming their name. The authorities at first refused. But under pressure, as the case went on, it was agreed that Doomadgee's tribal name of 'Mulrunji' would be used.

But Mulrunji and all like him have been reduced by force, as Simone Weil says, to the status of a thing, even in life. And, as such, their lives are irrevocably transformed, deformed, defaced and mutilated. Remember Weil's observation, clearly applicable here:

> Who can say what it costs moment by moment, to accommodate itself to this residence; how much writhing and bending, folding and pleating are required of it? It was not made to live inside a thing; if it does so, under pressure of necessity, there is not a single element of its nature to which violence is not done.[39]

Remember too Weil's conclusions about power: 'Force is as pitiless to the man who possesses it, or thinks he does, as it is to its victims.' This is what Chloe Hooper says: 'Can you step into this dysfunction and desperation and not be corrupted in some way? In a community of extreme violence, are you, too, forced to be violent? If you are despised, as the police are, might you not feel the need to be despicable sometimes?'[40]

At the end of the story of Troy, at the end of Malouf's *Ransom*, the women and children are taken away to slavery and exile; that is where the story of Palm Island begins. It was originally a convenient dumping ground, a holding settlement for natives who were unwanted by their local white communities. 'This was an island', writes Chloe Hooper, 'of stolen children'. She goes on:

> Across Australia, it is estimated, between one in three and one in ten Aboriginal children were forcibly removed from their families in the period 1910–1970 and transported to distant missions, orphanages or foster families ... They were often told that their parents had died, and they were given new names. One Palm Island woman, Bethel Smallwood, told me that her mother was haunted all her life by not being able to remember her own mother's appearance. She could picture her outline, but could never give her a face.[41]

All these children: David Malouf's nine-year-old self in a country at war; Podarces enslaved, ransomed and renamed as Priam; Bethel Smallwood's mother who cannot remember her mother's face. Cameron Doomadgee's own son, Eric, was fifteen when his father died in 2004. He was found hanged in 2006.

As Weil says, 'To be outside a situation as violent as this is to find it inconceivable, to be inside it is to be unable to conceive its end'. This too is part of the 'incurable bitterness' that is in the *Iliad* and all its later versions, including the story of Palm Island.

In his ANU speech David Malouf said:

> It has always seemed astonishing to me that the *Iliad*, standing as it does at the very beginning, twenty seven centuries ago, of our literary culture, should remain after all that time perhaps the greatest single work our culture has produced. Readers at every point since then have found something in it that speaks powerfully to their human concerns and anxieties, and directly to their feelings.[42]

It may be that the very saddest part of this story is that we have lost so many stories. The one hopeful thing is that Chloe Hooper has told a story that would otherwise have been lost: 'Cameron Doomadgee's sister Valmai said [to Hooper] "We're human". I am struck by how often I've been told that by Palm Islanders: *We are human too*.' Hooper has given Mulrunji an epithet, an epitaph, a proper name. But because of this peculiar collision of cultures over the last two hundred years, the world has lost something that it will now never know.

Describing the 'song lines or Dreaming tracks' of ancient Aboriginal culture, Hooper says: 'In the old days, when the Gulf Aborigines travelled, they remembered the layout of the land from song cycles about the Dreaming ancestors. This was akin to knowing the *Iliad* and the *Odyssey* by heart and then using that knowledge to make the land intelligible.'[43]

Later on in the book, waiting to witness one of Hurley's many trials, Hooper attended an evening prayer meeting on Palm Island:

> Outside the hall, the Gulf country's night sky was jammed with stars, the darkness vibrating. In 1850, up to a hundred Aboriginal languages were spoken across Queensland alone; now, around the nation, less than twenty are in good health. It is one of Australia's great tragedies that most of the song cycles about these stars have been lost since Europeans came. The songs contained knowledge about the Dreamtime, about the ancestral heroes' endeavours and epic travels – and therefore about Shooting Star Dreaming, Dingo Dreaming, Black Cockatoo Dreaming, Flying Fox Dreaming, Wind Dreaming, Hail Dreaming, Fog Dreaming, Sugarbag (wild honey) Dreaming, and Shark, Dugong, Louse, Moon, Water Lily, Barramundi, Wave, Mosquito, Kangaroo Dreaming – on and on. Song lines and ritual song cycles of phenomenal complication. There were songs to make people better, songs to make them sick, songs to sing to babies so as to 'make him good fella, strong fella', songs for crows to come and eat all the camp's scraps, songs about unrequited love, love magic songs, songs of the obscene, songs about fighting, songs for country, songs for hunting, songs for the dead, songs for mourning, songs for widows so that they might be set free, songs to change the weather, songs to make you move from one place to another 'ever more quickly' – epic songs with hundreds of verses that took all night to sing.[44]

The *Iliad* comes down to us from a long ago past, from an oral tradition, from a culture that is gone, from a way of life that has vanished. But through chance, and through scholarship, because of fashion, or the treasuring of specific cultural values, the *Iliad* speaks to us still, makes us still. So Weil can call the *Iliad* the 'loveliest of mirrors', helping us to understand and interpret force, violence, suffering and conflict into the twentieth century and beyond.

But we will never know the lost *Iliads* of Australia.

Bibliography

Golding, William (1954), *The Lord of the Flies*. London: Faber and Faber.

Hooper, Chloe (2006), 'The Tall Man', in *Monthly* (March 2006) and in Drusilla Modjeska (ed.), *The Best Australian Essays 2006,* 111–137. Melbourne: Black Inc.

Hooper, Chloe (2010 [2008]), *The Tall Man: Death and Life on Palm Island*. London: Vintage Books, first published by Penguin Books, Australia on 1 January 2008. In the US it was published by Simon & Schuster Inc. as *Tall Man: The Death of Doomadgee.*

Malouf, David (1974), *Neighbours in a Thicket: Poems*. St Lucia, Queensland: University of Queensland Press.

Malouf, David (1978), *An Imaginary Life*. London: Chatto and Windus.

Malouf, David (2009a), 'The Classics Today', speech at the official launch of the new ANU Bachelor of Classical Studies and the Classics Endowment at the Australian National University in Canberra, 11 September 2009: www.anu.edu.au › ANU Podcasts › Public Lecture.

Malouf, David (2009b), *Ransom*. London: Vintage.

Weil, Simone (2005 [1940]), 'The *Iliad:* or, the Poem of Force', *New York Review of Books.*

Willard, Myra (1967), *History of the White Australia Policy to 1920*. Routledge: London.

14

Young Female Heroes from Sophocles to the Twenty-First Century

Helen Eastman

In a third-millennial development, a new kind of hero, with a feminist as well as a social agenda, has emerged from the intersection of Greek mythical archetypes and fiction writing: the teenaged female, fighting for both her family (in particular, on behalf of siblings) and the moral heart of her civilization. However far we may believe we are on the path to gender equality, there is still something potent and unsettling in the image of the young female hero. Early myth cultures can provide us with some archetypes for female warriors, particularly hunters,[1] but later periods in the literary canon often lack pro-active female archetypes altogether, let alone fighters. Perhaps, therefore, it is inevitable that contemporary fiction writers should find themselves looking as far back as ancient Greece for progenitors of the rebellious teenage heroine.

This chapter compares the literary modelling of Nizam, the young Pashtun 'Antigone' figure in the Indian writer Joydeep Roy-Bhattacharya's 2012 novel *The Watch*, who is determined to bury her brother, with the figure of Katniss Everdeen in Suzanne Collins' *The Hunger Games* trilogy.[2] Katniss' struggle begins when she takes part in the lethal Hunger Games in place of her vulnerable younger sister, Prim. Both novels place an archetypal Antigone figure in a dystopic, conflict-ridden world. Roy-Bhattacharya's novel is set in contemporary Afghanistan and Collins' in the fictional post-apocalyptic land of Panem. However, as I will go on to discuss, the two novels function as acts of classical reception in radically different ways and for different audiences; while Roy-Bhattacharya's novel is primarily aimed at adults, Collins' novel started as a work for teenagers (though its reach has now far transcended the 'YA fiction' literary sub-genre).

In this chapter I ask how these novelists – one male, one female, one South-East Asian, one North American – use teen heroines to question patriarchy, the exclusion of many young adults from political agency, and the responsibility of the individual in a community to whose laws she has not given her assent. I explore how the resonance of classical mythology, in dialogue with recent feminist theory, helps the writers to add gravitas to the rebellious young women's plight and, in particular, explore the corporeality of female as opposed to male protest and to create 'feminine' as well as 'feminist' mythology of weaponry and violence.

Sophocles' *Antigone* has been prolifically produced and adapted throughout the twentieth and twenty-first centuries,[3] and transplanted to countless latter cultures and conflicts; Antigone has spoken out, on behalf of her unburied brother, in the context of the Irish troubles, Indian imperialism, Polish military law, and South African apartheid, and covered his dead body amidst countless geographical landscapes.[4] *The Watch* is explicitly labelled and marketed as a contemporary retelling of the *Antigone* story, transplanted to Afghanistan, and thus self-consciously places itself within the reception history of Sophocles' play. There are linguistic echoes throughout of Sophocles' original text: for example, Nizam's triplet of fears, that she will be left 'unmourned, unwept and unburied' (25), recalls Antigone's lament that she will remain 'ἄκλαυτος, ἄφιλος, ἀνυμέναιος' (876) (literally, 'unlamented, without friends, unmarried'). For the general reader, who may be unfamiliar with *Antigone*, Roy-Bhattacharya makes the relationship explicit from the outset. He uses an extract, in Greek, from the Sophocles play as a prologue to the novel and titles the first chapter not with the name of his character, Nizam, but with the name 'Antigone', her literary progenitor.

In this first chapter, written from Nizam's perspective, we see a young Pashtun woman arrive at a US military outpost and demand her brother's body for burial: 'I am here to bury my brother according to the tenets of my faith. That is all there is to it.' She describes what she must do:

> I will ask you for water to wash him, as is my right. I will dig the grave and place him in it, with his body facing the qibla. Then I will say a prayer, pour three handfuls of soil over him and recite: 'We created you from it, and return you into it, and from it we will raise you a second time.' After that I will leave, I promise. Do not deny me this duty that I must perform.[5]

The US soldiers believe her brother was not a Pashtun hero but rather a Talib terrorist and refuse to hand over the body. She refuses to leave. The ensuing debate echoes the fundamental conflicts at the heart of Sophocles' play; the soldiers are affronted not only by Nizam's individual act of rebellion against their authority but by her gender, retorting 'You are a woman. You have no role in Muslim burial' and 'This is a battleground. It isn't a place for women's hysterics'. She observes: 'Clearly I am a dilemma for them. I am a woman in their man's world, and they do not know how to proceed.' The essays in Mee and Foley (2011a) point out that receptions of Sophocles' *Antigone* sometimes emphasize her gender, focusing on the fact a woman is rebelling in a patriarchal society, and sometimes focus on her as an individual rebelling against a state, downplaying her gender but emphasizing her singularity.[6] Roy-Bhattacharya's scenario harnesses both.

Furthermore, *The Watch* engages with *Antigone*'s debate between religious and civic duty, where burial is not just a political act, but a religious one; Antigone is prepared to be perceived as wrong in the eyes of humans if she is right in the eyes of the gods. Nizam is immovable in her belief that her religious duty to bury her brother, and the ties of family, transcend all other loyalties; she repeats that she has a 'religious duty', frequently asserts her 'right' and reiterates that a corpse belongs 'only to God'; the Americans claim that duty to the State must override religious duty:

> And I have a duty to the state, the Amrikâyi says, which is also your state, by the way. I have a duty to abide by the rule of law, which are now your rules. Without laws, we'd be back to your tribal anarchy.[7]

In this quotation Roy-Bhattacharya identifies the cultural superiority assumed by the Americans in the novel; they perceive their society, governed by 'rules' as a progression from Nizam's 'tribal' society. Like Creon, they are inflexibly holding on to rules to try and preserve a fragile peace.

The literal debate at the heart of Sophocles' play, whether to bury a corpse, feels terrifyingly pertinent. As Blake Morrison put it, when translating *Antigone* for the stage in 2003:[8]

> No age is more fixated with corpses than the present; no age more preoccupied with the dignities and indignities of their disposal . . .
>
> Article 17 of the Geneva conventions in respect of the war dead states that they should be 'honourably interred', according to their religion . . . It's not clear that such standards were met in Iraq in 2003. The ethos of Creon – that the enemy, deserving no better, be left to jackals and vultures (including the jackals and vultures of the media) – is hard to dislodge.[9]

In *The Watch*, one of the reasons for not burying the body is the Americans' intention to display it as propaganda. This is an additional element to contemporary warfare, its global coverage through traditional and social media, and the battles played out in that arena will become an even more pervasive theme in Collins' work.

Roy-Bhattacharya explains in an interview, published on his own website, that he had decided to write about the Afghan war, then decided to use *Antigone* as a vehicle to do so.[10] Giving his reasons, he cites not only his fascination with the original play, and desire to create a strong female protagonist within the 'misogynistic Pashtun culture', but also the importance of using *Antigone* as a bait to draw in the Western reader, harnessing Sophocles' canonical play to bring readers to Roy-Bhattacharya's non-Western contemporary novel; clearly he feels that the classical association gives a gravitas to his novel and demands attention from a literary readership in the way a wholly original novel about the Afghan war might not. Furthermore, he explains his desire to place the play in a 'non-Western' context as partly to counter 'the partial use of classical Greek mythology to justify Western prejudices'. He gives examples of 'racist' use of the classics to present 'West' as good and 'East' as bad.[11] Roy-Bhattacharya's act of classical reception is therefore a political as well as artistic statement.

It is worth noting that Roy-Bhattacharya's claim in this interview to be placing *Antigone* 'for the first time, in a non-Western context' isn't true. There have been productions in the West which have set the play in non-Western cultures and, perhaps more importantly, there have been productions around the world which have actually been produced outside of the Western tradition, aesthetically and geographically (the production in Manipur, discussed in Mee (2011), would be an excellent example).[12] Recent classical reception scholarship has been acutely aware of the historic use of Classics to assert Western values, and has charted the reclamation of classical texts by postcolonial and non-Western cultures in volumes including Emily Greenwood's *Afro-Greeks* (2010) and *Classics in Post-Colonial Worlds*, edited by Lorna Hardwick and Carol Gillespie (2007); thus Roy-Bhattacharya's claim to be initiating this reclamation may seem naïve if passionate.

One of the problems with Roy-Bhattacharya's novel is, in fact, that it has not escaped the dominance of Western viewpoint. First, rather than locating the action within the civil conflict in Afghanistan, Roy-Bhattacharya makes the axis of his novel a Pashtun women versus Western, American, soldiers. In Sophocles' play, it is crucial that Creon and Antigone are related and that Antigone is making a stand against her own family and community, as represented by the chorus of elders. Sophocles' *Antigone* is unusual amongst Greek tragedy in that there are no foreign characters in it, no 'other'. It is a civil conflict, taking place within one insular community.[13] Where Roy-Bhattacharya might have had an opportunity to use *Antigone* as a vehicle for exploring a single, young woman's resistance against the patriarchy of her own Pashtun community, he has, instead, made it a cross-cultural East–West conflict.

Second, the novel is structurally dominated by an exploration of the internal psyche of the US soldiers. The novel is in eight chapters, each written from the perspective of a different character.[14] Thus, once we move past the first chapter, we lose our female protagonist's voice for the rest of the novel and the remainder of the text is from a variety of male, predominantly Western, perspectives. Ismene, Antigone's sister, is recast as a male, albeit gay, translator.[15] There is no Eurydice character. Having asserted that he wanted to create a female and feminist protagonist, Roy-Bhattacharya effectively silences her with his structure and devotes seven-eighths of the novel to male voices.[16] There is perhaps an argument that this male perspective on Antigone's actions may, to some extent, bring us closer to the true nature of the original, which was, after all, written, performed and watched by men.[17] One way of understanding why Greek tragedy is populated with strong, rebellious women, is to see it as an arena in which men explored their worst imaginings of what would happen if the women in their society were not repressed. If we regard Sophocles' work as a male imagining, for other men, of what might happen if a young woman flouted societal norms and rebelled against the patriarchy, Roy-Bhattacharya's novel may share more with its source than is initially apparent; what it doesn't do is give equal space to a female or non-Western voice.

As the novel progresses, the text contains increasingly overt meta-textual references to the source text. Roy-Bhattacharya uses the device that one of the US soldiers, Nick Frobenius, who was formerly a Classics major and met his wife at college while rehearsing a Sophocles' play.[18] This allows the original text to be quoted in flashbacks. The army 'medic' character also recalls seeing Irene Papas play Antigone on screen.[19] Frobenius has a copy of Sophocles with him amongst his few possessions, which he has passed on. Roy-Bhattacharya's overt citing of the original feels like one of the least successful features of the novel, a narrative device unsubtly introduced to allow *Antigone* to be directly referenced. Kamila Shamsie, reviewing in the *Guardian* (15 June 2012), is typical of reviewers in feeling that the opening chapter, in Nizam's voice, was let down by the direction the rest of the novel took: 'The movement away from a story that embodies Greek tragedy to one that invokes it dissipates some of the emotional power of the novel.'

By comparison, Collins' *Hunger Games* trilogy of novels, all written in the first person from the perspective of Katniss Everdeen, offer a more sustained exploration of the inner life of the female teenage rebel who is pitting herself against an unjust society. Collins' text has a less overt relationship with its classical sources, though she has been explicit in interviews about the two primary classical sources that inspired her: first, the ancient Greek Theseus/ Minotaur myth, particularly the detail of the selection of two Athenian child 'tributes' to be fed to the Minotaur every nine years to remind the Athenians of their subjugation; and second, the phenomenon of the Roman gladiatorial games. Collins fuses these two ideas into the 'Hunger Games', where two children from each crushed district of Panem, in penance for an attempted uprising, are chosen by lottery each year and made to fight to the death in a constructed 'gladiatorial' arena for the entertainment of the masses.[20] 'Panem', the name for the post-apocalyptic society in which the novel is set, is taken from Juvenal's phrase '*panem et circenses*' ('bread and circuses') (10.81), where he observes that the elite control the masses by providing them with food and trivial entertainment to distract them from political engagement. The Roman Empire is continuously referenced: the elite capital of Panem is named after the Roman 'Capitol' and the inhabitants have significant Greek and Roman names (examples include Plutarch, Cato, Octavia, Fulvia, Brutus, Cinna, Castor, Pollux); terms are borrowed from Latin (such as 'tesserae') or created from classical stems (for example the 'avox' are servants who have had their tongues cut out, the term created from the a- negative and 'vox'); many of the features of the Hunger Games are reminiscent of the gladiatorial games, including the chariots, processions and some weaponry.

Sophie Mills' recent article 'Classical Elements and Mythological Archetypes in *The Hunger Games*'[21] looks in detail at how these two key classical sources manifest in the first book of the trilogy, charting the many parallels, and there is not space (or need) to duplicate that analysis here. However, it is worth commenting on an important effect of Collins' choice to echo past cultures in her creation of a future dystopia; it creates a terrifying sense of the cyclical nature of human behaviour. The classical allusions expand the novel from being a comment on contemporary society (and the way it may progress in the future) into being a more fundamental comment on human behaviour throughout human history.

What Mills' article does not consider, and I am not aware of this being explored elsewhere, is the conscious, or unconscious, manifestation of the Antigone archetype in the *Hunger Games* novels. Katniss is a young female pitting herself against a Creon figure in the form of President Snow. He is affronted by her gender and her youth, and is determined not to appear weak in the face of her protest against authority. Katniss enters the Hunger Games to defend her sibling, for whom she is prepared to sacrifice her life.[22] Having lost their fathers both Katniss and Gale, her hunting partner and potential love, are fiercely protective of their siblings, just as sororal duty is a key theme of Sophocles' play.

Echoing Antigone, Katniss' first consciously political act, which is not merely an attempt to stay alive, is to give her own form of 'burial' to a body which the authorities rule should lie untouched. Rue, the youngest tribute in the arena, and Katniss' ally, is killed and Katniss feels she must make some statement in response, a gesture towards the corpse:

> . . . I remember Peeta's words on the roof. 'Only I keep wishing I could think of a way to . . . to show the Capitol they don't own me. That I'm more than just a piece in their Games.' And for the first time, I understand what he means. I want to do something, right here, right now, to shame them, to make them accountable, to show the Capitol that whatever they do or force us to do there is a part of every tribute they can't own. That Rue was more than a piece in their Games. And so am I.
>
> A few steps into the woods grows a bank of wild flowers. Perhaps they are really weeds of some sort, but they have blossoms in beautiful shades of violet and yellow and white. I gather up an armful and come back to Rue's side. Slowly, one stem at a time, I decorate her body in the flowers. Covering the ugly wound. Wreathing her face. Weaving her hair with bright colors [. . .] I step back and take a last look at Rue. She could really be asleep in that meadow after all.
>
> 'Bye, Rue,' I whisper. I press the three middle fingers of my left hand against my lips and hold them out in her direction. Then I walk away without looking back.
>
> The birds fall silent.[23]

Her garlanding of the body, witnessed throughout Panem through televized coverage, is a simple act of rebellion: an individual refusing to lose her humanity; a brief assertion of her own self in the face of a pervasive society and authority. In attending to Rue's corpse, she refuses to play by the rules of the Hunger Games. Just as Antigone insists that there is a higher, religious order to which she has a duty and which trumps newly made laws, Katniss insists on a basic humanity which cannot be destroyed or subjugated by the new state. The three-finger gesture she makes is an old and traditional gesture from District Twelve, where she grew up; likewise Nizam, we have seen, was accused of adhering to old tribal customs rather than the new, supposedly civilizing, laws. All three women are asserting the value of an older, or more traditional, order in the face of a new administration.

The significance of these acts is also in their repercussions. In the second book of the *Hunger Games* trilogy, *Catching Fire*, Peeta will recreate the garlanding of Rue's body in a painting on the training room floor as an act of protest. The people of Rue's district will use the three-finger sign as a cue for rebellion. Katniss' individual act of defiance will inspire others. It is important to note that neither Katniss' nor Antigone's actions actually create a physical or military threat to Snow or Creon. Both rebels are powerless in any real sense to evade authority, or death, should that be their punishment. They are dangerous because of what they represent: a challenge to authority. Katniss goes on to challenge the whole concept of the Hunger Games by threatening a simultaneous suicide with Peeta, cheating the public of a winner. Snow's concern is less with her action than what it might inspire in others:

> 'People viewed your little trick with the berries as an act of defiance, not an act of love. And if a girl from District Twelve of all places can defy the Capitol and walk away unharmed, what is to stop them from doing the same [. . .] What is to prevent, say, an uprising?'[24]

Katniss is depicted metaphorically as a spark which could spread:

> 'Your stylist turned out to be prophetic in his wardrobe choice. Katniss Everdeen, the girl who was on fire, you have provided a spark that, left unattended, may grow to an inferno that destroys Panem.'[25]

In *Catching Fire*, this is exactly what we see.

This is very different to the threat Nizam presents in *The Watch*; in the world of the novel, there is less concern about any precedent Nizam may set, and more genuine fear that she may be hiding a bomb. The Americans worry she might be a 'Trojan horse', harnessing another classical metaphor, hiding an explosive beneath her feminine appearance. The idea that her burka might be concealing a bomb is a potent juxtaposition of the feminine and deadly.[26] She may be prepared to martyr herself and the American soldiers are caught between their desire to show her humanity and their fear of a trap. She is depicted as disabled by a previous shelling which emphasizes her potential duality as both helpless victim and potential aggressor. When she sings at night the soldiers are drawn to her voice, but still feel she may be dangerous, like a deadly Siren.

Martyrdom is a powerful concept in both novels. In *Catching Fire*, Snow realizes he cannot kill Katniss overtly for fear of turning her into a martyr, and thus an even more dangerous symbol:

> 'Why don't you just kill me now?' I blurt out.
> 'Publicly?' he asks. 'That would only add fuel to the flames.'
> 'Arrange an accident, then,' I say.
> 'Who would buy it?' he asks. 'Not you, if you were watching.'[27]

Snow is offered, by the Head Games Maker, the solution of sending Katniss back into the Hunger Games to get her killed, without it being overtly his responsibility. Creon too creates a death for Antigone from which he can abdicate responsibility: he decides to have her entombed, without sustenance, and then leave her fate in the hands of the gods. If she dies he will not actually have killed her and, spiritually, his hands will be clean:

> ἡμεῖς γὰρ ἁγνοὶ τοὐπὶ τήνδε τὴν κόρην.
> μετοικίας δ' οὖν τῆς ἄνω στερήσεται. (889–890)

> [It makes no difference, since our hands are clean so far as regards this girl. But no matter what, she will be deprived of her home here above.]

Both Katniss and Antigone accept that their own death may be something they have to face, and have a developing relationship with their own mortality. Both are accused of morbidity but by accepting the possibility of their own death, they become a very specific problem for the authority figures against which they rebel; unlike a normal opponent, their threat is not literal and cannot be fought against with military might; killing them makes them a martyr and more potent symbol.

Moreover, the society's corporeal obsession with the tributes makes Katniss even more dangerous. Before the tributes in the Hunger Games are sent into the arena, they are rigorously styled by 'prep-teams'. Citizens of the Capitol are encouraged to take an obsessive interest in their appearance, their clothes, their bodies. Attractive tributes have a greater chance of survival as people will pay to send them gifts in the arena; given that the tributes are essentially children, being made to fight to the death by adults, this is an unsettling fetishizing of the teenage body. It backfires on the Capitol when the groomed and continuously televized Katniss becomes an attractive symbol of rebellion. In the first novel, we learn that the Capitol inadvertently created the 'mockingjay': they created a mutant bird, the 'jabberjay', intended to spy on the districts and repeat all it heard, but the jabberjay mated with the mockingbird to create something new and unexpected. Similarly, in creating a compelling, alluring female fighter in Katniss, they have unexpectedly created a symbol for the rebellion that they cannot control.

In the third book of the trilogy, also called *Mockingjay*, much space is devoted to the creation of propaganda by both sides and Katniss' allies are as keen to use her symbolically in the media war as her opponents. It was, in fact, the juxtaposition of reality television and war coverage that first inspired Collins; she describes:

> 'I was channel surfing between reality TV programming and actual war coverage when Katniss's story came to me. One night I'm sitting there flipping around and on one channel there's a group of young people competing for, I don't know, money maybe? And on the next, there's a group of young people fighting an actual war. And I was tired, and the lines began to blur in this very unsettling way, and I thought of this story.'[28]

Thus Collins highlights, throughout, how the public experience of a war is mediated through the media and the gaze of the camera, continuously comparing this to the way we mediate 'reality' in reality television, where editing creates deliberate narratives and manipulates emotions. In this visual medium, the corporeality of the female warrior is brought into even greater focus; Katniss herself is continuously aware of how she must be appearing on screen, and at times consciously tries to manipulate the wider perception of her actions (deciding not to cry at certain points, or to 'play' at being in love with Peeta for the camera).

The archetype that Katniss evokes visually is perhaps less Antigone and more Artemis (or Diana to the Romans), goddess of the hunt. The bow is Katniss' weapon. Most female mythical ancient warriors, whether Atalanta or the Amazons, were associated with the bow, which therefore carries feminine overtones in the mythology of weaponry; many more recent young female heroines, from Philip Pullman's Lyra in the trilogy *His Dark Materials* (1995–2007) to Merida in the 2012 Disney movie *Brave*, sport bows as their weapon of choice. Father Christmas, in the C. S. Lewis Narnia stories, gives the brothers, Peter and Edmund, swords and then gives Susan a bow and arrow (and Lucy a medical kit).

It is, of course, a gender-levelling weapon, as it is not dependent on mere strength, but rather skill, and therefore allows a woman to take out a stronger man. It also, as feminist theorists have pointed out, allows a female warrior to be depicted as distant from actual interactive combat; she does not get her hands dirty. She can be calm and intelligent rather than passionate and aggressive; she can still be portrayed as graceful, petite and beautiful rather than muscly or brawny. Thus female archers can be killers while still conforming to traditional ideas of feminine beauty which allow them to be simultaneously alluring.

The hunter archetype is often also associated with virginity and opposition to marriage. Katniss is certainly portrayed as having a purity; in the second book of the trilogy she is being teased for this by other tributes. Peeta has to explain it to her:

> 'They're playing with you because you're so . . . you know.'
>
> 'No, I don't know,' I say. And I really have no idea what he's talking about.
>
> 'It's like when you wouldn't look at me naked in the arena even though I was half dead. You're so . . . pure,' he says finally.
>
> 'I am not!' I say. 'I've been practically ripping your clothes off every time there's been a camera for the last year!'
>
> 'Yeah, but . . . I mean, for the Capitol, you're pure,' he says, clearly trying to mollify me. 'For me, you're perfect. They're just teasing you.'.[29]

Katniss Everdeen is caught (like her namesake Bathsheba Everdene in Hardy's *Far From the Madding Crowd* of 1874) in a love triangle, but cannot contemplate committing to either man for most of the trilogy. She continually rejects the idea of marriage, to either Gale or Peeta, claiming it is impossible to think of such things when fighting for justice. She also refuses a maternal role: 'I know I'll never marry, never risk bringing a child into the world.'.[30]

While Katniss is instinctively rejecting being a love interest, this is exactly the narrative the Capitol demands she plays. Snow gives her a last chance: if she can convince people her suicidal act with the berries was out of love, not a gesture of rebellion, she may survive. There is then a concerted effort to recast her, by her stylists, and by her mentor Haymitch and Peeta, as a young, unthreatening teenage girl in love, but by this point she has become a symbol of revolution for too many people. Collins has been rightly praised for creating one of the first YA novels with a female protagonist which is read as widely by boys as girls, and Collins clearly has a feminist agenda in the writing of the book. This juxtaposition of the real Katniss, who symbolizes rebellion and is uninterested in marriage or maternity, and the Katniss the patriarchal society demands she pretends to be (young, romantic and completely disempowered), allows Collins to create a direct comparison between her feminist heroine, and the type of heroines often encountered in teen novels: love interests for their male counterparts. In Sophocles' play, Antigone has to make a fundamental choice between the competing priorities of burying her brother, and her commitment to her lover, Haemon. She chooses to reject the romantic role and to make a political stand, knowing she will die 'ἀνυμέναιος' ('unmarried'). Thus Antigone becomes a rare and powerful archetype for a young woman who chooses the political over the romantic role in the narrative of her life.

Collins states that her aim was to tackle the subject of war for a young adult readership: 'I don't write about adolescents. I write about war for adolescents.' (She had already produced books which attempt to make sense of war for even younger readers.) Similarly to the case of Roy-Bhattacharya, Collins' impulse to write about contemporary warfare preceded the choice to do so through a classical prism. Both writers, however, present us with compelling examples of why contemporary writers might use a classical archetype to tackle this subject, though they pursue radically different approaches. Roy-Bhattacharya overtly uses the classical allusion to draw readers to his book, citing *Antigone* both within the book and in the book's marketing. He uses the act of classical reception to confer a status on his novel and place it in a literary tradition, which he believes he is reclaiming for the non-Western cultures he wishes to celebrate in his work. Collins' work stands alone for a reader with no classical knowledge and while she happily acknowledges the classical sources in interview, they are not meta-textually referenced in the novel. This guarantees the accessibility of her work to a young readership with no classical education, but for those who can observe the use of archetypes and sources in the work, it presents a frightening circularity in human behaviour: history is repeating itself. What both books highlight is that Greek mythology offers us a rare archetype, in Antigone, of a young woman who pursues the political above the romantic, and will rebel against authority and make herself a symbol of rebellion against injustice. Such teenage female archetypes are rare in later literature and our writers look two and a half thousand years backwards to find Antigone in the Western canon. Her reincarnation in contemporary literature may herald a new era of feminine, and feminist, heroines, refusing to conform to authority.

Bibliography

Blasingame, James (2009), 'An Interview with Suzanne Collins', *Journal of Adolescent and Adult Literacy*, 52 (8) (May): 726–727.

Collins, Suzanne (2008), *The Hunger Games*. New York: Scholastic.

Collins, Suzanne (2009), *Catching Fire*. New York: Scholastic.

Collins, Suzanne (2010), *Mockingjay*. New York: Scholastic.

Foley, Helene P., ed. (1981), *Reflections of Women in Antiquity*. New York: Gordon and Breach.

Garriott, Deirdre Anne, Whitney Elaine Jones and Julie Elizabeth Tyler, eds (2014), *Space and Place in the Hunger Games: New Readings of the Novels*. New York: Barnes & Noble.

Hall, Edith, Fiona Macintosh and Amanda Wrigley, eds (2004), *Dionysus Since 69: Greek Tragedy at the Dawn of the Third Millennium*. Oxford and New York: Oxford University Press.

Hall, Edith (1989), *Inventing the Barbarian: Greek Self-Definition through Tragedy*. Oxford: Clarendon.

Hall, Edith (2004), 'Introduction: Why Greek tragedy since the late 1960s?', in Edith Hall, Fiona Macintosh and Amanda Wrigley (eds), *Dionysus Since 69: Greek Tragedy at the Dawn of the Third Millennium,* 1–46. Oxford and New York: Oxford University Press.

Hall, Edith (2006), *The Theatrical Cast of Athens.* Oxford: Oxford University Press.

Hall, Edith (2010), *Greek Tragedy: Suffering under the Sun.* Oxford: Oxford University Press.

Hall, Edith (2011), '*Antigone* and the internationalization of theatre in antiquity', in Erin Mee and Helene Foley (eds), *Antigone on the Contemporary World Stage*, 51–63. Oxford: Oxford University Press.

Honig, Bonnie (2013) *Antigone Interrupted.* Cambridge: Cambridge University Press

McClure, Laura (1999), *Spoken Like a Woman: Speech and Gender in Athenian Drama.* Princeton, NJ: Princeton University Press.

Mee, Erin (2010), 'Classics, cultural politics, and the role of *Antigone* in Manipur, North-East India', in Edith Hall and Phiroze Vasunia (eds), *India, Greece & Rome 1757–2007* [*Bulletin of the Institute of Classics Studies* supplement 108], 131–42. London: ICS.

Mee, Erin (2011), 'Antigone in Manipur, North-East India', in Erin Mee and Helene Foley (eds), *Antigone on the Contemporary World Stage*, 107–126. Oxford: Oxford University Press.

Mee, E. and H. Foley, eds (2011a), *Antigone on the Contemporary World Stage.* Oxford: Oxford University Press.

Mee, E. and H. Foley (2011b), 'Mobilizing Antigone', in *Antigone on the Contemporary World Stage*, 1–47. Oxford: Oxford University Press.

Meyer, Adrienne (2015), *The Amazons: Lives and Legends of Warrior Women Across the Ancient World.* Princeton, NJ: Princeton University Press.

Mills, Sophie (2015), 'Classical Elements and Mythological Archetypes in *The Hunger Games*', *New Voices in Classical Reception Studies* 10: 56–64.

Roy-Bhattacharya, Joydeep (2012), *The Watch.* New York: Hogarth.

Sampson, Fiona (2012), '*Antigonick*, by Anne Carson; *The Watch*, by Joydeep Roy-Bhattacharya', *Independent* (26 May).

Shamsie, Kamila (2012), '*The Watch* by Joydeep Roy-Bhattacharya – review', *Guardian* (15 June).

Steiner, George (1979), *Antigones.* Exeter: University of Exeter Press.

Wilmer, John, and S. E. Wilmer, eds (2005), *Rebel Women: Staging Ancient Greek Drama Today.* London: Methuen.

Zeitlin, Froma I. (1996), *Playing the Other: Gender and Society in Classical Greek Literature.* Chicago: University of Chicago Press.

15

Generation Telemachus: Dinaw Mengestu's *How to Read the Air*

Justine McConnell

Dinaw Mengestu is a rising star of the contemporary literary scene. His first novel, *Children of the Revolution* (2007), garnered a series of accolades, including the *Guardian* First Book Award; his second, *How to Read the Air* (2010), contributed to his selection for both the *New Yorker*'s '20 under 40' writers of 2010 and a MacArthur 'Genius Grant' Fellowship in 2012; while his third, *All Our Names* (2014), won the CBC Bookie Award for International Fiction and was included in the *New York Times*' '100 Notable Books of 2014'. The three novels taken together form a kind of loose trilogy,[1] exploring the experience of diaspora and migration that can continue to haunt subsequent generations.

Mengestu grows tired of the label 'immigrant literature', which has so often been applied to his work and which relies in part on his own biography (he was born in Ethiopia, before moving to the United States when he was two years old, as his family fled the violence of the Communist Revolution and the Ethiopian Civil War). The term's segregation from the American novel is problematic:

> I'm also very aware of the idea of 'immigrant literature' and how it is excluded from the traditional category of the American literary novel; there's the American literary novel and then there's the immigrant novel, which is seen as a derivation, and not a natural extension of what someone like Saul Bellow and other American immigrants traditionally have been doing.[2]

Mengestu is right, of course: the great American novel must incorporate 'immigrant literature', just as modern literature must. Migration has become a dominant feature of life in the contemporary era; as the cultural theorist Stuart Hall put it, 'I can't go back to any one origin – I'd have to go back to five; when I ask anybody where they're from, I expect nowadays to be told an extremely long story'.[3]

While this kind of migration, born of the globalized world in which we now live, of the history of forced displacements brought about by the slave trade, and the multiple identities that colonialism foisted onto people (both colonizers and colonized),[4] may feel like a very modern concern, Mengestu identifies it with antiquity too. As he has explained, 'Whether it's Aeschylus's *Oresteia* or Homer's *Odyssey*, exile inevitably dominates the works I love the most'.[5] Exile, and indeed the *Odyssey*, dominates his second novel too, for *How to Read the Air* reads very much like a 'Telemachy', with a smattering of the *Oresteia* thrown in too. The latter is seen in the way the protagonist's family troubles and mistakes pass from one generation to the next, like the curse on the House of Atreus; while the Telemachy manifests itself in the journey that the central character takes, both in imagination and reality, to retrace his father's earlier travels and seek out his own sense of identity.

Mengestu has elaborated further on the influence of Homer on his imagination, which is interwoven with his tale of modern migration and African diaspora:

> [Patmos is] a dreamlike landscape, similar to the one I imagined after first reading the *Iliad*, and that I've continued to imagine with each rereading of my favourite Greek tragedies, texts that over the years have been as pivotal to my understanding of the world as the stories of Ethiopia my father once told me.[6]

Patmos is, of course, the Greek island where St John had the apocalyptic visions that became the Book of Revelation, and in this respect too, Mengestu draws a link with his own Ethiopian origins, reflecting that his Coptic Orthodox grandmother would have been 'perfectly at home' on the island. Patmos is also a place of asylum for those seeking refuge from places such as Afghanistan, Eritrea and Somalia in the modern day, which, in Mengestu's imagination, consolidates his long-held sense of the impermanence of home. Yet with its religion and its traditional tales, the Greek island reminds him of his homeland of Ethiopia nevertheless.

Mengestu's comparison of Greek myth with Ethiopian folklore recalls Ralph Ellison's similar discussion of Ulysses and Brer Rabbit in 'Change the Joke and Slip the Yoke' (1958),[7] although Mengestu here asserts an equality that Ellison denied in that essay. Ellison's prioritization of Greek myths over African American ones, and of white writers over black,[8] contributed to his poor reception among African-American critics when *Invisible Man* was first published in 1952. The constellation of his influences, however, is more nuanced than that, with ancient literature, nineteenth- and twentieth-century novels, and African American folklore all playing crucial roles.[9] Mengestu has spoken of the impact of Ellison on his literary imagination, and as I shall discuss, *How to Read the Air* contains a number of allusions to Ellison's only completed novel.

If 'world literature' is a highly contested term,[10] then Mengestu's novel exemplifies some of the most incisive capacity of the designation. For *How to Read the Air* is of multiple places simultaneously,[11] and moves beyond the circulation of its primary nation, as well as engaging with literary predecessors which are likewise 'actively present within a literary system beyond that of its original culture'.[12] The American and the Ethiopian, the ancient Greek and the modern Midwest, all have currency within the novel.

Dislocation and displacement dominate Mengestu's fiction, even to the extent that, while all three of his novels have been well received in critical circles, it has escaped nobody's attention that there are some strong similarities between them.[13] *Children of the Revolution* (2007), like *How to Read the Air*, features an emigrant who has moved to the United States from the political turmoil of 1970s Ethiopia, and who is caught between memories of life in his homeland and disillusionment with his present, American life. He too, as we will see of *How to Read the Air*'s protagonist, is haunted by memories of his father. This debut novel was renamed for the American market because publishers feared that North American readers would be put off by the political turn of the title, and would not recognize the allusion to the 1972 hit by the rock band, T. Rex,[14] after which Mengestu's characters nickname themselves.[15] Thus in the United States it was retitled as *The Beautiful Things that Heaven Bears*, deploying a quotation from the end of Dante's *Inferno* (Canto 34.137–138) which recurs throughout the novel as a favourite phrase of one of the protagonist's friends, Joseph, an immigrant from Zaire.[16] The quote, which is taken from the moment Dante finally leaves Hell, evokes the protagonist's journey from war-torn Ethiopia to America. Casting this kind of emigration as a *katabasis* will likewise be important to *How to Read the Air*, particularly to its exploration of father-son relationships, and its engagement with canonical literature. Yet one wonders that Mengestu did not object more forcefully to this renaming, given that he has lamented the way that Africa is so often described and depicted as a hellish place.[17]

Lurking in the background of Mengestu's first two novels, and the cause of the absence of both protagonists' fathers, is the conflict that wracked Ethiopia from 1974 until 1991. After the Marxist Derg, supported by the Soviet Union, overthrew Emperor Haile Selassie in 1974, civil war ensued. The rule of Selassie, who had annexed Eritrea in 1961, had increasingly come to be perceived as imperialist; the Derg, on the other hand, were Marxist in name, but military in style. In 2006, the Derg's chairman, Mengistu Haile Mariam, who had ruled

Ethiopia for seventeen years, was convicted *in absentia* of genocide, in relation to his commands during 'the Red Terror' of 1977–1978. It is from this crisis that Dinaw Mengestu's family fled in 1980, joining his father who had escaped two years earlier, just before Mengestu's birth. As Mengestu has said, the revolution 'split the family cleanly down the middle', as some were high-ranking members of the Derg, while others had been wealthy landowners whose property was confiscated by the new Communist administration; one of his uncles was arrested and executed, other family members fled the country when they could.[18] This, then, is the autobiographical echo that reverberates through the novel: *How to Read the Air* features a protagonist whose father also escaped to Europe, and eventually America, before his birth.

The traces of the *Odyssey* within Mengestu's work may be only one element, but they are crucial to it. By interacting with the Homeric epic, Mengestu positions his novel as the latest in a prodigious line of canonical literature that begins with Homer, and extends through Dante, Tennyson, Joyce, Ellison and Walcott, to name only a few. The archetypal themes of homecoming, storytelling and identity that have long since been recognized as fundamental to the *Odyssey* are therefore already foreshadowed in Mengestu's work; a foreshadowing which the novel will amply fulfill.

How to Read the Air is structured as a new 'Telemachy'. The novel interweaves the stories of several journeys, which are each physical as well as psychological. The primary one is that of the narrator, Jonas Woldemariam, and his relationship with Angela, who he meets, marries and separates from over the course of the novel. The second journey is that taken by Jonas' parents thirty years earlier, which he re-traces as his own marriage falls apart. The third, and the one in which Mengestu's engagement with the *Odyssey* is most prominent, is that undertaken by Jonas' father, Yosef, as he fled Ethiopia after being imprisoned for his political views. The reader learns of this journey through the fictionalized narrative that Jonas tells his students, though Yosef never shared the story with his son. Following his father's death, Jonas 'needed a history more complete than the strangled bits that he [Yosef] had owned and passed on to me' (180), so he invents a story to fill the void.

The ill-fated road trip through the American Midwest taken by Jonas' parents came to define the violent and destructive pattern that their marriage was to follow. As he retraces his parents' steps, Jonas is like the Homeric Telemachus searching for news of his absent father; but unlike his Homeric predecessor, his search will be in vain. Lacking a Nestor, a Helen or a Menelaus who can tell him stories of the father he scarcely knows, Jonas does a very Odyssean thing: he invents. The shift of focus and role is more complete than anything found in Homer: the Telemachean Jonas is not striving to walk in his father's shoes, nor is his father the central figure. Jonas is not only the novel's protagonist, he is also its unreliable narrator, thereby fulfilling the role traditionally taken by Odysseus, most especially in the part of his travel narrative which he relates himself in books 9–12 of the *Odyssey*. Thus, when Jonas begins to tell his own stories, he exceeds the Homeric model: the classical Telemachus listens to stories, but scarcely tells his own. Expanding on the ancient Telemachus' ability to string the bow that we see in book 21 of the *Odyssey*, Jonas has acquired the Odyssean trait of storytelling.[19]

Jonas repeatedly emphasizes that his narration should not be taken at face-value. Echoing Oscar Wilde, he declares,

> History sometimes deserves a little revision, if not for the sake of the dead, then at least for ourselves.
>
> (74)[20]

His job at an immigration centre utilizes his flair for departing from the truth, as he embellishes the stories of the immigrants seeking asylum and citizenship in the United States: in Jonas' account to the authorities, economic migrants come to have suffered brutal violence, and brutalized immigrants see their stories exaggerated to fever pitch, conforming to what Jonas describes as 'common assumptions that most of us shared when it came to the poor in distant, foreign countries' (27). His 'exaggeration' of the truth, in these instances, has a direct purpose, much as Odysseus's Cretan Lies do; later in the novel, this kind of direct purpose will be implemented to more destructive effect when Jonas lies about a promotion at work in order to reassure Angela and impress her boss.

In fact, the reader is repeatedly reminded of Jonas' unreliability as a truthful storyteller: for example, he breaks off midway through an episode relating his parents' road trip to remark, 'There are two directions the story can go in at this point' (150), weighing up the possibilities of what might have happened next, and which imagined version he will choose. Remarking that telling lies, or fictional tales, comes naturally to him, Jonas observes,

> I thought of this as a distinctly American trait – this ability to unwind whatever ties supposedly bind you to the past and invent new ones as you went along.
>
> (104)

One of the most distinctly Odyssean traits, therefore, is also a distinctly American one, and is part and parcel of the potentiality of the American dream. Think of F. Scott Fitzgerald's *The Great Gatsby* (1925), which explores this very idea, notwithstanding that novel's warnings of the dangers of doing so.[21] In addition, Jonas' musings recall the way that the American tales of Brer Rabbit developed from the African folklore brought over by the enslaved victims of the Middle Passage: new stories can be invented, but Jonas' retelling of his father's tale, just like Gatsby's fate, suggests that they are never entirely cast off.

Storytelling is, of course, at the heart of the *Odyssey*, both as a means by which Odysseus achieves his *kleos* (fame) and his *nostos* (return home) – by charming and impressing the Phaeacians with the tales of his fantastical adventures – and as a narrative device. The internal narrations enable the structural complexity of the epic, which in turn poured praise on the bard performing the tale in ancient times, and by extension, on Odysseus himself. But a focus on storytelling as a practice and as a theme would not be enough to claim Homer as a central intertext for Mengestu: it is the journeys he relates, and the *nostos* and katabatic travels that these entail, that make the identification unmistakable.

Two of Jonas' major narratives concern his parents: his father's odyssey through Africa and Europe to America, and, interwoven throughout, the story of that road trip his parents once took. The narration of the earlier story is prompted by Yosef's death, and is retrospectively defined as a *katabasis* in his wife's mind too: following a car crash, she contemplates her husband's migration to America: 'If he died now it wouldn't be a stretch to think that it was for the second time' (257). Jonas, too, imagines his father musing on 'the River Styx and the final passage we all must make out of life' (161), and in keeping with the Telemachean focus of the novel, it is Jonas who retells this nekuian adventure. Yosef's voyage itself not only resonates with hellish motifs, but is introduced by an Underworld scene in which Jonas imagines that the ghost of his father is with him, 'haunting' him, as he heads to work on the subway. This imagined scenario allows Jonas, for the first time, to be the speaker in a conversation, and his father the listener (176). Thus, in a reversal of the Homeric scenario – or more precisely, the Virgilian one, given that it is his father, not his mother, with whom Jonas converses – it is the living who have the answers, not the dead.[22] Furthermore, the postcolonial connection between *katabasis* and *nostos* that Gregson Davis has posited,[23] is apparent here; Yosef's journey out of Ethiopia, as well as his son's in the United States, are both simultaneously descents to an underworld and journeys to a place they can call home.

Mengestu, therefore, plays with a central tussle of the later reception of the *Odyssey*: is Odysseus a centripetal or a centrifugal character (to employ Joyce's designation in the 'Ithaca' chapter of *Ulysses*[24]); a man driven to return home, or always driven onwards? Jonas' father has been only centrifugal; yet although

Yosef will never return to Ethiopia, for his son, 'this is how I like to picture him, whether it's accurate or not: as a man in search of a home' (73).[25] The nekuian journey on which son and ghostly father go, likewise leads *from* Jonas' home to the school where he works. This is a feature of Jonas' life: like Tennyson's Ulysses, he is always leaving, always 'pushing off' to new places.[26]

Although Yosef never returns to Ethiopia, in this he is cast less as a centrifugal Odyssean character (once he reaches Illinois, he is content to stay there until his death), and more as an Achillean one. Like Achilles who makes a choice that precludes him ever returning home but is seen to regret this in the afterlife (*Od.*11.489–491), so too Jonas imagines Yosef wanting to say to his wife,

> If I could start all over again I would. I'd go back to my father's house and I'd stay there forever. I'd become a farmer. I'd die in the same place as I was born.
>
> (211)

Yosef may have none of the heroism that we expect from Achilles, but he certainly has the anger, as seen in his repeated violent treatment of his wife.

Mengestu's novel explores the condition of second-generation African immigrants, self-identifying as African Americans, and valuing their connections to both continents. An early conversation between Angela and Jonas lightheartedly underlines the mapping of each continent onto the other and the layers of identity that this denotes; she explains that '"being of African American descent and all ..."' (20), her greatest empathy is with the immigrants from West Africa, while Jonas with his Ethiopian roots, empathizes with those from East Africa. Abbreviating this, the two playfully taunt each other with a victory for 'the West side' or 'the East side' each time one of their refugees is successfully granted asylum (21). Later, the darker repercussions of such layers of identity are exposed in a scene in which the racial suspicion – racism masquerading as curiosity – of the contemporary United States is foregrounded. At the interview for a teaching job at a privileged private school, the following exchange takes place:

> 'Where's that accent of yours from?' the dean of the academy had asked me during our first interview, after I had said all of eight words to him: Hello. It's a pleasure to meet you.
>
> 'Peoria,' I told him.
>
> He hesitated a second before moving on, and I could see him wondering if it was possible that there was more than one Peoria in this world, another situated perhaps thousands of miles away from the one he had heard of in the Midwest and therefore completely off his radar.
>
> (58)

This central theme of dual identity gives rise to the other layer of 'reception' found in the novel. Martindale, deploying Eliot, coined the term, 'chain of receptions';[27] so here, in Mengestu's novel, it is not only the *Odyssey* and Greek myth that are being responded to, but also Ralph Ellison's 1952 classic novel, *Invisible Man*. Indeed, Mengestu could hardly read the *Odyssey* free of the Ellisonian 'accretions'; they have become inextricably entangled with Homer. Given *Invisible Man*'s canonical status, *How to Read the Air*'s allusions to it need not surprise. Mengestu has cited Ellison, along with James Baldwin, Toni Morrison, and Ernest Gaines as one of 'those writers [who] kind of helped validate my own identity very much'.[28] In the wake of Ellison's novel, it has become impossible not to recall his protagonist who is 'invisible . . . simply because people refuse to see me';[29] when a character remarks upon his own 'invisibility' in a novel that is much preoccupied with identity, Ellison is evoked. Junot Díaz, contemporary of Mengestu, fellow 2012 winner of a MacArthur Fellowship, and another candidate for the category of 'Generation Telemachus', has also spoken of his immense respect for Ellison, and employed the imagery of invisibility to describe Latinos in the United States in the generation before him.[30]

Mengestu simultaneously evokes, yet modifies, Ellison. For example, Jonas wishes that he had responded to his wife's accusation that he has no sense of identity, with an explanation that she was only partially correct:

> I may not have had a solid definition of who I was, but that was only because for so long I had concentrated my efforts on trying to appear to be almost nothing at all – neither nameless nor invisible, just obscure enough to always blend into the background and be quickly forgotten.
>
> (107)

'Neither nameless nor invisible' implies that Jonas has not been striving to emulate Ellison's unnamed protagonist. At the same time, he rejects one of the major driving forces of the Homeric Odysseus, that of *kleos*, with his wish to remain 'obscure' and 'be quickly forgotten', but in doing so, he is simultaneously rejecting the right to be the hero even of his own story.

Ellison's novel is evoked by Mengestu at a number of other moments: for example, just as Invisible Man burns the papers he has been carrying with him,[31] which have bound him to a course that he had not himself chosen, so too does Yosef. After fleeing through first Africa and then Europe as an illegal immigrant, Yosef reaches London, from where he has been instructed to send for the daughter of the man who helped him in Sudan, and to claim that she is his wife. Standing on Hampstead Heath with 'London at his feet' (309), Yosef burns the fake marriage licence and the photo of the daughter, and is thereby free – like Invisible Man, after his own incendiary moment – to choose his own path. Similarly, in *Children of the Revolution*, Mengestu plays with another pivotal moment of *Invisible Man*, when the tricksy advice of Invisible Man's grandfather (to 'overcome 'em with yeses, undermine 'em with grins, agree 'em to death and destruction')[32] is echoed by the protagonist's uncle who may '"sir" his way through the day', but makes sure his nephew also sees the defiance that lies beneath.[33] The influence of *Invisible Man* is, in fact, scarcely less pervasive than that of Homer. Far from being derivative, these discreet echoes deliberately help situate Mengestu's novel in a line of foundational texts, suggesting that his trilogy of the African diaspora explores an experience as fundamental to the twenty-first century as the dying out of the Iliadic mode of heroism was to the eighth century BCE, and the incipient Civil Rights Movement was to 1950s America.

Ellison's protagonist builds a home for himself underground, which is perhaps the most literal manifestation of the trope that Davis has identified in the work of Aimé Césaire and Derek Walcott: the conflation of home and the Underworld, of *nostos* with *katabasis*.[34] Mengestu's employment of this theme is less emphatic, but the almost subterranean location of the flat Jonas shares with Angela is an important feature of their home together:

> It's often said that a city, especially one as vast and dense as New York, can be a terribly lonely and isolating place. I had felt that before, even at the happiest points of my marriage to Angela, even when we deliberately hid ourselves nearly underground in the five-hundred-square-foot confines of our apartment, just the two of us, alone and with nowhere to go for days at a time.
>
> (198)

Towards the end of the novel, Jonas has come to sense the dismal, suffocating undertones of such a home, and when he makes an effort to save their marriage, he knows that he must not do so in the house: to even enter the flat before they speak will doom his efforts (198–199). It is not only the apartment itself that is nekuian, but all that happens there: the progression of their relationship has been a katabatic journey, and Jonas is trying to lead the relationship back out of the underworld and into the light.

Further Homeric elements can be seen in Mengestu's novel, so that as well as the themes of *nostos* and *katabasis*, and the fundamental interest in the role and power of the storyteller and the questionable truth of his tales, there is a scene that recalls the famous *teichoscopia* ('viewing from the wall') of the third book of the *Iliad* (3.146–244). The battlefield observed has an emphatic absence of heroes, reflecting the enlarged nature of modern conflict, the technological advances that have led to planes and tanks, not men, warranting description, and the turn away from the heroization of war. Nevertheless, the observers of this battle, the father Yosef and his companion Abrahim, watch the battle unfold from a very similar physical perspective to that from which Helen, with an interjection from Antenor, points out the Greek warriors to Priam. Up on the rooftop of their boarding house, they see the rebel army advancing, and moments later, they watch as they are wiped out: 'at least seven bombs were dropped directly onto rebels, whose convoy disappeared into a cloud of smoke and sand' (248). Mengestu's journalistic experience in Sudan and Chad informed his writing of these scenes, and in that sense his descriptions are of the contemporary world, stuffed into the era of 1970s Ethiopia.[35] The 'inaccuracy' is apt because this whole narration is voiced by Jonas, who has never been to Africa and has barely been told a word of the story of his father's travels out of Ethiopia: Jonas' imagination would inevitably set the story in the modern era, informed by his impressions gained from the news and media.

Nevertheless, the revolution from which Jonas' father escapes was a real one, and the narrative Mengestu and Jonas give to it here serve an important purpose that again belong both to the author and to his fictional creation: that of telling a tale of Africa not often told. Mengestu has described how his father found it infuriating in 1980s Illinois that no one knew of the Communist Revolution from which his family had fled, but were only aware of the famine which had, naturally, been contributed to significantly by the political turmoil of the country.[36] It is this narrow-minded vision of Africa that Jonas attempts to overturn in the tales he tells his students of his father's escape from Ethiopia.

During the second half of the twentieth century, a number of fascinating anticolonial and postcolonial responses to the *Odyssey* depicted protagonists who embodied, and frequently flitted between, their Odyssean and their Cyclopean roles and natures.[37] A generation later, the twenty-first century has begun to see what I have suggested could be termed 'Generation Telemachus'. The intellectual 'children' of postcolonial artists (engaging with their literary forebears such as Ellison and Walcott), the actual children of migratory parents, find themselves torn between two worlds still, but this time from the perspective of the child, trying to understand and communicate with their literary and literal ancestors.

The term 'Generation Telemachus' functions as a kind of shorthand for a trend that I see among a number of African diaspora, young contemporary novelists; not just Mengestu or Díaz, but also, for example, Paul Beatty, author of

The White Boy Shuffle (1996) and Teju Cole, who wrote the highly acclaimed *Open City* (2011). By gathering them together thus, I do not intend to imply that the Homeric epic is a core, or even a primary, inspiration for their work. But these writers do form a kind of network by which their works can be illuminatingly compared to each other; such networks have been at the heart of 'world literature' since Wieland invented – and subsequently Goethe adopted – the term (*Weltliteratur*) in the early nineteenth century.[38] Further adding to the appropriateness of the designation, each has written a kind of *Bildungsroman*, in which a key part of the protagonist's development is his relationship with his (absent) father.

Dinaw Mengestu's Telemachy (and the ones that we see in Junot Díaz's fiction as well),[39] are not merely about rewriting the Homeric epic from the son's perspective, nor about updating a founding work of the Western canon for the twenty-first century, or even claiming the right to appropriate these myths. That battle was won by their predecessors, and nobody any longer would claim that the ancient Greek and Roman classics belong any more to one group of people than to another. The deployment of Greek myth in their fiction, however, not only illuminates the tales of modern experience, migration, and conflict, but it also exemplifies that most Damroschean feature of world literature: a work that has moved beyond its culture of origin,[40] and thereby warrants its designation as 'world literature'.

Bibliography

Apter, Emily (2013), *Against World Literature: On the Politics of Untranslatability*. London & New York: Verso.

Atwood, Margaret (2005a), *The Penelopiad*. Edinburgh: Canongate.

Atwood, Margaret (2005b), *Eating Fire: Selected Poetry, 1965–1995*. London: Virago.

Casanova, Pascale (2005), 'Literature as a World', *New Left Review* 31 (Jan–Feb): 71–90.

Césaire, Aimé (2000 [1955]), *Discourse on Colonialism*, trans. Joan Pinkham, with an introduction by Robin D. G. Kelley. New York: Monthly Review Press.

Céspedes, Diógenes, Silvio Torres-Saillant, and Junot Díaz (2000), 'Fiction Is the Poor Man's Cinema: An Interview with Junot Díaz', *Callaloo* 23 (3) (Summer): 892–907.

Chamberlain, Kendra R. (2012), 'Bearing Gaines', *DIG* (1 February) – http://old.digbatonrouge.com/article/bearing-gaines-4363/

Charles, Ron (2010), Review of *How to Read the Air*, *The Washington Post* (3 November).

Damrosch, David (2003), *What is World Literature?* Princeton, NJ: Princeton University Press.

Davis, Gregson (2007), '"Homecomings without Home": Representations of (Post) colonial *nostos* (Homecoming) in the Lyric of Aimé Césaire and Derek Walcott', in Barbara Graziosi and Emily Greenwood (eds), *Homer in the Twentieth Century: Between World Literature and the Western Canon,* 191–209. Oxford: Oxford University Press,.

Duffy, Carol Ann (1999), *The World's Wife*. London: Picador.

Ellison, Ralph (1995), *Shadow and Act*. New York: Vintage International.

Ellison, Ralph (2002 [1952]), *Invisible Man*. New York: Random House.

Fitzgerald, F. Scott (2004 [1925]), *The Great Gatsby*. New York: Scribner.

Hall, Edith (2008), *The Return of Ulysses*. London and Baltimore, MD: I. B. Tauris & Johns Hopkins University Press.

Joyce, James (1961 [1922]), *Ulysses*, with a foreword by Morris L. Ernst; and the decision of the United States District Court rendered by Judge John M. Woolsey. [The Modern Library]. New York: Random House.

La Force, Thessaly (2010), 'At Work: Dinaw Mengestu', *The Paris Review* (28 October) – http://www.theparisreview.org/blog/2010/10/28/dinaw-mengestu/

McConnell, Justine (2013), *Black Odysseys: The Homeric Odyssey in the African Diaspora since 1939*. Oxford: Oxford University Press.

Martindale, Charles (1993), *Redeeming the Text: Latin Poetry and the Hermeneutics of Reception*. Cambridge: Cambridge University Press.

Mengestu, Dinaw (2007), 'Children of War', *New Statesman* (14 June).

Mengestu, Dinaw (2008), *Children of the Revolution*. London: Vintage.

Mengestu, Dinaw (2011a), 'The Q & A: Dinaw Mengestu, Novelist', *The Economist* (26 April).

Mengestu, Dinaw (2011b), 'My Personal Greek Myth', *The Wall Street Journal* (2 July).

Moretti, Franco (2000), 'Conjectures on World Literature', *New Left Review* 1 (Jan–Feb), 54–68.

Rankine, Patrice D. (2006), *Ulysses in Black: Ralph Ellison, Classicism, and African American Literature*. Madison, WI: University of Wisconsin Press.

Rohter, Larry (2010), 'A Novelist's Voice, Both Exotic and Midwestern', *The New York Times* (16 October), C1.

Walcott, Derek (1990), *Omeros*. New York: Farrar, Strauss & Giroux.

Walcott, Derek (1993), *The Odyssey: A Stage Version*. London: Faber & Faber.

Weitz, Hans-J. (1987), '"Weltliteratur" zuerst bei Wieland', *Arcadia* 22, 206–208.

Wendland, Tegan (2012), 'Dinaw Mengestu Wins Ernest Gaines Literary Award', *WRKF 89.3* (25 January) – http://wrkf.org/post/dinaw-mengestu-wins-ernest-gaines-literary-award

Wilde, Oscar (2007 [1891]), 'The Critic as Artist', in *The Collected Works of Oscar Wilde*. Hertfordshire: Wordsworth Editions, 963–1016.

Notes

Introduction

1 Hall (2005).
2 Hall (2005) 24–25.
3 Unsworth, in a 2008 email to Edith Hall.
4 Auerbach (1971) 19–20.
5 The notes are undated, and a number of revised editions of Wieland's translation were published (in 1782, 1790, and posthumously in 1816), but his death in 1813 makes it clear that his use of the term preceded Goethe's, to whom the coinage is often attributed – see Weitz (1987).
6 Goethe (1850) 351 (vol. 1) detailing a conversation that Eckermann recorded as having occurred on 31 January 1827.
7 'World Lite: What is Global Literature?,' *n+1* 17 (2013); Moretti (2000); Apter (2013); Damrosch (2003).
8 Gilroy (1993) 19.
9 Hall (1991) 57.
10 Hall (1999).
11 Maire and Edward Said, in introduction to Auerbach (1969), 1.
12 Goethe (1973) 8.
13 Auerbach (1969) 2.
14 Auerbach (1969) 7.
15 Etiemble (1974); Spivak (2003). See also Park (2015) and Reynolds, Omri and Morgan (2015) for further discussion of the perpetuation of this Western dominance.
16 See Young (2011) 214 both on these simultaneous developments and the way that the idea of 'world literature' was first developed as 'a way of bringing classical and modern texts together'.
17 Reynolds, Omri and Morgan (2015) 152–153, citing a Frederic Jameson talk on world literature at Duke University in 2008, identify this as key: those studying comparative literature are 'exploring how writers and artists have reconciled the ambition to go beyond their borders with the desire to remain singular'.
18 Casanova (2004). On Casanova's misappropriation of the fifteenth-century concept of a 'Republic of Letters', see Buescu (2011).
19 On cosmopolitanism in the final days and in the aftermath of the Cold War, see, for instance, Hannerz (2006).

20 Hall (2009).
21 Hall (2009) 24.
22 Etiemble (1974).
23 Auerbach (1969) 17.

1 From Anthropophagy to Allegory and Back: A Study of Classical Myth and the Brazilian Novel

1 Amado (1993) 104.
2 Cavalcanti (1992) 107 recounts, between 1964 and 1974 'military justice arrested, tortured, and tried 7,367 Brazilians for subversive activities . . . To those numbers were added 10,034 individuals reported by civilians, 6,385 of whom went through preliminary military interrogation and trial'.
3 See Bartsch (1998) and Rudich (2013).
4 For a general overview of this prevalent aspect of Amado's work, see Hamilton (1967) and Nunes (1973).
5 It ended in 1985, but the first post-dictatorship president would not be firmly installed until 1989. The date 1989 is not incidental: the threat of communism had fuelled the military takeover in Brazil.
6 As Smallman argues, 'the Brazilian military has long used terror during moments of crisis' (2000: 119). He points to the treatment of rebels in the navy in 1910 (suffocation, summary assassination).
7 Vieira (1989).
8 Hamilton (1967).
9 Butler (24).
10 See Freyre (1964).
11 Butler (1998) 31–32.
12 Cavalcanti calls this 'the sort of intolerance [that] could rarely be comfortable with a pluralistic, democratic form of government' but that is 'more compatible with an authoritarian model of political regime' (1992: 103).
13 Smallman (2000).
14 Butler (1998) 33.
15 See Vieira (1989).
16 *War of the Saints*, 225.
17 See Stam (1997).
18 Butler (1998) 34.
19 Butler (1998) 34.
20 See Flynn (1991) for a rich overview of the various stages of the dictatorship.
21 Namorato (2006).

22 Namorato (2006).

23 Namorato (2006).

24 There are several references to Judaism throughout, often coupled with the shame of being a centaur. The references culminate in the assertion that 'the Jews killed Christ, the Jews are avaricious' (76).

25 The role of cities in progress is central to the narrative but a topic space does not allow me to cover here. The city is a space of heightened modernization and open-minded advancement, or so it would seem. Guedali's father decides to leave the countryside and make his way to the city, Porto Alegre, where 'nobody will stare at you. City people don't care about anything' (37).

26 Some passages are reminiscent of Freyre's *Masters and Slaves,* where sexual miscegenation between slaves and their masters is the everyday taboo.

27 For Pirott-Quintero (2000), the narrator 'shuns chronological time' (768), but I find this strong, given the temporal markers throughout that arc indicative of the regime – and hint chronologically.

28 Lindstrom (1984) talks about this in terms of 'the unexpected persistence' of such remnants left behind as Jewishness.

29 She also has an affair, and Pirott-Quintero (2000) characterizes these affairs as 'bourgeois restlessness' (769). Pirott-Quintero characterizes the dissenting narrative viewpoints between Tita and Guedali as *themselves* a centaur (the narrative itself as centaur).

30 Richard A. Preto-Rodas (1990) 285.

31 Shaw (1998).

32 Shaw (1998) sees this as Noll's 'implicit denunciation of the country's social problems' (294).

33 Serbin (2001).

34 Vieira (1996) questions the effectiveness of the satire, which has the effect of misogyny and a deep sexism.

2 Ibrahim Al-Koni's Lost Oasis as Atlantis and His Demon as Typhon

1 al-Kawni (2002), 97–98. (There are two possible scholarly transliterations of his surname: al-Kawni or al-Kuni. His novels in translation have been published with his name as al-Koni. In recent emails he has used the spelling Al Koni.)

2 *Decline of the West* (*Der Untergang des Abendlandes*), first published in two volumes in 1918 and 1923. He also referenced Hegel in al-Kuni (2004a) 33.

3 al-Kuni (2001 and 2008) I, 96–98. This work was continued in al-Kuni (2004, 2005, 2006).

4 al-Kuni (2005–2006) I, 7.
5 Ibrahim al-Koni, email, dated 9/4/2014, to William Hutchins.
6 al-Kuni (2001 and 2008) III, 53.
7 Ibrahim al-Koni, email, dated 9/4/2014, to William Hutchins.
8 Spengler (1932 [1918–1923]) vol. 2, 147.
9 al-Kuni (2001 and 2008) I, 97, and Spengler (1932 [1918–1923]) vol. 2, 153–154.
10 al-Kuni (2001 and 2008) I, 98.
11 Ibrahim al-Koni, email, dated 9/4/2014, to William Hutchins.
12 Ibrahim al-Koni, email, dated 9/4/2014, to William Hutchins.
13 al-Kuni (2012–14) III, 398.
14 al-Kuni (2001 and 2008) III, 29–30.
15 al-Kuni (2004–2006) III, 22.
16 Herodotus, *Histories* 4.189, trans. Holland (2014) 331.
17 Cartledge in Holland (2014) 675, n. 146.
18 Herodotus, *Histories* 4.188 and 2.28, in Holland (2014) 331 and 118.
19 al-Kuni (2001 and 2008) III, 7.
20 al-Kuni (2001) 196.
21 Kerényi (1951) 127. Kerényi's ancient source for these traditions was Pausanias' *Guide to Greece* 1.18.2 and 1.27.2–3.
22 Scully (2013) 155, 169.
23 al-Kuni (2001 and 2008) III, 8.
24 al-Kuni (2001) 193.
25 al-Koni (2008) 52.
26 al-Koni (2008) 89.
27 al-Koni (2008) 120.
28 Hesiod, *Theogony* 295ff., translated in Schlegel and Weinfield (2006) 32–33.
29 Kerényi (1951) 51. Kerényi's ancient sources on Echidna include Hesiod, Theogony 270–300, Pausanias, *Guide to Greece* 8.18.2, and the Orphic fragment number 58 in Kern (1922) 138–140.
30 al-Koni (2014) 128.
31 al-Kuni (2001 and 2008) III, 31.
32 al-Kuni (2001 and 2008) III, 32.
33 al-Kuni (2001 and 2008) III, 33.
34 al-Kuni (2001 and 2008) III, 35.
35 al-Kuni (2001 and 2008) I, 91.
36 al-Kuni (2001 and 2008) I, 71.
37 al-Kuni (2001 and 2008) III, 42.
38 al-Kuni (2004–2006) III, 59.
39 al-Kuni (2004–6) III, 60–61.
40 al-Kuni (2001) 196.

41 al-Kuni (2001 and 2008) I, 91.
42 al-Kuni (2004) 153.
43 al-Kuni (2004) 72.
44 Translator's note in Fähndrich (2002) 66.
45 al-Kuni (2001) 61.
46 Almrtdi (2014) 38.
47 Deheuvels (2002) 31ff.
48 al-Kuni (2004b) 92.
49 al-Kuni (2001 and 2008) IV, 264.
50 al-Kuni (2001 and 2008). See also: Plato's *Critias*, 114a ff.
51 Herodotus 4.184 in Holland (2014) 329–330.
52 al-Kuni (2001) 310–318.
53 al-Kuni (2001) 310.
54 al-Kuni (2001 and 2008) IV, 218.
55 al-Kuni (2001) 311.
56 al-Kuni (2001) 311.
57 al-Kuni (2001) 314.
58 al-Kuni (2001) 313.
59 al-Kuni (2001) 313.
60 al-Kuni (2001 and 2008) 153.
61 al-Kuni (2001 and 2008) 155. Plutarch's text is contained in sections 384–394 of his *Moralia*, reproduced and translated in Babbitt (1936).
62 Wehr (1994) 121.
63 al-Kuni (2004–2006) I, 9.
64 al-Kuni (2001 and 2008) I, 9.
65 al-Koni (2005) 17.
66 al-Koni (2005) xv–xvii.
67 Scully (2013) 11.
68 al-Kuni (2001) 111–113.
69 al-Koni (2014) chapter 16, 138–140.
70 al-Kuni (2001) 51ff.
71 al-Kuni (2001) 11; Scully (2013) 11.
72 al-Kuni (2001) 287.
73 Ibrahim al-Koni, email, dated 9/4/2014, to William Hutchins.
74 Hesiod, *Theogony* 824–825 and 835 in Schlegel and Weinfield (2006) 48–49.
75 Kerényi (1951) 26.
76 al-Koni (2008) 191.
77 al-Kuni (2004–2006) I, 89,
78 al-Kuni (2004–2006) I, 89.
79 al-Kuni (2004–2006) I, 50.

80 Wilkinson (2003) 197.
81 Hesiod, *Theogony* 837–838, in Schlegel and Weinfield (2006) 49.
82 Hesiod, *Theogony* 869, 878–880 in Schlegel and Weinfield (2006) 50.
83 al-Kuni (2004–6) I, 50–51.
84 Ibrahim al-Koni, email, dated 9/4/2014, to William Hutchins.
85 It may be a coincidence, but the word *tyafa/tyafatan* is defined as 'fétichisme . . . culte de fétiches or 'fetishism . . . the cult of fetishes' in Prasse *et al.* (2003) vol. 2, 778.
86 al-Kuni (2001) 322.
87 al-Kuni (1998) 127.
88 al-Kuni (1998) 196.
89 al-Koni (2008) 75.
90 al-Koni (2008) 143.
91 Ibrahim al-Koni, email, dated 9/4/2014, to William Hutchins.
92 al-Koni (2008) 129.
93 al-Kuni (2005) 14–15, 236.
94 Te Velde (1967) 13–26.
95 Budge (1969) vol. 2, 367.
96 al-Musbahi (2012) chapter 5, 144.
97 al-Kuni (2004–2006) III, 51–52. The text and a translation of *Isis and Osiris* are included in Babbitt (1936).
98 Assman (2008) 44.
99 al-Kuni (2004–2006) III, 53.
100 al-Kuni (2004–2006) III, 54.
101 al-Kuni (2004–2006) III, 53.
102 al-Kuni (2001 and 2008) III, 126.
103 al-Kuni (2001 and 2008) III, 127.
104 Plutarch, *Isis and Osiris*, chs 30–1, 3 in Babbitt (1936) 75ff.
105 al-Kuni (2004–2006) I, 62.
106 Te Velde (1967) 29.
107 Te Velde (1967) 55.
108 Ibrahim al-Koni, email, dated 9/4/2014, to William Hutchins.
109 al-Kuni (2001 and 2008) III, 87, 89.
110 al-Kuni (2001 and 2008) III, 172–173.
111 al-Kuni (2001 and 2008) III, 210.
112 al-Kuni (2004b) chapter 13, 'Al-Khatar', 149–160.
113 al-Kuni (2004b) 29ff.
114 al-Kuni (2004b) 186–190.
115 al-Kuni (2004b) 248.
116 al-Kuni (2004b) chapter 20, 'al-Wahaq; ('The Lasso') 211–219.

117 Ibrahim al-Koni, email to William Hutchins dated November 15, 2013. See al-Kuni (2012–14).

118 al-Kuni (2012–14) III, 400–401.

119 See Hutchins (2003).

3 Greek Myth and Mythmaking in Witi Ihimaera's *The Matriarch* and *The Dream Swimmer*

Thanks to Edith Hall, Katie Billotte, and Justine McConnell for organizing this volume, and the conference from which it derives, with characteristic *kharis* and *aretê*. Thanks also to my first audience at the conference and to subsequent audiences at Victoria University of Wellington, Otago University and the University of Auckland for comments and suggestions. Staff at the Beaglehole Room in the V.U.W. library provided much-appreciated assistance with Ihimaera's MSS. I gratefully acknowledge the contribution of Samuel Howell and the V.U.W. Summer Scholarship which supported him in the summer of 2012/13. Most importantly, to Witi Ihimaera himself: e hoa, nga mihinui ki a koe mo tou tautoko me tou awhina.

1 One book-length exception, on J. K. Baxter, proves the rule: Miles, Davidson, and Millar (2011). In addition to Baxter, I adduce, e.g., C. K. Stead (various poems), Ian Wedde's *Commonplace Odes* (2001), Anna Jackson's *Catullus for Children* (2003) and *I, Clodia* (2014) and Harry Love's *Hūrai* (2011). See also Jackson (2009); Harrison (2009b); Perris (2013).

2 According to the author's note in the revised edition of *The Matriarch*, the diptych in fact began as one long manuscript which grew out of a single short story entitled 'The Mother' (2009: 495).

3 Ihimaera's own tribal groups are represented in a wider claim presented to the Waitangi Tribunal (WAI 814) concerning land confiscated from Maori in the Turanganui (Gisborne) area in contravention of the Treaty of Waitangi. The other iwi involved finalized settlements in 2012; but Ihimaera's iwi (nation) and hapu (tribe), Te Aitanga a Mahaki and Te Whanau a Kai, were still negotiating a Deed of Settlement as of August 2015.

4 Perris (2013).

5 Regarding the 2009 revised edition of *The Matriarch*, I will here discuss only substantive differences relevant to my argument. In the text and notes, the equivalence symbol (≈) denotes such parallel passages. For further detail, see Perris (2013).

6 Agathe Thornton argued along similar lines in *Maori Oral Literature as Seen by a Classicist* (1999). Cf. West (1966: 212) on the Ouranos–Gaia/Rangi–Papa parallel.

7 Williams (1990) 119–120.
8 Jannetta (1990: 21–22) briefly notes classical references in *The Matriarch*; Crawford (2004: 45) notes 'extensive referencing of the *Oresteia* in *The Matriarch* and *The Dream Swimmer*'. Vigier (2008: 117, 173) treats Greek tragedy as one among many paradigms.
9 Calvert (2002) 73–77.
10 Thomson (1998) 80.
11 Fox (2006) 9. According to Fox (2008) 136, however, 'Both the Verdian and the Greek intertexts serve to reveal a self that is internally divided'. I would rather subordinate the operatic intertexts to the Greek material, inasmuch as a 'conceptual framework' necessarily supersedes the 'connotative associations' provided by the Verdian intertexts (Fox (2006) 16).
12 MS in box 549/7 in the Witi Ihimaera collection housed at the Beaglehole Room, Victoria University of Wellington.
13 The Latin and Greek titles for Euripides' earlier Iphigenia play are *Iphigenia in Tauris* = *Iphigeneia hê en Taurois* = 'Iphigenia among the Taurians'.
14 Perris (2013) 21–26, 32–38.
15 In Maori, *e* + personal name = vocative *O* in Greek/Latin/English.
16 A. S. Murray (189) mentions different accounts of the Erinyes: daughters of Night; daughters of Earth and Darkness; daughters of Kronos and Eurynome. Vergil's *Aeneid* is the earliest known literary source to name the Furies (Tisiphone, Allecto and Megaera).
17 The character name 'Regan' immediately calls to mind *King Lear* and thus echoes elements in the main narrative including interrupted succession, inter-generational conflict, and blinding. Tama's daughters also have Shakespearean names, one of which further echoes Ihimaera's main plot and one of which does not: Miranda (*The Tempest*) and Bianca (*Othello*). Thus, these names both burnish the tragic pedigree of Ihimaera's story and also align it with global literary and dramatic canons.
18 I thank Witi Ihimaera for gently pointing this out to me. See Ewans (2007) 69–70.
19 Mastronarde (2002: 8) 'Medea can usefully be read as a revision or extension of the model of Clytemnestra.'
20 Fox (2006) 5. Ihimaera includes an explanation of the Verdi connection in *The Matriarch* (2009) 272.
21 *The Matriarch* (2009) 441; cf. *The Dream Swimmer* 92–95.
22 Perris (2013) 25–26.
23 See also Perris (2015) on Ihimaera's engagements with the Great Mother/Dread Goddess archetype.
24 See Belfiore (2000).
25 Witi Ihimaera, personal communication. See note 3 for the land claims of those tribal groups with which Ihimaera is affiliated.

26 See *The Matriarch* (2009), 'author's note', 496.
27 Quoted in an interview with Diana Wichtel in the *New Zealand Listener*, 8 October 2011 http://www.listener.co.nz/culture/books/witi-ihimaera-interview/ [accessed 22 February 2013].
28 Quoted in Millar (1998) 255.
29 Quoted in Millar (1998) 255.
30 Williams (1990) 119.
31 Ihimaera's lone picaresque masterpiece *Bulibasha* (1994) is an outlier.
32 Heim (2007); Fox (2008) 184–188, 208–210.
33 Ihimaera (2000) 343.
34 Ihimaera (2005) 322.
35 Millar (1998) 255–256.
36 I owe this trenchant observation to Professor Jeff Tatum.

4 War, Religion and Tragedy: The Revolt of the Muckers in Luiz Antonio de Assis Brasil's *Videiras de Cristal*

1 See interview with José Pinheiro Torres, available at http://assisbrasil.org/luizanto.html.
2 See also, Rankine in this volume (Chapter 1).
3 See Valente (1993) 54–55: 'Faced with the realization that the optimistic definition of Brazil based on harmony and unification, as forged in the nineteenth century and manipulated by military rulers from 1964 to 1985, conflicts with the reality of a society that is fragmented politically and socially, Brazilian writers have turned to the past in search of explanations for the divisions they perceive in the present. Moreover, the historical novels of the 1970s and 1980s must be seen as interlocutors in an intertextual dialogue with a literary and cultural tradition that dates back to the decades immediately following political independence and continues into the twentieth century. This tradition is exemplified by fictional and nonfictional works like Euclides da Cunha's *Os Sertoes* (1902, published in English in 1944 as Rebellion in the Backlands), Mario de Andrade's *Macunaima* (1928, published in English in 1984 under the same title), Sergio Buarque de Holanda's *Raizes do Brasil* (1936, *Roots of Brazil*), and others. Much like their nineteenth-century counterparts, recent historical novels serve as vehicles for understanding and defining Brazil. In my view (which differs somewhat from that of Jean Franco), it is not the notion of Brazil as a single nation that is being contested but an officially endorsed version of Brazil based on discredited myths and ideologies. Ultimately, these novels aim to redefine the collective past and present of Brazil in terms that can account for the heterogeneity and difference that may paradoxically constitute the essence of "Brazilianness"'.

4 Silverman (1998) 26.
5 Silverman (1998) 27.
6 Valente (1993) 41: 'Brazilian fiction has been characterized by the search for alternative angles from which to reconstruct the country's past and give forgotten or marginalized groups a voice.'
7 For a full development of this theme, see Barreto (2001).
8 See Masina (1992).
9 On the tendency for modern adaptations of *Medea* to fuse pagan and Christian motifs and also to associate divine forces with social imperatives, see Hall (2014).

5 Translating Myths, Translating Fictions

1 Rose (2011) 106.
2 Wolf (1998b).
3 Ngũgĩ (2012) 61.
4 For further discussion of the theory and practice of global translocation of performance, see Hardwick (2015).
5 Bassnett (2014) 173.
6 Hopman (2012).
7 I will not be concerned here with the finer points of translation from Wolf's original German text into English. That would be a separate paper, but it might well start with consideration of the different resonances of the Greek and German words for sacrifice used by Wolf ('burnt offerings' might be a better English translation than 'sacrifice'; the resonances with the Holocaust are very different from those of religious duty).
8 Colton (1994) 207.
9 For early and influential explorations of the idea of 'crisis' in modern literature, see Frank (1963) and Craig and Egan (1979). More recently see e.g. Pozorski (2014), which explores cultural responses to the crisis of 9/11.
10 Wolf (1998b). Elizabeth Cook in her *Achilles* (2001) 104, presents a variant on the physical metaphor: 'A game of Chinese whispers. A hot word thrown into the next lap before it burns. It has not been allowed to set. Each hand that momentarily holds it, weighs it, before depositing it with a neighbour also, inadvertently, moulds it: communicates its own heat.'
11 Wolf (1998b).
12 Wolf (1998b).
13 In his 1995 poem 'The Eternity of the Prickly Pear', Mahmoud Darwish focalizes the response of the displaced father to his son's question 'why did you leave the horse alone?': 'To be company for the house my son,/ For houses die when their

inhabitants leave them' tr. Shaheen (2014) 29. Translocated myth is one example of a living but prickly pear.

14 Steinmeyer (2003) 156.

15 van Wyk (1997) 79–80.

16 This is part of a larger trend. Translation of classical material and its role in the writing of new performance narratives in post-apartheid South Africa are discussed in Van Zyl Smit (2010) and Hardwick (2010).

17 Johnston (2013) xviii. Affiliation Studies were first developed by legal anthropologists seeking to explore the experience of indigenous peoples, especially relating to the disruption of ancient burial sites in North America, and have been applied more recently to the study of groups in historical archaeology.

18 Ngũgĩ (1986). For detailed discussion of Ngũgĩ's approach and its implications for translation studies, see Bassnett (2014) ch. 2, especially 42–44.

19 Wolf (1998b).

20 This question has been explored in reference especially to novels responding to the tragedies of Euripides, with an extended discussion of the multivocal form chosen by Wolf, in Hall (2009).

21 For further discussion on this, see Gaskin (2013), and on the rediscovery of the authorial 'subject' as a response to the literature of trauma survival, Hall (2007).

22 'Multiple frames' was the term used at the conference of the Oikos research project *Framing Classical Reception Studies* held in Nijmegen in June 2013 (Proceedings forthcoming).

23 All quotations are taken from the English translation by Van Heurck (1984).

24 Wolf (1984) 142.

25 Wolf (1984) 142.

26 Wolf (1984) 178.

27 Wolf (1984) 262.

28 Wolf (1984) 288. For the text of Schiller's poem, see Schiller (1983) 258; there is an English translation by Daniel Platt available online at http://www.schillerinstitute.org/transl/schiller_poem/cassandra.html.

29 Bridge (2004).

30 See Clauss and Johnston (1997).

31 Mastronarde (2002) 8.

32 In her essay on variations of the story of Medea, Margaret Atwood observes that 'we owe the slain children to the oddly sympathetic play by the Greek tragedian Euripides' (Atwood (1998)).

33 Atwood (1998).

34 Wolf (1998b).

35 Wolf (1998b).

36 Wolf (1998b).

37 For a rather different answer to these questions, see Hall (2009).
38 On the mythological alternatives and their relationship with Medea's psychological state, see Mastronarde (2002) 20–22.
39 Easterling (1977). Mastronarde (2002) 63 n. 102 considers the scholiasts' suggestion that Euripides was paid by the Corinthians to make Medea rather than the Corinthians the killers. Whatever the truth of the matter, this is evidence that it matters who kills them and helps to explain the priority that Wolf gives to the issue.
40 Eur. *Medea* 264 discussed by McCullum-Barry (2014) 24–26; for discussion of the wider significance of the cult in the context of the religion of *Medea*, see Hall (2014).
41 Wolf (1984) 185–186.
42 Wolf (1998) 285–289.
43 Graves (1994); Lu (2004).
44 Graves (1994) 5.
45 For example, Jason's comments on the show trials; Wolf (1998a), 164.
46 Mastronarde (2002) 8–15.
47 The exploitation of Greek and Roman texts and ideas has also been a significant element in postcolonial literature and its 'writing back' to dominant imperial cultures (see the essays and extensive bibliography in Hardwick and Gillespie (2007)).
48 Rose (2011) 106.
49 Shaheen, in Darwish (2014) 3.

6 Echoes of Ancient Greek Myths in Murakami Haruki's novels and in Other Works of Contemporary Japanese Literature

1 Japanese names are given in the normal Japanese order, with the family name preceding the personal name.
2 *The Mikado* was first performed at the Savoy Theatre, London.
3 See Miner (1966) 55–61 on the cultural significance of *The Mikado* and the Japanese vogue on the English and American stage.
4 For a detailed analysis of Yano Ryūkei's novel, see Ghidini (2013).
5 Inose Naoki with Sato Hiroaki (2012) 718.
6 Plato, *Phaedo* 62c, translated by Fowler (1914).
7 'Edge' was published posthumously as no. 42 in the collection *Ariel* (1965).
8 Mishima (1982a) 73–132.
9 Mishima (1982b) 108.
10 For Greek influence on Mishima, see also 'Girisha', in Matsumoto, Satō, and Inoue (2000) 482–483.

11 Mishima (2006), 84. Kawabata Yasunari, who was Mishima's mentor, apparently did not share this view. In one of his short stories, 'Nāshissasu' ('Narcissus', 1927) he choose, in one of the most unusual version of this myth, to make Narcissus a female character; see Kawabata (1981) 417–439. This short story is extensively analyzed in Starrs (1998) 77–87.
12 My interpretation is confirmed by the homoerotic undertones of this essay, even though they are not easy to detect in the English translation, where several passages are abridged.
13 Kurahashi (1984) 254.
14 For an analysis of the Oedipus myth in Kurahashi Yumiko's *To Die at the Estuary* and in Murakami's Haruki's *Kafka on the Shore*, see Cardi (2014).
15 The numbers in the text here and henceforward refer to the pages in Murakami (2005).
16 In his poem 'Responsibilities', published in Yeats (1914) 172–174.
17 Lichtig (2005).
18 Komori (2006), 23–28.
19 Polese (2008).

7 'It's All in the Game': Greek Myth and *The Wire*

1 Hornby (2007).
2 Hornby (2007).
3 The scholarly literature on this is vast. See, for example, Reinhold (1984), Sellers (1994) and Richard (1994).
4 Rawlings (2013).
5 Letter of 18 June 1813, to James Monroe in Jefferson (2009) 257.
6 Dubois (1920) 25.
7 Kennedy was slightly misquoting Edith Hamilton's translation of Aeschylus' *Agamemnon,* 179–183, in her *The Greek Way* (1930) 156. Kennedy's words, which can be heard at http://www.npr.org/2008/04/04/89365887/robert-kennedy-delivering-news-of-kings-death, are quoted from Schlesinger (1978) 875 and 1020 n.84, who also describes how Kennedy encountered Hamilton's book at 616–620.
8 See, for example, novels by Percival Everett, Toni Morrison, Jesmyn Ward among many others.
9 There is an excellent list of resources produced by the University of York available online at http://www.york.ac.uk/media/sociology/curb/publications/The%20Wire%20resource%20list.pdf.
10 Chou (2011); duBois (2004).
11 Love (2010) 496.

12 See especially Hall (2011).
13 Unless otherwise indicated, quotations are from *The Wire: The Complete Series* (New York: HBO Video, 2008), DVD.
14 Love (2010) 499.
15 MacDougall (2006).
16 Watkins (2014).
17 Love (2010) 502.
18 Love (2010) 503.
19 Directed respectively by Alan Parker (1988) and Martin Scorsese (1985).
20 Love (2010) 503.
21 A version of this was subsequently published as Žižek (2012).
22 Ducker (2006).
23 Moore (2010).
24 Obama's statement was made in January 2012 on Bill Simmons' podcast *The B.S. Report*. Bill Simmons asked Obama to settle an office debate: 'Best *Wire* character of all time?' Obama answered 'It's got to be Omar, right? I mean, that guy is unbelievable, right? . . . And that was one of the best shows of all time.'
25 Translated by the editors.
26 Translated by the editors.
27 Weil (1956) 5. The translation is by Mary McCarthy of the French text which first appeared in December 1940 and January 1941 issues of *Cahiers du Sud*. On Weil's essay, see also Reynolds, this volume.
28 Anderson (2010) has argued that phrases in *The Wire* like 'The Game is the Game' both offer and conceal meaning. You can only know what the game is by playing it. And to play the game, whether as politician, cop or drug dealer, means that you will lose, eventually.
29 By 'Panglossian', I mean the type of extreme and unrealistic optimism associated in Voltaire's *Candide* with the figure of Dr Pangloss.
30 See Goodman (2012).
31 Alvarez (2004) 4.
32 Simon (2000) 3.
33 Rowbotham (2012).
34 See further the discussion in Bolf-Beliveau and Beliveau (2015) 217.
35 Bryant (2009).
36 There is a fuller analysis of some of these moments in Lavik (2011).
37 E.g. Zeitlin (1994); Hall (2009).
38 Jameson (2010) 362.
39 See for example http://dossierjournal.com/read/theory/baltimore-as-world-and-representation-cognitive-mapping-and-capitalism-in-the-wire/.
40 Fitzgerald is here misquoted, as he is often. What he actually wrote, in a story unpublished in his lifetime, printed in Fitzgerald (1965), called 'My Lost City', was

much more optimistic: 'I once thought that there were no second acts in American lives, but there was certainly to be a second act to New York's boom days.'

41 He uses both Sophocles' *Oedipus Tyrannus* and Petronius' *Satyrica* (which used to be known as the *Satyricon*) in *The Great Gatsby* (1925), for example.

42 Moore (2010).

43 Skillz (2008).

44 Curry (2013). It is interesting in this context to juxtapose an article by black Baltimore writer D. Watkins (2014) in which he describes Baltimore as two cities barely able to communicate the one with the other: 'My black friends call it Baldamore, Harm City or Bodymore Murderland. My white friends call it Balti-mo, Charm City or Smalltimore . . . I just call it home.' Watkins describes his various journeys between white Bolton Hill and black Marble Hill, and how he gradually learns to communicate between the two. He describes this process as assembling a set of fictional reference points till he is able to tell stories that, briefly, span the divide. He becomes *The Wire*. He recognizes that this process of communication is fragile, and won't last – the connection, such as it is, occurs in telling the story. As Watkins puts it: 'the two Baltimores felt like one – but only for that night. Because after the show, I travelled back to my Baltimore and they returned to theirs.'

45 The quotations from Simon's talk are taken from a report by Chris Barton, which can be read online at http://latimesblogs.latimes.com/showtracker/2008/03/the-wire-david.html.

8 Writing a New Irish Odyssey: Theresa Kishkan's *A Man in a Distant Field*

1 Kishkan (2004) 65–6. All subsequent references to the novel appear in parentheses in the text following the citation.

2 First published in 1843 and 1924 respectively.

3 Presumably one of the several Loeb editions of the text with translation by A. T. Murray, first published in 1919.

4 On hedge schools, see Stanford (1976) 25–30; Macintosh (1994) 2.

5 Kiberd (1992).

6 Foster (2014) 87–90.

7 Joyce's Cyclops, the Citizen in Episode 12 of *Ulysses*, is a racist nationalist who rails in the pub against the Jews in front of Leopold Bloom.

8 Gregory (1902).

9 Notably by Arbois de Jubainville (1899). For comment, see Macintosh (1994), especially 10.

10 Thomson (1929); Huxley (1969); Luce (1969); O'Nolan (1969).

11 Synge (1982) 44–184.
12 Macintosh (1994) 35–6.
13 Cf Synge (1982) especially 74.
14 Stanford (1976) 211.
15 Joyce (1971) 367.
16 See the excellent study of American lyrical responses to Homer by Platt (2015).
17 Mahon (2005) 57–9.
18 Longley (1991) 33, 35.
19 Macintosh (2015) on the emblematic figure of Erin.
20 Foster (2014).

9 The Minotaur on the Russian Internet: Viktor Pelevin's *Helmet of Horror*

1 Ljunggren and Rotkirch (2008) 84–85.
2 See, for example, Andrei Konchalovsky's *The Odyssey* (1997); another earlier and more refined and important example is Marcel Camus' *Black Orpheus* (1959). For a substantial recent bibliography on late twentieth- and twenty-first-century uses of classical mythology in contemporary media and culture, see Moog-Grünewald (2010).
3 An anglophone edition of OBERIU writings translated by Eugene Ostashevsky, Matvei Yankelevich, Genya Turovskaya, Thomas Epstein and Ilya Bernstein was published as *OBERIU: An Anthology of Russian Absurdism* by Northwestern University Press in 2006. OBERIU's pioneering works have extended an influence over Russian culture out of all proportion to the briefness of their actual activities, and are often cited as influences by contemporary dissident performers including the feminist pop group Pussy Riot.
4 Brodsky (1989).
5 Genis (1999) 217.
6 See the extensive discussion of aesthetic strategies of the late Soviet unofficial art in Bobrinskaya (2013).
7 For the 'void' as an artistic concept, see Bobrinskaya (2013) 261–67. There is an important collection of essays on Moscow Conceptualism available in English translation, published as Groys (2010).
8 Quotes from *The Helmet of Horror* are taken from Pelevin (2006).
9 See the discussion of the code of behaviour in the Russian rave-subculture of the 1990s (an ironic parody in Russian is called 'stiob') in Alexei Yurchak, 'Nochnye tancy s angelom istorii. Kriticheskie kultural'nye issledovanija post-socializma: http://www.academia.edu/393241/./ Accessed 20.03.2014/.

10 An excellent English translation of Michel Foucault's essay 'Des espaces autres', by Jay Miskowiec (1984), is available online at http://web.mit.edu/allanmc/www/foucault1.pdf.

11 Kerényi (1951) 111.

12 This episode begins 95 minutes into Fellini's *Satyricon*, and is briefly discussed by Armstrong (2011) 120–21.

13 The author expresses gratitude to Edith Hall for communicating this information.

14 Federico Fellini's *Satyricon* is widely known and celebrated in Russia, having been shown both in cinemas and on TV. Victor Pelevin is also acquainted with both *Star Wars* and *The Matrix*, and prefers the first film in the latter series (Ljunggren and Rotkirch (2008) 85). On the impact of *The Matrix* on the contemporary Russian literature, see also Ågren (2010). Sergei Eisenstein, as a reader of C. G Jung, shaped a Teuton knight as an image of the archaic which makes possible a connection to the Minotaur. On Eisenstein's reading in psychoanalysis, see Lövgren (1996) 16–19.

15 Victor Pelevin was working with materials on oriental mysticism for the journal *Science and Religion* [*Nauka i religiya*] in the 1980s. He frequently uses patterns borrowed from the Buddhist learning in his works and interviews and answers the question about his connection to Buddhism in a following manner: 'When *and how did you become acquainted with Buddhism?* – It was about two thousand years ago in Benares. I don't remember the exact circumstances' (Ljunggren and Rotkirch (2008) 78, 85).

16 For some other contemporary novelists' use of Greek myth in exploring the philosophical status of subjectivity, see Hall (2007).

17 See the notion of 'errative' describing the internet 'anti-norm' was introduced in: Gasan Guseinov, 'Berloga webloga. Vvedenie в erraticheskuiu semantiku', http:/speakrus/.ru/gg.microprosa_erratica-1.htm [2006]; "Zametki k antropologii russlog interneta: osobennosti jazyka i literatury setevych ljudej", (Novoe literaturnoe obozrenie N43. Moskva 2000), 289–321. Http:/ magazines. russ.ru.nlo/2000/43/main.8.html. / Accessed 20.03.2014/.

18 Cf. speaking in unison as a device in OBERIU (The Association for Real Art): see Daniil Charms' play *Elizaveta Bam* (1972, first published 1927) and Aleksandr Vvedinskii's play *Elka u Ivanovykh* [Christmas at the Ivanovs] (1938).

19 Ljunggren and Rotkirch (2008) 86.

10 Diagnosis: Overdose – Status: Critical. Odysseys in Bernhard Schlink's *Die Heimkehr*

1 Leopold (2006); unless otherwise indicated, all translations of German texts are the author's.

2 Cavelty (2006).

3 For example, Cavelty (2006): 'Bernhard Schlink's "Homecoming" is a Gordian knot, a fabric woven of discourses, lies, twists and turns.' Or Leopold (2006): 'Schlink could have written a nice and neat novel based on each individual strand of the narrative. But he seems not to have wanted that. He wanted everything.'
4 For example, Weidermann (2006): 'Earlier on the novel has already rushed through German history like a tornado – the end of World War II, the fall of Breslau, flight from the East, post-war misery, finally the fall of the Wall, reunification and 9/11. The book leaves nothing out and, on top of it all, every single strand of the narrative is forced into the template of Homer's *Odyssey*, the ur-story of all homecoming.'
5 For example, Schmitz (2012): 'The artfully interwoven, cleverly constructed tales of homecoming are intellectually intriguing but ultimately leave the reader cold . . . Otherwise coherent narrative strands lose their dramatic force in tiring digressions about law . . . In Schlink, emotions are effectively suffocated by historical references, legal discourses and philosophical reflections.'
6 Weidermann (2006).
7 See Beßlich *et al.* (2006).
8 See Fischer and Roberts (2007) and Krauss (2008).
9 See Emmerich (2008) 26.
10 Sebald's *Luftkrieg und Literatur* (1999) and Grass' *Im Krebsgang* (2002) are hallmarks of this development. On representations of German wartime suffering since 1945, see Schmitz (2007).
11 Müller (2003).
12 See Emmerich (2008) 27.
13 See, for example, Mauelshagen (1995), Vogt (1998), Schlant (1999) 80–99, and Fuchs (2008) 20–44.
14 See Fuchs *et al.* (2006) and Fuchs (2008), esp. 203.
15 '*The Reader* is about Germany as victim. It is a victim of its history of murder, to be sure, but then, even the murderers themselves are victims, and those they ultimately victimize are the next generation of Germans. It is a German fate.' Bartov (2000) 34; cf. Knobloch (2007).
16 Friedrich (2008) 215–217.
17 On the resulting discrepancy between official/public and private memory, see Assmann (2006a), esp. 21–118 and 205–216, and Assmann (2006b), esp. 25.
18 Friedrich (2008) 218.
19 See Friedrich (2008) 218–222. The controversy surrounding Jörg Friedrich's *Der Brand. Deutschland im Bombenkrieg 1940–1945* (2002) with its overt and markedly collective *victima* rhetoric illustrates the persisting resistance against narrativizations of German wartime suffering that go beyond strictly 'personal' accounts; see Fulda (2006).
20 See Fuchs (2008) 203.
21 Friedrich (2008) 221.

22 Fuchs (2008) 204.

23 Stephan (2007), esp. 172; notwithstanding significant post-war reactions against myth as discredited by extensive Nazi appropriations, see Bohrer (1983), esp. 10. For discussions of this trend, see Schrödter (1991), Emmerich (2005), and Fischer and Roberts (2007) 171–222; key examples include Strauß's *Ithaka* and Wolf's *Medea: Stimmen* (both 1996), on the latter of which see Hardwick's chapter in this volume.

24 See Stephan (2007) 172–173 and Fuchs (2008) 203–204.

25 On continuities and differences between the fathers' literature of the 1970s and 80s and more recent generational novels, see Eigler (2005).

26 *Die Heimkehr* (=*DH*; page references to German/English editions), 73–75/52–53; cf. Hom. *Od.* 10.1–27.

27 *DH* 81–82/56–7; cf. Hom. *Od.* 11.84–224.

28 *DH* 84–86/58–60; cf. Hom. *Od.* 5.151–267.

29 *DH* 94–96/65–67.

30 On Schlink's not unproblematic portrayal of deconstruction, see Börnchen (2008).

31 The writings are collected in Hamacher *et al.* (1988); see Hamacher *et al.* (1989) for early responses by de Man's supporters. The critique of deconstruction as ethically and intellectually dubious articulated, not least against the backdrop of this controversy, in Evans (1997), esp. 233–238, resonates in Schlink's novel.

32 *DH* 289/201.

33 *DH* 139/97.

34 *DH* 140–143/98–100.

35 *DH* 141/98; cf. Hom. *Od.* 10.80–132, 1–24 and 135–547, respectively.

36 *DH* 130/92.

37 *DH* 289–290/201.

38 *DH* 206–207/144.

39 *DH* 27/18.

40 *DH* 32/22.

41 *DH* 32/22.

42 *DH* 326/226.

43 *DH* 255/176.

44 *Der Vorleser* (=*DV*; German/English editions), 42–43/40.

45 *DV*, 174/181.

46 *DV*, 192–194/201–203.

47 Cf. Taberner (2002) 34 and Niven (2003).

48 A realist novel about a German soldier's return from internment in Siberia, whose exculpating portrayal of the protagonist as a Nazi-sceptic 'good German' contrasts with the picture emerging from Schlink's novel.

49 Note Peter's extensive reflections on the implications, possibilities, and problems of such Homer receptions at *DH* 78–80/54–56 and 95–99/65–69.

50 See *DH* 130/92, 139–143/97–100, 175/121, 289/201, 368/255. Together with his presence as an intrafictional storyteller (at *DH* 124–125/6 and 174–175/120–121) and unreliable narrator (who reveals at *DH* 132/93 that the preceding chapter was an idealized, fictional account that is now corrected), Peter approximates the type of character engaged with 'overt fictionalization' discussed by Paver (1999), esp. x–xii and 1–19.
51 *DH* 200/140.
52 *DH* 202–204/141–142.
53 *DH* 207/144.
54 *DH* 309/214–215; another reference to de Man, whose complicated post-war family life in America has already been fictionalized by Henri Thomas in his 1964 novel *Le parjure*.
55 *DH* 362–364/251–253.
56 See *DH* 228–229/158–159, 272–273/186–187, and 375/260.
57 See Wöhrle (1999), esp. 11–48 and 117–144.
58 See *DH* 314–315/218–219.
59 On '[t]he *Odyssey*'s status as the archetype of all fiction' (Hall (2008) 46), which predestines it for taking on this role, see Calvino (1981).
60 On this seminal text and its influence on the reception of the *Odyssey*, see Hall (2008) 94–95, 100, 207.
61 'The instrument by which the self survives adventure, casts itself away in order to preserve itself, is cunning.' Adorno and Horkheimer (1947) 114.
62 Porter (2010) 204; cf. Adorno and Horkheimer (1947) 130–131.
63 *DH* 314–315/218.
64 *DH* 292/203.
65 Adorno and Horkheimer (1947) 139–140.
66 Porter (2010) 202.
67 Cf. e.g. Arist. *Poetics* 1451b:19–26, 1453b:22–26, and Blumenberg (1979) 34.
68 Cf. e.g. Moritz (1791) and Blumenberg (1979) 3–33.
69 Typologies of myth reception which distinguish between variation of myth (in details), correction of myth (in its core), and critique of myth (through wholesale rejection), as in Vöhler *et al.* 2005 (esp. 7), fail to accommodate a response like Schlink's, which *continues* mythological writing and *thereby* critiques/rejects it.
70 See *DH* 130/96 (Barbara as Penelope), 236/163 (the couple's reconciliation compared with the nation's reunification) 254–255/176 (reunification compared with a couple moving in together, followed by a nod to the couple's Homeric furniture secret).
71 See Williamson (2004), esp. 293–299.
72 A charge held against Schlink's *Vorleser* by Adler (2002) and others.
73 Adorno and Horkheimer (1947) 118.
74 Frye (1957) 57.
75 Adorno and Horkheimer (1947) 141

11 Narcissus and the Furies: Myth and Docufiction in Jonathan Littell's *The Kindly Ones*

1 The numbers in the text here and henceforward refer to the pages in Littell (2010), the Vintage edition of the English translation by Charlotte Mandell.

2 Mercier-Leca (2007); Grethlein (2009) and (2012); Mendelsohn (2009).

3 For a discussion of the challenges involved in the artistic representation of the Holocaust, see Schwarz (1999). For some other uses of Greek myth, and especially Homer and Greek tragedy in negotiating the portrayal of the death camps and the other horrors of World War II, see Hall (2004) 191–193, (2007), and (2008) 208–210. On Greek myth in fiction dealing with World War II, see especially Hall (2009); for film, Michelakis (2004) 209–210.

4 This highlights the extremely fraught clash between German history and classical mythology explored by Matzner, this volume.

5 For other invitations to conceive the action described in the novel as a theatrical performance, see pp. 6, 141, 172, 401, 403, 447, 476–477.

6 *A Report on the Banality of Evil* was the celebrated subtitle of Arendt's *Eichmann in Jerusalem* (1963).

7 Mönniger (2006). See the negative reception of Schlink's novel, also described is 'kitsch', in the first newspaper reviews discussed by Matzner, this volume.

8 LaCapra (2011), 'Abstract'.

9 Radisch (2008): 'Warum sollen wir dieses Buch eines schlecht schreibenden, von sexuellen Perversionen gebeutelten, einer elitären Rasseideologie und einem antiken Schicksalsglauben ergebenen gebildeten Idioten um Himmels willen dennoch lesen? Ich muss gestehen: Pardon, *chers amis français*, aber auf diese Frage habe ich keine Antwort gefunden.'

10 Lanzmann (2006), who continues: 'In spite of the best efforts of the author, these 900 stormy pages are completely unconvincing . . . The book as a whole is simply a scene setter and Littell's fascination for the villain, for horror, for the extremes of sexual perversion, work entirely against his story and his character, inspiring discomfort and repulsion, even though it's hard to say against who or what.'

11 Lanzmann (2007).

12 Manne (2009).

13 For the cultural resonances of this famous sentiment, see Hall (2010) 'Introduction.'

14 On the importance in classical reception of these famous lines from *IA*, see further Hall (2005).

15 See e.g. Michaud (1832) 289.

16 Hagemann (1936), a review in the Catholic journal *Germania* for 6 August 1936, cited and further discussed in Fischer-Lichte (2008) 493.

17 Rosenberg (1930) vol. 1, 37–45.

18 Stobl (2007) 7; Hall (2013) 216–227.
19 Stobl (2007) 8.
20 Stobl (2007) 191.
21 Stobl (2007) 3; Gadberry (2004).
22 Stobl (2007) 212
23 Hostetter (2004) 196.
24 Hofstetter (2004) 197.
25 Hofstetter (2004) 198.
26 Quoted in Delvaux (1992) 43–44.
27 Bourguignon (2007) 38; see Hall (2013) 209–230.
28 Waldemar von Radetsky was indeed a brutal Baltic SS Officer who participated in the Ukrainian exterminations and was later convicted of war crimes.
29 Clemens' account fuses details from *The Libation Bearers* which are drawn both from the nurse Cilissa's speech about looking after Orestes when he was a baby (749–56), and from the actual confrontation between Orestes and his mother before he kills her, when she does indeed show him her breast (896–8).
30 On the coercive and unsatisfactory conclusion of *Eumenides*, see further Hall (2015).
31 See e,g, Hall (1998) xxii.
32 See Hall (2013) 5 with Fig. I.i and 209 with fig. X.2.
33 See further Hall (2013) 180.
34 See Näcke (1899), and the history of the Narcissus myth within psychiatry and psychoanalysis in Engels (2013), especially 78.
35 See McGuire and Hull (1977).
36 Hyland, Boduszek and Kielkiewicz (2011).
37 Above all Grethlein (2012).
38 Blumenthal (2006).
39 Blumenthal (2006).

12 Philhellenic Imperialism and the Invention of the Classical Past: Twenty-first Century Re-imaginings of Odysseus in the Greek War for Independence

1 A word found in local nineteenth-century texts that connotes the chase of a chimera, a chase over and beyond the possible, according to the author.
2 Historical novels have blossomed on the Greek literary scene for at least two decades now. They provide history from (and in) literature to an audience that seems ever growing. The novels seem to feed, and are fed by, a national historical introspection. This literature turns to the past as a source both of illumination and puzzlement, locating individualized and epic narrative, in predominantly recent Greek history

(late-nineteenth century onwards). In these novels, nation and individual are experienced alongside each other, but often in conflict. Isidoros Zourgos has emerged in the last ten or so years as a major contributor to this literature. In particular, his insistence on questioning the certainties of collective narratives has become a landmark feature of his work: his protagonists, often humble personalities, are impressive in their tenaciousness, individuals pitted against trends, history, cultural values and traditions. In *Aidonopita*, ancient Greek mythology, and, to a lesser extent, Christian imagery, both prove inadequate as guidance for the hero. As a result the climax of the story is not to be found in epic success and 'arrival', but in intense solitary moments and personal choices that the hero makes against a background of narrative and historical forces that seem to work against him.

3 Discussing the trajectory of the unified nation state in the years since the Greek revolution, John Koliopoulos and Thanos Veremis suggest that 'Northern European liberals and Romantics constructed and promoted a view of modern Greece that corresponded to their own sensibilities and satisfied their Western intellectual requirements. Modern Greeks, for their part, created their own Europe. Those at least who chose the West European liberal nation-state as a model for Greek national development created a Europe that satisfied the ideological requirements of its creators' (Koliopoulos and Veremis (2002) 283). See also Tzanelli (2008), especially 1–16, on the exclusionary techniques that surrounded Greek nation-building in the nineteenth century, expected by Europe and adopted by a Greek state eager for recognition.

4 For a detailed account of America's involvement in the Greek Revolution, see Lazos (1983).

5 When addressing the Romantic idea of Ancient Greece as transcendent truth, one thinks above all of Percy Bysshe Shelley, and his verse drama *Hellas*, written in 1821 as news of the Greek revolution was breaking out in Europe. On this, and on the challenges that the Greek revolution posed to this idealistic view of ancient Greek civilization, see Beaton (2014).

6 Leontis (1995) 41; also 40–66 for a broader look at the heterotopoias generated through arriving at (and writing about) the Acropolis, with an ample bibliography (especially 41, notes 4 and 5).

7 See also note 1 above.

8 To borrow a phrase from the travelogue by Lady Mary Wortley Montague, one of the early British travellers to Greece; see Koundoura (2004).

9 I deliberately allude here to one of the most iconic accounts of visiting the Acropolis: that of Sigmund Freud in 1936. Once again Gabriel leads us through the looking glass; violently shaken out of his dream of the land of classical heroes striding across a proud land in a forced co-existence with far less impressive copies of the old, he reflects Freud's own, frequently discussed, shock at the moment when

the ideal turns out to have a very material (and less elevated) incarnation on the rock of the Acropolis and its surroundings. On this encounter, see Gourgouris (1996) 122–128.

10 Throughout his work Zourgos has regularly opened his narrative to classical themes, as well as to iconic themes from beyond the Greek repertory. European symbols and literature have been important in his work since his first novel (Zourgos 1995), modelled on the myth of Faust, while a consciously epic-heroic element runs through the *Bildungsroman* of a group of boys growing up against a background of war-torn Cyprus in 1974 in Zourgos (2000). Zourgos (2011) is a fascinating contemporary tale of male escape, in constant, explicit and playful dialogue with Homer. Finally, his most recent book (Zourgos 2014) is a substantial travelogue across countries, cultures, religions, and politics in seventeenth- and early eighteenth-century Europe.

11 All English translations from Zourgos' novel in this article are mine. The pages in brackets refer to the Greek original.

12 Cf. here *Od.* 6.127–137.

13 *Od.*17. 336–341.

14 http://www.americanphilhellenessociety.com/history.html. Accessed on 24/04/2014.

15 The often contingent function of Philhellenism and, in association, classical Hellenism within the different national agendas of nineteenth-century European powers has been scrutinised in recent scholarship with postcolonial orientation; cf. Gourgouris (1996), especially 122–154; Most (2008); Marchand (2009a); Marchand (2009b), especially 53–101; Miliori (2009); van Steen (2010).

16 A lengthy semi-autobiographical narrative written in four cantos in Spenserian stanzas recounting the adventures of the jaded aristocratic youth of the title around the Iberian Peninsula, Italy and the Aegean Sea. Significantly, the *Pilgrimage* was a kind of Bible for young Gabriel in Zourgos' novel, the one book he kept in his bag together with his diary.

17 Byron [McGann] (1986) 98.

18 Byron [McGann] (1986) 95–96. On Byron's political masterminding and his conviction that the Greek War of Independence had a significant role to play in the geopolitical developments across Europe, see Beaton (2013), especially 211–227.

19 The reference here is to Augusta Leigh, his half-sister.

20 Gourgouris (1996) 131.

21 On the challenge that this enforced reciprocity poses for contemporary Europe, see Tzanelli (2008) 177–188.

22 For a reflection of the idea of Europe caught between 'one and many', see Vestraete (2010), especially 20–40.

23 Cf. Yerasimos Kaklamanis, quoted in Gourgouris (1996) 173: 'Hellenic culture comes to the West after centuries of elaboration and historical wear in the domains of the

Eastern Mediterranean, in a tremendously extensive composite nature. The West does not inherit solely the ancient Greeks; along with the ancients it inherits the spirit of the Byzantine quarrels about them, as well as the Arab problematization of them.'

24 In its rejection of a resolution, Zourgos' epic story is reminiscent of diverse Odyssean reworkings such as Tennyson's *Ulysses* and Kazantzakis' *Odyssey*.

13 The 'Poem of Force' in Australia: David Malouf, *Ransom* and Chloe Hooper, *The Tall Man*

1 Malouf (1974) 13.

2 Golding (1954). The ethnonym 'Myrmidons' itself suggests swarming, being etymologically from the same root as the Greek word for an ant, *myrmēx*,

3 The SS *City of Benares* was launched in 1936. In September 1940 she was sailing for Canada with ninety evacuated children aboard. She was struck by a torpedo from a German submarine and sank off Rockall. The ship was abandoned but many of the children died, lost at sea.

4 Malouf (2009a).

5 In the years after the Second World War, Australia became concerned about the rise of Communism in South East Asia. In 1962 Australia sent a small group of military advisors to assist the government of South Vietnam in their struggle with Communist-run North Vietnam. Over the following decade as the conflict escalated to war, approximately 60,000 Australians served in Vietnam. 521 were killed, and more than 3,000 were wounded. Australian troops were finally withdrawn in 1973. American president Lyndon B. Johnson made an official visit to Australia in October 1966 and 'All the way with LBJ' figured in demonstrations supporting the war.

6 At Anzac Cove in 1915 the stretcher-bearer John Simpson used donkeys to transport wounded soldiers to the shore for evacuation, before himself being killed.

7 Plebiscites on conscription were carried out in Australia in October 1916 and December 1917. Both were rejected, the second by a large margin. At the beginning of the Second World War, conscription was introduced for unmarried men aged twenty-one but they were required to serve in Australia or its territories only. Under the National Service Act (1964), compulsory military service for males aged twenty was introduced.

8 The protest group called Save Our Sons was formed in Sydney in 1965. Many other groups joined it and they helped conscientious objectors to make their case. In April 1971 five SOS women were sentenced to 14 days in Fairlea Women's Prison for distributing anti-conscription leaflets to men registering for national service. The

charge was trespass. The plight of the 'Fairlea Five' attracted great attention and the women were released after eleven days.

9 The Joint Defence Facility Pine Gap – usually just called Pine Gap – is a satellite tracking station about eighteen kilometres south-west of the town of Alice Springs, Northern Territory, in the centre of Australia. It is operated by both Australia and the United States, so that it is partly run by the US Central Intelligence Agency (CIA), US National Security Agency (NSA) and US National Reconnaissance Office (NRO). The Facility is a key contributor to the global surveillance network ECHELON.
10 Malouf (2009b) 31.
11 Malouf (2009b) 27.
12 Malouf (2009b) 59.
13 Malouf (2009b) 70.
14 Malouf (2009b) 75.
15 Malouf (2009b) 98–99.
16 Malouf (2009b) 174 and 184.
17 Malouf (2009b) 192, 186, 208, 216.
18 Weil (2005 [1940]) 3. Weil's essay was first published in 1940 in *Cahiers du Sud* as 'L'*Iliade,* ou le poeme de la force', copyright 1989 Editions Gallimard. English translation by Mary McCarthy first published in the November 1945 issue of *Politics.*
19 Malouf (2009a).
20 Weil (2005 [1940]) 3.
21 Weil (2005 [1940]) 4.
22 Weil (2005 [1940]) 5.
23 Weil (2005 [1940]) 9.
24 Weil (2005 [1940]) 11.
25 Weil (2005 [1940]) 23.
26 Weil (2005 [1940]) 30 and 31.
27 Malouf (2009b [1940]) 218.
28 Weil (2005 [1940]) 31.
29 Weil (2005 [1940]) 35.
30 Malouf (1978).
31 Maolouf (2009a).
32 This primarily related to immigration and had been in force since the early twentieth century. The 'White Australia' slogan was 'Australia for Australians'. From 1949 to 1966 successive governments lifted the restrictions on migrants from countries other than Britain and in 1973 under the premiership of Gough Whitlam laws were passed to ensure that race was disregarded with regard to immigration to Australia. For the background to the policy, see Willard (1967).

33 In spite of the curious wording of this legislation the Indigenous Peoples were, in fact, counted in the censuses before 1967. However it was widely believed that they were not, and at the time of the 1967 referendum many people understood that they were not. The original purpose of the wording of Clause 127 relates to the calculation of the population for the purposes of returning members of parliament to the federal government and the clause was designed to stop Queensland and Western Australia – where both states then had large Aboriginal populations – acquiring too many seats.

34 'I move: That today we honour the Indigenous peoples of this land, the oldest continuing cultures in human history. We reflect on their past mistreatment. We reflect in particular on the mistreatment of those who were Stolen Generations – this blemished chapter in our nation's history. The time has now come for the nation to turn a new page in Australia's history by righting the wrongs of the past and so moving forward with confidence to the future. We apologize for the laws and policies of successive Parliaments and governments that have inflicted profound grief, suffering and loss on these our fellow Australians. We apologize especially for the removal of Aboriginal and Torres Strait Islander children from their families, their communities and their country. For the pain, suffering and hurt of these Stolen Generations, their descendants and for their families left behind, we say sorry. To the mothers and the fathers, the brothers and the sisters, for the breaking up of families and communities, we say sorry. And for the indignity and degradation thus inflicted on a proud people and a proud culture, we say sorry. We the Parliament of Australia respectfully request that this apology be received in the spirit in which it is offered as part of the healing of the nation.' Kevin Rudd, 'Apology to Australia's Indigenous Peoples', 13 February 2008: www.dss.gov.au/our.../apology-to-australias-indigenous-peoples. The 'Stolen Generations' refers to the ethnic cleansing practice of removing mixed Aboriginal children from their birth families. In February 2009, on the first anniversary of the Apology, all Australian schools received a large reproduction of the Apology Motion calligraphy artwork 'as a permanent reminder of our shared Journey of Reconciliation'. I have seen this Apology prominently displayed in the reception area of a school in Sydney.

35 Hooper (2006).

36 Hooper (2006) 117.

37 Hooper (2010 [2008]) 22.

38 Hooper (2010 [2008]) 26.

39 Weil (2005 [1940]) 5.

40 Hooper (2010 [2008]) 74.

41 Hooper (2010 [2008]) 52–53.

42 Malouf (2009a).

43 Hooper (2010 [2008]) 102.

44 Hooper (2010 [2008]) 228–229.

14 Young Female Heroes from Sophocles to the Twenty-First Century

1 Adrienne Meyer's recent *The Amazons: Lives and Legends of Warrior Women Across the Ancient World* (2015) provides an excellent introduction to the topic.

2 The three installments were published in 2008 (*The Hunger Games*), 2009 (*Catching Fire*) and 2010 (*Mockingjay*). The trilogy has subsequently been adapted into four internationally successful films.

3 For an overview of the performance history and broader intellectual and philosophical reception history of the play see Mee and Foley (2011a) in conjunction with Steiner (1979). Wilmer and Dillon (2005) also includes important material on 'rebel women' in contemporary productions of Greek tragedy more broadly.

4 See Mee and Foley (2011a) for studies of many late twentieth-century theatrical receptions of the play, and Hall (2004) 18 for a list of wide-ranging examples.

5 Roy-Bhattacharya (2012), 9.

6 Mee and Foley (2011b) 22.

7 Roy-Bhattacharya (2012), 17.

8 Blake Morrison translated *Antigone* for Northern Broadsides' 2013 production.

9 *The Guardian* (4 October 2003).

10 http://joydeeproybhattacharya.com/interviews.html (last visited 3 March 2015).

11 On the representation of the East, or 'foreign' in Greek tragedy, see Hall (1989).

12 Mee (2011), a revised version of her earlier discussion of *Antigone* in India and Manipur (Mee, 2010) in the volume *India, Greece and Rome* edited by Hall and Vasunia.

13 On the 'insular, parochial, introverted' portrayal of Thebes in the play, see Hall (2011) 54. Edith Hall also argues here that the local nature of the play (all the characters are from one city) makes it one of the easiest Greek tragedies to topicalize or acculturate elsewhere.

14 It is perhaps worth commenting that in the transition from a dramatic source text to a prose version, this is a useful way of preserving the dramatic nature of the first person.

15 The translator, 'Ismene', and the Antigone character were the only two Afghan characters in the novel and were generally perceived to be the least credible: 'these two Afghan characters are the least believable' (Sampson (2012)).

16 The novel has also been criticized for omitting the voices of the male Afghan soldiers, the ANA: 'The absence of Pashtun male voices in a novel about the Afghanistan war is a perplexing decision in a novel that is structured to embrace a multiplicity of voices' (Shamsie (2012)).

17 On the phenomenon of the strong female characters that appear in fifth-century drama, despite it being authored and performed by men, see Shaw (1975), Foley (1981), Zeitlin (1996), McClure (1999), Foley (2001), Hall (2010) Chapter 3 section 3; on whether women were in the audience, see the summary of the debate in McClure (1999), particularly Chapter 1.

18 It is possible that the name was inspired by that of Leo Frobenius (1873–1938), famous archaeologist and ethnologist whose areas of interest included India and South-East Asia. His work has an acutely ambivalent reputation in former colonial territories, since it both emphasized the great antiquity of some non-Western cultures, especially in Africa, and assumed that western culture was superior.

19 Presumably in the 1961 Greek movie *Antigone* directed by Yorgos Javellas.

20 She explains these two inspirations in several interviews, for example Blasingame (2009).

21 Mills (2015).

22 For more on sororal sacrifice, see Honig (2013). There may also be echoes of the Iphigenia of Euripides' *Iphigenia in Tauris*, who is prepared to die to save her younger sibling Orestes from sacrifice, and shares many features with her divine avatar Artemis, the female god of hunting and archery.

23 Collins (2008), 236–237.

24 Collins (2009), 21.

25 Collins (2009), 23.

26 The imagery of the dangerous yet feminine veils of Islam was identified as a key trope in western colonial discourse as early as the Antillean psychiatrist Frantz Fanon's seminal article 'Algeria unveiled'. This was first published in 1959 at the height of the Algerian struggle for independence. See further Hall (2006) 193: female headgear symbolizes danger, plots and secret resistance, which demand unveiling and extirpation.

27 Collins (2009), 23.

28 Interview with Collins, at http://world.clubs-kids.scholastic.co.uk/clubs_content/18832 (last accessed 1 February 2015).

29 Collins (2009), 216.

30 Collins (2008), 311.

15 Generation Telemachus: Dinaw Mengestu's *How to Read the Air*

1 Rohter (2010) quotes Mengestu as saying that the third novel 'seems to be the last component of this cycle'.

2 La Force (2010).

3 Hall, in *The Stuart Hall Project* (2013), directed by John Akomfrah.

4 On the reciprocal impact of colonization, see Césaire (2000) on the 'boomerang effect of colonization', by which the colonizers are dehumanized by their inhuman treatment of the people they colonize.

5 Dinaw Mengestu (2011b).

6 Mengestu (2011b).

7 Ellison (1995 [1958]) 58: 'I knew the trickster Ulysses just as early as I knew the wily rabbit of Negro American lore, and I could easily imagine myself a pint-sized Ulysses but hardly a rabbit, no matter how human and resourceful or Negro . . . My point is that the Negro American writer is also an heir of the human experience which is literature, and this might well be more important to him than his living folk tradition.'

8 Ellison (1995) 140.

9 McConnell (2013) 76.

10 See, for example, the various theorizations offered by Moretti (2000), Damrosch (2003), Casanova (2005) and Apter (2013), and the discussion of these in the introduction to this volume.

11 Moretti (2000), 65 adapting Fredric Jameson sees works of world literature as embodying a 'triangle: foreign form, local material – *and local form*'.

12 Damrosch (2003) 4.

13 See, for example, Lasdun (2011) on the similarities of the first two novels.

14 Mengestu (2011a): 'I think in America they thought the first title would sound too political. Americans might not have caught the irony or the music reference. I think the publishers thought that people would come to the readings thinking this was a political novel about communism'.

15 Mengestu (2008) 47 and *passim*.

16 Mengestu (2008) 100 and *passim*.

17 Mengestu (2007).

18 Rohter (2010).

19 Feminist responses to ancient literature have enacted a very similar kind of appropriation, giving voice to the previously silenced. Margaret Atwood (2005a and 2005b), for example, gave Penelope and Circe their own narratives, and Carol Ann Duffy does likewise with a range of female counterparts to renowned male figures in *The World's Wife* (1999).

20 Wilde (2007), 979. Charles observes a 'nod to *The Great Gatsby*', another iconic novel of the American literary canon.

21 Fitzgerald (2004) 110: '"Can't repeat the past?" he cried incredulously. "Why of course you can!"

He looked around him wildly, as if the past were lurking here in the shadow of his house, just out of reach of his hand.

"I'm going to fix everything just the way it was before"'.

22 The 'accretions' of later receptions are evident here. Quite possibly, Mengestu is channelling the *Odyssey* via not only Virgil's response to *Odyssey* 11 found in *Aeneid* 6, but also Derek Walcott's, both in *Omeros* (when Achille meets his ancestor Afolabe in a katabatic reverse Middle Passage episode) and in *The Odyssey: A Stage Version*, where Odysseus' Underworld is the London Underground.
23 Davis (2007), 196–198; 204–206 on Césaire's *Cahier d'un retour au pays natal* and Walcott's poem, 'Homecoming: Anse La Raye'.
24 Joyce (1961) 704, the historic revised Random House edition.
25 Cf. Mengestu (2008) 175, where the narrator contemplates this very same contrast.
26 Cf. Mengestu (2010), e.g. 129: 'The guard looks up at me and says, "The park closes in about an hour. You'll have to leave soon."

I nod my head. I smile at him. Don't worry, I want to tell him, these days I always do.'
27 Martindale (1993) 7: 'our current interpretations of ancient texts, whether or not we are aware of it, are, in complex ways, constructed by the chain of receptions through which their continued readability has been effected. As a result we cannot get back to any originary meaning wholly free of subsequent accretions.' And T. S. Eliot, 'Tradition and the Individual Talent' (1919): 'the past [is] altered by the present as much as the present is directed by the past.'
28 Wendland (2012).
29 Ellison (2002) 3.
30 Céspedes, Torres-Saillant and Díaz (2000), 896.
31 Ellison (2002) 428.
32 Ellison (2002) 13.
33 Mengestu (2008) 141.
34 Davis (2007).
35 Mengestu (2011a)
36 Chamberlain (2012).
37 Rankine (2006); Hall (2008) ch. 7; McConnell (2013).
38 For references, see further Weitz (1987).
39 McConnell (2013) 1; 37.
40 Damrosch (2003) 4.

Index